SIDNEY WEINTRAUB

Free Trade between Mexico and the United States?

THE BROOKINGS INSTITUTION
Washington, D.C.

Library of Congress Cataloging in Publication data:

Weintraub, Sidney, 1922–
    Free trade between Mexico and the United States?
    Includes bibliographical references and index.
    1. Mexico—Commercial policy. 2. United States—
Commercial policy. 3. Free trade and protection—
Free trade. I. Title.
HF1481.W44   1984   382'.0972'073   84-1923
ISBN 0-8157-9286-7
ISBN 0-8157-9285-9 (pbk.)

1 2 3 4 5 6 7 8 9

Foreword

FOR MOST of the twentieth century U.S. foreign policy has focused on distant more than on neighboring countries. The United States has fought wars in Europe and Asia, and U.S. trade policy has been based primarily on relations with the European Community and Japan. But in recent years national attention started to shift toward the south, stimulated primarily by the 1973–74 oil crisis and the discovery of huge quantities of oil in Mexico. By the late 1970s, Mexico had become the third-ranking U.S. trading partner after Canada and Japan. The economic stabilization program that Mexico undertook in 1982 to correct its balance-of-payments deficits led to a sharp decline in Mexican imports and to a loss of jobs in U.S. export industries. After peso devaluations in 1982 and 1983, the number of undocumented Mexicans crossing the long border to work in the United States increased substantially. Thus it became obvious to all observers that what happens in Mexico affects the United States, and vice versa.

Trade between the two countries is important in its own right and for its social and political implications. The structure of industries in both countries and their levels of income and employment are influenced by their trade with each other. Diplomatic relations between the two governments are dominated by trade issues.

This study is an analysis of the possibility that Mexico and the United States can move gradually toward free trade in substantially all goods. It examines the political impediments to such a movement, but it concentrates on economic issues, especially on whether the benefits of free trade would be shared equitably or would tend to favor the more advanced U.S. economy. In this connection, it is worth noting that in specific industries—such as steel, petrochemicals, automobile production and assembly—it is possible that by the year 2000 the United States

vii

rather than Mexico will shy away from free trade. This is already the case in labor-intensive industries such as the manufacture of clothing and electronic components.

Sidney Weintraub began his research for this book as a senior fellow in the Brookings Foreign Policy Studies program. He is now Dean Rusk Professor at the Lyndon B. Johnson School of Public Affairs of the University of Texas at Austin and a member of the Brookings associated staff. His study reflects extensive discussion with public officials and private citizens in Mexico and with U.S. experts on Mexican affairs. Though too numerous to list here, they all contributed to the analysis. Joseph Grunwald stimulated Weintraub's interest in undertaking the study; its format and content owe much to counsel from John D. Steinbruner, Jorge Dominguez, Abraham Lowenthal, and Clark Reynolds. Jean Rosenblatt edited the manuscript, Alan G. Hoden verified its factual content, and Ward & Silvan prepared the index.

This study was financed in part by the William and Flora Hewlett Foundation. The views presented here are solely those of the author and should not be ascribed to the persons whose assistance is acknowledged above, to the William and Flora Hewlett Foundation, or to the trustees, officers, or other staff members of the Brookings Institution.

BRUCE K. MACLAURY
President

January 1984
Washington, D.C.

Author's Preface

I HAVE BEEN STUDYING Mexico for many years, from the time I lived there more than thirty years ago. Since then I have observed some remarkable achievements such as maintenance of political stability under a structure that is uniquely Mexican and high growth rates sustained over a long period. Mexican leaders must have done many things right to have attained this record. But there also have been defects in the Mexican miracle, as Mexico's success has sometimes been called. The main defect, in my view, has been the inequitable distribution of Mexico's economic growth, made evident by, for example, skewed benefits in favor of well-to-do persons, the high level of unemployment and under-employment, the lack of opportunities in rural areas, and the allocation of federal funds that has contributed to these inequalities.

These are largely Mexican affairs, and for the most part I have remained a witness rather than a commentator. However, they are not purely Mexican. It is clear that what happens in either Mexico or the United States affects the other country. U.S. recession restricts imports from Mexico; high U.S. unemployment stimulates protectionism of U.S. industry. Mexican growth leads to more imports from the United States; inequalities and underemployment in Mexico stimulate emigration to the United States. Prosperity in either country is good for both. Prosperity and reasonable equity in both is ideal for both. These are my starting premises.

What stimulated me to write this book was a certain perversity in outlook. I had heard repeatedly from Mexican and American colleagues that the economic differences between the two countries precluded taking any formal steps toward trade integration. The polarization, or "backwash," thesis first set forth by Gunnar Myrdal was, by general consensus, accepted as inviolable. How could a country with a low per capita income move toward free trade with one with a high per capita income without damage to the former? The assumed conclusion was that the rich country would become richer and the poor country poorer. But I doubted that in such a relationship the rich country really could get richer without the poorer country also getting richer. Poor countries in Europe enter into free-trade or customs-union relationships with richer countries in both the European Community and the European Free Trade Association, and the rich country does not necessarily benefit at the expense of the poor. Both benefit. The outcome depends not only on the relative starting levels of per capita income but also on the degree of industrialization of the poorer country and on its physical and human infrastructure.

I was not certain that bilateral free trade would lead to the convergence of the Mexican and U.S. economies at higher levels for each, but I felt the possibility deserved analysis. Though I am still not certain what the outcome of bilateral free trade would be, I tend to believe that economic convergence is more likely than economic divergence. The main purpose of this book is to stimulate debate on the subject so that the divergence hypothesis will not be automatically accepted.

Another stimulus for the book was my rebellion against the idea that because of their different histories each country would be unable to ever accept any formal agreement leading to bilateral free trade. It may be that political sentiment in each country will preclude a deep analysis of the economics of free trade, but I would like to give the technicians a chance to explore the issue.

A final stimulus was my conviction that the bilateral relationship is, in fact, unavoidable. Mexico and the United States are linked together. This connection affects their trade, their investment relationships, the movement of their people, and their cultural exchanges. I asked myself whether this inevitable interaction would proceed best if some common goals were set—such as to reach free trade by, say, the year 2000—and if both individual and joint measures were taken to make the most of growth and employment in each country. In the book I explore the options open to each country, particularly Mexico, to accomplish these objectives through trade policy. Trade relations really serve as an analytic proxy for the entire bilateral relationship. The issue for the two countries, in my view, is not whether they can limit their dependence on each other—since I do not believe they can, except at an unacceptable cost in income and employment—but how they can best profit from this interdependence.

When I started to write this book in 1981 the Mexican economy was growing at about 8 percent a year, or close to 5 percent per capita per year, and enough jobs were being created each year not only to absorb the new entrants into the labor force but also to reduce the number of openly unemployed and underemployed Mexicans. By the end of 1982 the boom had collapsed. Economic growth was zero or negative, open unemployment and underemployment were growing, and Mexico was unable to meet scheduled servicing on its external debt, which, at about $80 billion at the end of 1982, was one of the highest of any country in the world. The Mexican peso had collapsed. When I started writing, it took 20 to 25 pesos to buy a U.S. dollar; at the end of 1982, the free-market rate was about 150 pesos per dollar.

I do not know whether it is better to release this book at a time of economic crisis in Mexico or at a time of boom. In any case, events dictated the choice. Just as the good time did not last forever, neither will the current bad time.

I have discussed the issues contained here with many colleagues from Mexico, the United States, and other countries. Not all agree with my analysis (this is an understatement), but almost all encouraged me to proceed. The analysis owes much to these discussions. I wish especially to thank those persons who reviewed the draft of the manuscript. I incorporated many of their suggestions, and the final product is better for it.

s.w.

Contents

Text Tables

Contents

CHAPTER ONE

Introduction

THE PURPOSE of this study is to examine whether a slow but steady movement to free trade between Mexico and the United States would benefit both countries. The theme is controversial. Detractors in Mexico will interpret it as the latest U.S. device to exercise political and economic hegemony over Mexico. Detractors in the United States will object that, at best, free trade would lead to a flow of goods into the United States made with cheap Mexican labor and, at worst, would encourage Mexican labor to emigrate. Impartial economists in both countries will question whether it is feasible for two countries vastly unequal in economic strength to have free trade without the economic progress of the weaker country being held back. Each of these issues will be analyzed in the following chapters.

There has been considerable study of the effects of free trade between Canada and the United States but none of any significance about what the economic consequences might be if Mexico and the United States began to move toward free trade.[1] Such study never seemed worthwhile. The conventional wisdom has been that the economics of free trade between Mexico and the United States would benefit only the United States because of the greater efficiency and higher productivity of its industry. The instinctive expectation in Mexico has been that if free trade actually did encourage greater specialization in each country, the

1. Examples of studies on U.S.-Canadian free trade include Ronald J. Wonnacott and Paul Wonnacott, *Free Trade between the United States and Canada: The Potential Economic Effects* and *U.S.-Canadian Free Trade: The Potential Impact on the Canadian Economy;* Sperry Lea, *A Canada-U.S. Free Trade Arrangement: Survey of Possible Characteristics;* Canadian-American Committee, *A Possible Plan for a Canada-U.S. Free Trade Area;* Canadian Parliament, Senate, *Canada–United States Relations,* vols. 2 and 3: *Canada's Trade Relations with the United States;* Sidney Weintraub, "Fear of Free Trade," pp. 9–12. Full references to the works cited appear in the bibliography.

United States would specialize in high-technology industry and Mexico in simple processing of raw materials and unsophisticated assembly.[2]

Even if these economic misgivings could be dispelled, the political obstacles to getting Mexican politicians and intellectuals to consider free trade are immense.[3] To draw an analogy, before Germany and France came together in the European Coal and Steel Community (ECSC) and then in the European Communities generally, an emotional barrier of mutual suspicion and even hatred had to be surmounted. The experience of two devastating world wars and the desire not to repeat them helped accomplish this. There is no such driving force to help the United States and particularly Mexico overcome their emotional and psychological barriers. Inequality in the power of the two countries has deeply influenced Mexican thinking.[4] Mexico fears that free trade would solidify a dependent-hegemonic relationship. This is so much taken for granted that the issue has not been meticulously examined.[5] Whether such a

2. This has been Canada's concern as well, typified in the phrase that a free-trade area with the United States would convert Canadians into "hewers of wood and drawers of water." The literature on customs unions is replete with analysis of unequal benefits among partners at different degrees of development. For example, see Stuart I. Fagan, *Central American Economic Integration: The Politics of Unequal Benefits;* Donald C. Mead, "The Distribution of Gains in Customs Unions between Developing Countries," pp. 713–36; David Morawetz, *The Andean Group: A Case Study in Economic Integration among Developing Countries;* Peter Robson, "The Distribution of Gains in Customs Unions between Developing Countries: A Note," pp. 117–19; David Segal, "On Making Customs Unions Fair: An East African Example," pp. 115–60.

3. These misgivings are typified in separate writings by Castañeda, who qualifies as both a politician and an intellectual. He wrote the following in 1958: "Since the first Pan-American conference (Washington, 1889–90), the United States has proposed—and Latin America rejected—the creation of a customs union embracing the entire hemisphere, which would have ruined any future possibility of industrialization in Latin America and would have condemned it to the never-ending extraction of raw materials for industry in the United States. The differences in viewpoints have not lessened with time." Jorge Castañeda, *Mexico and the United Nations,* p. 170. In "En busca de una posición ante Estados Unidos," p. 297, written shortly before he became Mexico's foreign minister, Castañeda argued that Mexico must cement its relations with other developing countries—like-minded middle-income countries and socialist countries— since "no one in Mexico any longer believes seriously that there is or can be a 'special relationship' between the United States and Mexico."

4. For example, one of Mexico's distinguished scholars of the bilateral relationship, Mario Ojeda, in *Alcances y límites de la política exterior de México,* uses the phrase "the hegemonic power" (*la potencia hegemónica*) repeatedly (pp. 8, 163, 177) when referring to the United States.

5. In a brief article on the subject, "Prospects for Further Development of Economic Relations among Mexico, Canada, and the United States," pp. 1–4, Victor L. Urquidi simply asserts the familiar argument that free trade among economic unequals would lead to unequal benefits for the stronger country.

relationship would develop depends on the economic outcome of free trade.

This examination will not argue the case for a gradual movement toward free trade between the two countries but rather will attempt a dispassionate analysis of the issue. If it were determined that free trade would benefit both countries, they could move toward it over a protracted but defined period. Such movement would not necessarily lead to other steps toward integration, such as free movement of labor between the countries, freedom by U.S. companies to take over Mexican industry, or some form of political integration. Free trade would benefit both countries if it raised their incomes and welfare above what they otherwise would be and if the advantages were evenly distributed between the two countries.[6]

The Economic Issues

The main economic issues that require analysis are familiar from customs-union theory. The most important is the effect a movement toward free trade would have on the location and development of industrial production in the two countries. Harry Johnson has asserted that there is a collective preference in most countries for industrial production and that electorates are prepared to spend resources to increase the level of industrialization.[7] In one of the pioneering analyses of customs unions in developing countries, Cooper and Massell accepted the thesis that industrialization was a legitimate policy goal and proceeded to examine how two or more countries could stimulate a given amount of industry at the lowest possible real cost.[8] This emphasis on industry is particularly strong in Latin America, growing out of the work

6. In an interview with James Reston, José López Portillo, then president of Mexico, was reported as saying that a North American common market was a dream that might eventually become a reality if the nations worked on practical problems one at a time. "Mexican Wants Full Review of Ties in Carter Talks," *New York Times,* February 8, 1979. The free-trade eventuality was hedged in this statement, but not completely dismissed.

7. Harry G. Johnson, "An Economic Theory of Protectionism, Tariff Bargaining, and the Formation of Customs Unions," pp. 256–83.

8. C. A. Cooper and B. F. Massell, "Toward a General Theory of Customs Unions for Developing Countries," pp. 461–76.

started in the 1950s of the Economic Commission for Latin America.[9] It has been precisely this desire to stimulate industrialization that has caused most developing countries to fail at economic integration, since no satisfactory method has been devised for partner countries to share equitably in the division of new industrial investment.

There undoubtedly was a time when Mexico's inability to protect infant industry would have had—to use Myrdal's term—a "backwash" effect impeding Mexican industrialization, but this time may have long since passed.[10] The increased number of assembly plants along the U.S.-Mexican border and elsewhere in developing countries has shown that a large wage differential between the United States and Mexico can be an important stimulus to industrial location. Much of this industry in Mexico has involved only the last stages of assembly, but in other countries, such as Taiwan and South Korea, it has proceeded beyond this.

Mexico's automotive industry and petrochemical production might well prosper at the expense of similar production in the United States; or both could flourish through specialization if investors could depend on a large, combined, tariff-free market—not just for the final product but for parts as well. Indeed, misgivings about the future location of such industries might be greater in the United States than in Mexico as long as significant wage differentials that could not be nullified by greater U.S. productivity persisted between the two countries. Mexico might be to the United States in these industries, and in others such as steel, nonelectrical machinery, and consumer durables, what the South has been to the North in the United States in recent years. The internal U.S. common market that for so long favored northern industrial production at the expense of the South is history; it may be that Mexico would be similarly benefited in U.S.-Mexico free trade. This possibility is worth examining in general and for several key industries.

Movement toward free trade would allow investors to make decisions

9. The initial conceptual work was United Nations Economic Commission for Latin America, *The Economic Development of Latin America and Its Principal Problems*, p. 2. The essay specifically states that industrialization is "the principal means, at the disposal" of the periphery—developing countries—for "progressively raising the standard of living of the masses."

10. Gunnar Myrdal, *Economic Theory and Under-Developed Regions*, especially pp. 27–33. What Myrdal had in mind was that a developing country that left its market freely open to imports would be unable to develop an industrial base—the country would remain a backwash.

knowing that plants of optimum scale could be placed to take advantage of a large market. The internal U.S. market is already large enough to achieve optimum scale for most industries. Mexico's internal market is not; its gross national product is roughly one-twentieth that of the United States.[11]

If free trade were to mean a progressive dismantling just of tariffs, some Mexican products to be sold in the United States would be significantly affected, but the reductions would not be large across-the-board. Nominal and effective U.S. tariffs are sometimes significant, but they are no longer overwhelming.[12] That they matter for some products, however, is evident from the assembly industries established in Mexico and elsewhere whose products benefit from the necessity to pay duty, upon reentry into the United States, only on the value added outside the United States.[13] Free trade that would also involve the progressive elimination of nontariff restrictions on industrial products would be much more significant for many Mexican products, such as textiles and apparel.[14]

The other side of the coin is that Mexican tariff and nontariff barriers are substantially greater than those of the United States, and U.S. exports to Mexico could be stimulated with the dismantling of these barriers.[15] The argument in favor of gradually reducing import barriers

11. According to the *1981 World Bank Atlas* (Washington, D.C.: World Bank, 1982), p. 20, Mexico's GNP at market prices in 1980 was estimated to be $144 billion and that of the United States $2,852 billion. U.S. per capita GNP in 1980 ($11,360) was 5.3 times that of Mexico's ($2,130).

12. Nominal U.S. tariffs will be 7.0 percent, measured by a simple average, or 4.4 percent, when tariffs are weighted by most-favored-nation imports after the Tokyo round of tariff reductions take full effect in 1987. Thomas R. Graham, *The Impact of the Tokyo Round Agreements on U.S. Export Competitiveness*, p. 22.

13. Under sections 806.30 and 807.00 of the U.S. tariff schedule. In early 1979 there were 470 border plants and 60 in-bond plants in the Mexican interior. About 40 percent of these produced electric and electronic products and 20 percent textiles and apparel. U.S. Department of Labor, *Profile of Labor Conditions: Mexico*, p. 3. By the end of 1980, there were about 575 plants, counting both those at the border and in the interior.

14. Mexican exports of these products to the United States are now restricted, as are exports of other countries, pursuant to the Arrangement Regarding International Trade in Textiles. The operative textile agreement between Mexico and the United States was designed to cover the period May 1, 1978, to December 31, 1981 (U.S. Department of State, Press Release 61 [March 9, 1979]), and was extended by an exchange of letters dated December 23 and 24, 1981, which became effective January 1, 1982 (U.S. Department of State, Press Release 42 [February 2, 1982]).

15. An excellent analysis of Mexico's protectionism can be found in Gerardo Bueno, "The Structure of Protection in Mexico," in Bela Balassa, ed., *The Structure of Protection in Developing Countries*, pp. 169–202.

is that this will encourage Mexican industry to become more competitive, which is a Mexican objective regardless of any free-trade arrangement with the United States. The differences between the two types of dismantlings, selective or comprehensive, are that in a bilateral free-trade arrangement the reduction of import barriers would affect substantially all products and be more pervasive over time but would affect only imports from the United States rather than those from all sources.

The United States already is Mexico's dominant trading partner. Until the last few years, between 60 and 65 percent of Mexico's imports have come from the United States and a slightly higher percentage— between 65 and 70 percent—of Mexico's exports were sent to the United States. The import proportion has not changed significantly during the last few years. Based on nine-month data for each year, 67 percent of Mexico's imports in 1981 and 60 percent in 1982 came from the United States. Total Mexican imports in 1981 (twelve months) amounted to $23 billion; this value seems to have declined by as much as 30 percent in 1982 as a result of import restrictions imposed on balance-of-payments grounds. The proportion of exports to the United States, however, did decline to 53 percent during the first nine months of both 1981 and 1982. The main reason for this decline was the diversification of Mexico's petroleum exports. For all of 1981, Mexico's exports amounted to $19 billion, a value that seems to have remained stable during 1982.[16]

The Mexican market is important for the United States—in recent years it has become the third largest export market, after Canada and Japan—but not as important as the United States market is for Mexico. In 1981, U.S. exports to Mexico of $17.8 billion constituted 7.6 percent of total U.S. exports ($234 billion). U.S. imports from Mexico of $13.8 billion made up 5.3 percent of total U.S. imports ($261 billion).[17] This asymmetry in market dependence, overwhelming for Mexico and merely significant for the United States, contributes to Mexico's feeling of dependency on the United States and explains in part why U.S. officials prefer to use the word "interdependence" to describe the U.S.-Mexico relationship.

16. The data are from Mexican sources. Annual trade figures are from Banco de México, *Informe Anual, 1981*, p. 153, and nine-month data from the American Chamber of Commerce of Mexico, "Foreign Trade," p. 15. The latter data are based on information provided by the Mexican Foreign Trade Institute. Mexican and U.S. trade data are not consistent.

17. U.S. Bureau of the Census, *Highlights of U.S. Export and Import Trade*, FT 990, December 1981 (Government Printing Office, 1982), pp. 11, 36, 71, 86.

As the more developed country, the United States has advantages in attracting investment. Related industries, both suppliers and buyers, are more abundant; skilled workers are more available; market-oriented industries are closer to the most important market; transportation and communications facilities are superior; and the total infrastructure of government and private services is more conducive to investment in the more developed economy. If the Mexican infrastructure were starting from scratch, these advantages favoring the United States would be so overwhelming that they would justify dismissing totally the idea of moving toward bilateral free trade. But this is not the case any more, and Mexican disadvantages would diminish even more if the move toward free trade were sufficiently extended.

Although the United States has limitations on foreign direct investment, particularly in defense industries, transportation, and broadcasting, it is generally open to foreign investment.[18] Mexico, on the other hand, has extensive restrictions on foreign investment. Some industries, such as petroleum, basic petrochemicals, electricity, and railroads, are run exclusively by the state; others, such as radio and television, urban transport, air and maritime transport, and gas distribution, are reserved for Mexicans and Mexican companies. More generally, foreign persons or corporate bodies may not hold more than 49 percent of the equity of business enterprises without specific exceptions.[19] Although free trade does not require freedom of capital movements, exploitation of the U.S. commercial market would probably be enhanced if U.S. investors had greater freedom to invest in Mexico. However, the mere expression of this thought would arouse a suspicion in Mexico that a movement toward free trade was a cover for the gradual Americanization of Mexican industry. Mexican concern about investment by foreign—that is, U.S.—multinational corporations is a central reason for the Mexican feeling of dependency on the United States.[20]

The United States would have a counterpart concern, namely, that a free-trade agreement would be a cover for free movement of Mexican

18. See Foreign Investment Review Agency of Canada, Policy, Research and Communications Branch, "Barriers to Foreign Investment in the United States."

19. These restrictions are spelled out in the Law to Promote Mexican Investment and to Regulate Foreign Investment (*Diario Oficial*, March 9, 1973) and in various laws relating to specific activities.

20. A good exposition of Mexican attitudes toward foreign investment in Mexico is Bernardo Sepúlveda Amor, Olga Pellicer de Brody, and Lorenzo Meyer, *Las empresas transnacionales en México*.

labor to the United States. Mexican workers often make possible the continued economic viability of certain activities in the United States, such as agriculture that requires hand harvesting and some construction and service industries in the Southwest. The need for cheap Mexican labor might intensify in agriculture if U.S. import protection against Mexico were to disappear. For the Mexicans, one quid pro quo for a gradual movement to bilateral free trade might be the abandonment of U.S. efforts to restrict the inflow of undocumented Mexican workers and, over time, their legalization.

Just as free trade does not require complete freedom of foreign investment, so it does not require the free movement of labor. However, the integration of the two economies would be more efficient if, along with freedom of capital movement, labor could move more freely. The issue is a sensitive one, mostly because of fear in the United States that free trade will lead to the free movement of labor and Mexico's desire that the United States not impede labor movement.

Despite the emphasis developing countries place on industry when considering customs unions and free trade, economic development obviously must encompass more than these. Perhaps the central short-coming of the Mexican development "miracle" of the past twenty-five years is that it overemphasized, or at least overprotected, industry. The result has been an inevitable inward turning of industries generally unable to compete in world markets.[21] The protection given to these industries against competition within the Mexican market has required that other sectors pay for this subsidization. Agriculture and mining have paid the heaviest price. From 1970 to 1979, compound annual growth rates were 5.6 percent for the economy as a whole, 5.9 percent for industrial production, 2 percent for agricultural production, and 3.6 percent for mining, excluding petroleum. Population growth rates were about 3.5 percent a year.[22] Mexico must ask itself, as it began to do under the administration of President José López Portillo (1976–82), if it is wise to insist that agriculture, in effect, subsidize industrialization.

How should agriculture be treated in a prospective free-trade arrangement between the two countries? The problems of agricultural trade in other economic integration schemes are well known. The European

21. This is discussed in Gustav Ranis, "¿Se está tornando amargo el milagro mexicano?" pp. 22–23.
22. Computed from Banco de México, *Producto interno bruto y gasto, cuaderno 1960–1977.*

Community (EC) opted for communitywide producer-support programs for many commodities at the expense of the European consumer and potentially of agricultural exports of third countries. The European Free Trade Association (EFTA) excluded agriculture from the free-trade process and justified this on the grounds that a free-trade area is required by international agreement to eliminate duties and other restrictive regulations of commerce only on "substantially" all the trade in products originating in the constituent territories.[23]

In recent years, many of the most contentious trade problems between the United States and Mexico have been over agricultural trade. These have involved, among other issues, high seasonal duties on Mexican tomatoes and other winter fruits and vegetables, marketing orders that regulate the size, grade, and quality of many of these products that can be sold in the United States, and allegations that these products are being dumped by Mexico in the U.S. market. For its part, Mexico maintains even greater restrictions on the import of agricultural products that compete with Mexican production. Although this examination focuses on industrial policy, some analysis of these sensitive agricultural problems is included.

Mexico's development plan has been criticized on two other related grounds: it has resulted in one of the most unequal patterns of income distribution in Latin America and among developing countries generally,[24] and it has failed to create enough jobs for those of age in the Mexican labor force.[25] For Mexico, the crucial question may be whether a gradual movement toward free trade with the United States could improve these problems. The beneficiaries of past Mexican industrialization have been primarily the owners of industries and that portion of the labor force able to obtain jobs in the protected industrial sector. For about 40 percent of the economically active population that is either underemployed or unemployed, there has been no Mexican miracle.[26] The weakest part of the argument of those who assert that Mexico must

23. General Agreement on Tariffs and Trade, *Basic Instruments and Selected Documents*, vol. 1, article 24:8(b), p. 54.

24. Hollis Chenery and others, *Redistribution with Growth*, p. 8.

25. U.S. Department of Labor, *Profile of Labor Conditions: Mexico*, p. 3, gives a figure of 700,000 persons entering the labor force each year.

26. The 40 percent figure is given in ibid. Saúl Trejo Reyes, "La política laboral," in Gerardo M. Bueno, *Opciones de política económica en México*, states that the combined percentage of unemployed and underemployed fluctuates between 35 and 44 percent of the economically active population (p. 150).

retain its ability to develop industry behind protective walls is that this has benefited only a minority of Mexicans. Gradual exposure to greater competition, with the attraction of a large market as the potential reward, might benefit many more Mexicans. With such exposure, some U.S. industries and workers might be hurt, at least in labor-intensive activities, in which the United States may be at a comparative disadvantage.

One other probable Mexican suspicion is that the launching now of trade integration between the two countries is part of a U.S. plan to encourage maximum exploitation of Mexican oil and natural gas. After all, Mexico discovered oil and the United States discovered Mexico. However, just as free trade need not lead to legalized free movement of labor, to complete freedom for foreign direct investors in Mexico, or even to any further steps toward economic integration let alone political integration, free trade certainly need not remove control from Mexican authorities over decisionmaking on oil and gas policy. As the United States decontrols its pricing and regulation of oil and gas, the issue of tariffs or other barriers to Mexican-U.S. trade in these products becomes mostly moot. Mexico's energy policy can continue to be made in Mexico in light of its own development policy. Decisions on energy policy may have to be altered to the extent that free trade alters development policy, but this says nothing more than that decisions in one economic sector affect decisions in other sectors.

The Structure of the Study

The question that will be examined here is whether it is in the economic interest of both the United States and particularly Mexico to move gradually toward free trade over a period of, say, twenty-five years. The precise number of years is negotiable; what is crucial is that the process allow time for adjustment in both countries to lessen hardships resulting from changing comparative advantages. In principle, free trade would encompass all trade, but exceptions may be necessary despite a lengthy transition. The most probable exceptions would be in agriculture, but there may also be exceptions to free trade in industry, mining, and other sectors. The intention would be to make the agreement compatible with, or at least defensible under, the provisions of the General Agreement on Tariffs and Trade (GATT). Although this study looks specifically at a U.S.-Mexico free-trade area, nothing suggested here would preclude its expansion into a North American free-trade area to include Canada and possibly other countries as well, although this is harder to envision.

The designation *free-trade area* was chosen deliberately since it is hard to contemplate a customs union, with a common external tariff, between the two countries. Mexico may still wish to give tariff protection to certain industries in which the United States is not the main competitor, and a customs union would require that the U.S. tariff go up jointly with that of Mexico, which is unnecessary. If the two countries moved jointly to a common tariff against third countries in the traditional way of averaging current tariffs (or the tariff equivalents of Mexican and U.S. nontariff barriers), substantial increases in the U.S. tariff would result. This would be unwise. In preferring a free-trade area over a customs union between Canada and the United States, the Canadian-American Committee pointed out that a customs-union agreement probably would be a more direct assault on the prerogatives of the U.S. Congress in setting trade policy.[27] The fear is that the U.S. Congress tends to react to special-interest pressure to raise tariffs and other barriers against imports.[28] Such actions need not violate a free-trade agreement—as long as the barriers are not raised against Mexico—under which the separate countries have their own external tariffs.[29] A free-trade area obviously introduces other types of problems, such as the need for rules of origin to prevent reexports from the low- to the high-tariff country, but the world has had some experience in dealing with this complication.

In theory, separate sector or industry agreements on most goods might be easier to negotiate than free trade. A sector agreement could lead to free trade, as it did in Europe following the formation of the

27. Canadian-American Committee, *A Possible Plan for a Canada-U.S. Free Trade Area*, p. 19.

28. One of the major legislative issues in 1982 and 1983 growing out of the U.S. recession and the decline in the U.S. automotive industry is the imposition of a requirement that automobiles sold in the United States contain a minimum percentage of total value added in the United States.

29. Jacob Viner, *The Customs Union Issue*, pp. 124–25, points out: "There might be important *political* significance . . . in the difference between a complete customs union and a 'free-trade area,' especially if one of the members was much larger than the other. Since the members of the latter could, in theory at least, have different tariff policies toward outside countries, and would have to maintain the tariff wall between themselves in order to guard against the entrance free-of-duty of dutiable goods originating in outside countries, there would be less call for common tariff policies and for unified customs administration and less pressure on the smaller country, therefore, to conform to the legislation of the larger."

ECSC, or it may not, as it did not in North America after the United States and Canada entered into their automotive agreement. Sectoral free trade would require one or more waivers by the United States from the GATT articles.

This examination will focus on economic issues, since their outcome is the crux of the benefits and costs of free trade to the two countries. Politics, however, rears its head, sometimes as an inducement but mostly as an impediment to the type of agreement that will be examined, and some background analysis of political issues will be provided. Little or no attention will be devoted to institutional arrangements for carrying out free trade, although these obviously can be important. They are better left to intergovernmental negotiation, if the issue ever comes to that.

CHAPTER TWO

The Politics of U.S.-Mexican Trade Integration

INGRAINED habits of thinking, instilled from childhood, among Mexicans and Americans impede analysis of the economics of a movement toward free trade and would complicate conclusion of a bilateral agreement even if the economic considerations weighed in its favor.[1] It is not possible to do justice in a brief discussion to the origins of these national differences, but neither can they be ignored in a serious analysis. Most of this book deals with economic issues, but economics as practiced between nations is also politics. This chapter examines the reciprocal political attitudes and concerns and their implications for a movement to free trade.

Disparate power and conflicting histories are obstacles to greater trade integration between Mexico and the United States. However, other countries with mutual antagonism and distrust have concluded trade and economic integration arrangements despite these or, in the case of Germany and France, because of them. Distrust may even remain as trade is freed, which is what happened with Ireland in relation to the United Kingdom and with the Netherlands in relation to Germany, when each country sought the benefits of membership in the European Community. The French need not love the Germans to cooperate with them economically. Despite a continuing territorial dispute, Peru and Ecuador cooperate in the Andean Group, and even a war between El Salvador and Honduras did not lead to the withdrawal of either from the Central American Common Market. Trade arrangements can transcend political tensions.

1. An excellent analysis of how these habits of thinking are instilled in Mexican children can be found in Rafael Segovia Canosa, *La politización del niño mexicano*.

Mexican Political Concerns

The major political impediments to greater U.S.-Mexican integration, even in a limited area such as trade, flow from a combination of specific incidents—some a century or more in the past and others more recent—and vastly different patterns of thought. An undercurrent of animosity towards the United States is endemic in Mexico and, like a sleeping volcano, sometimes erupts and becomes visible. Daily perusal of Mexican news media can leave no doubt of this.

The animosity has historical roots. U.S. behavior toward Mexico during the past 150 years started badly with imperialism and the annexation of Mexican territory and continued poorly with blatant intervention in Mexican affairs, domination of large segments of the Mexican economy, and condescension in economic and political relations. This behavior has deeply affected Mexico's thinking about its relationship with the United States. The Mexican attitude is reflected in what former President José López Portillo described as "international postulates that are inherent to Mexico—self-determination and peaceful solutions to controversies, nonintervention, and prohibition of the use of force."[2] President Miguel de la Madrid Hurtado emphasized the same foreign policy in his inaugural address.[3]

A good starting point in a description of some events that have conditioned Mexican thinking is the 1846–48 war between the United States and Mexico. Its origins resemble those of the Soviet-Finnish war of the 1930s, when the Soviet Union invaded Finland as it declared the need to defend itself from Finnish invasion, and of the German invasion of Poland in 1939, which began with a similar declaration from Germany. In his request to the Congress for a formal declaration of war against Mexico, U.S. President James K. Polk asserted: "But now, after reiterated menaces, Mexico has passed the boundary of the United States, has invaded our territory, and shed American blood on American

2. From José López Portillo, "Sixth State of the Nation Report to the Mexican Congress," p. 254. The speech was made September 1, 1982, and the translation is from Banco Nacional de México (BANAMEX).

3. Reprinted in English in Miguel de la Madrid, "President de la Madrid's Inaugural Address," pp. 339–418.

soil."[4] The Treaty of Guadalupe Hidalgo, which ended the war in February 1848, confirmed U.S. title to Texas and deprived Mexico of the California and New Mexico territories, thereby reducing Mexican territory by half. One history of Mexico widely used in U.S. universities, written by U.S. authors, notes that this war and the consequent peace treaty left Mexico with a "virulent, almost pathological, Yankeephobia."[5] This anti-Americanism has been perpetuated in Mexican textbooks, folk songs, and national shrines such as the Niños Heroes (Boy Heroes), a monument in Mexico City to the defense by boy cadets against the U.S. invaders. Annual pilgrimages are still made there.

U.S. intervention in Mexican internal affairs has often had profound influence on the course of Mexican history. The agreement under which Victoriano Huerta joined the rebellion against Francisco Madero in 1913 is referred to as the "Pact of the Embassy," because the negotiations were conducted under the aegis of the U.S. ambassador to Mexico, Henry Lane Wilson.[6] The period of this rebellion against Madero, which led to his overthrow and subsequent death, is known in Mexico as the *decena trágica* (ten tragic days), and the complicity of the U.S. ambassador in the plotting is amply documented.[7]

As most Mexican school children know, U.S. marines occupied Veracruz in 1914 in an action that led to hundreds of Mexican casualties.[8] Two years later, in 1916, a U.S. force of about 6,000 men engaged in a punitive expedition into Mexico in response to raids into U.S. territory by Mexicans under the command of Pancho Villa. The U.S. expeditionary force remained in Mexico for ten months, until January 1917, without ever catching up with and punishing the Mexican raiders.[9]

U.S. intervention has also taken more subtle form than occupation by troops. There were many reasons for the popular fervor in Mexico that greeted the nationalization of the Mexican oil industry by President Lázaro Cárdenas in 1938. The dominant role of the industry in the economy and its foreign ownership were basis enough for the popularity of the action, which followed the refusal of foreign-owned companies to

4. Cited in Michael C. Meyer and William L. Sherman, *The Course of Mexican History*, p. 345.
5. Ibid., p. 352.
6. Ibid., p. 520.
7. See Stanley R. Ross, *Francisco I. Madero: Apostle of Mexican Democracy*, pp. 276–92.
8. Meyer and Sherman, *Course of Mexican History*, p. 532.
9. Ibid., pp. 540–42.

obey a Mexican Supreme Court decision in its entirety after a labor dispute.[10] There is also a history of official U.S. interference in Mexican affairs on behalf of the U.S. owners of the oil companies, as well as of other business interests. U.S. refusal to recognize the regime of President Alvaro Obregón from 1920 to 1923 is traceable to the unwillingness of Mexican authorities to provide written assurance of the protection of property rights in Mexico of U.S. nationals. Diplomatic recognition of Mexico came only as part of the agreement in 1923 that dealt with future Mexican relations with the oil companies.[11]

Mexican concern about U.S. domination of the Mexican economy is best explained by the substantial participation of the United States in Mexico's foreign trade and the commanding position of U.S. companies in key sectors of Mexico's production and trade. Mexico's feeling of vulnerability is no longer based on the expectation of hostile acts by the United States, but on the degree of dependency on the United States as a market and source of capital. A slowdown in the U.S. economy will normally curtail the volume of imports and put downward pressure on prices of industrial raw materials. Development of a market in the United States for Mexican products can lead and has led to pressure for and actual import controls. (The constant agitation by U.S. tomato growers and their representatives in Congress to curtail tomato imports from Mexico is discussed in chapter 3.) Restrictions on U.S. textile and apparel imports from Mexico can be particularly troublesome because the United States represents such a large part of Mexico's export market.

Mexican policy statements deplore this trade dependence. That Mexicans have found it inescapable is aggravating rather than comforting. The energy policy set during the López Portillo administration recognized the concern about trade dependency by decreeing that no more than 50 percent of oil exports should go to any one country (that is, to the United States). As with trade generally, the Mexican sense of dependency need not be based on a hostile U.S. act against Mexico to curtail energy imports for political reasons, but the dominance of a single market makes Mexico vulnerable to economic fluctuations in that market. That dominance also probably reduces Mexican bargaining

10. A Mexican account of the oil expropriation can be found in Lorenzo Meyer, *Mexico and the United States in the Oil Controversy, 1917–1942.*
11. Meyer and Sherman, *Course of Mexican History,* pp. 577–79.

power, since the United States is less dependent on the Mexican source than Mexico is on the U.S. market.

Surveys of Mexican attitudes suggest that the United States is seen as treating Mexico unfairly in both trade and the pricing of energy. In a survey of opinion in Mexico City commissioned in 1979 by the U.S. Information Agency (USIA), 59 percent of those questioned thought it was easier for the United States to export its goods to Mexico than it was for Mexico to export goods to the United States. Only 12 percent thought the latter. In that same survey, 58 percent of the persons polled thought that the United States was offering too little for Mexican oil and natural gas, and only 1 percent thought that Mexico was asking too much.[12] In a 1981 survey of better-educated Mexicans, most felt that Spain and Japan paid a "good" price to Mexico for oil, but, despite the same basic price, opinion was divided as to whether the United States did.[13]

The trade dependency is troublesome but less upsetting to Mexican intellectuals than the dominance by foreign corporations, overwhelmingly from the United States, in critical sectors of the Mexican economy. Foreign corporations accounted for 21 percent of the value of all Mexican exports in 1977 and between 42 and 46 percent of manufactured exports. The proportions were extremely high—over 75 percent—for such categories as chemicals and machinery and equipment.[14] Of exports by Mexican firms in 1977, about 35 percent were manufactures; for foreign firms the percentage for manufactures was 71 percent.[15] In 1972, half of the 300 largest industrial firms in Mexico were foreign controlled and two-thirds were based in the United States. Foreign firms generated about 23 percent of all value added in manufacturing in Mexico in 1970; U.S. firms alone contributed almost 18 percent of value added in manufacturing that year. In some sectors—tobacco, rubber, and chemicals—the U.S. contribution was more than 50 percent. For firms with

12. U.S. International Communication Agency (hereafter USICA, as USIA was then called), "Mexico, Reluctant Friend of the U.S.: Mexico City Opinion on Bilateral and International Issues," Research Memorandum, prepared by William J. Millard (USICA, September 12, 1979), pp. 7, 29.

13. USICA, "Better-Educated Mexicans Have Serious Misperceptions of U.S," Briefing Paper, prepared by William J. Millard (USICA, September 8, 1981).

14. Rogelio Ramírez de la O., "Las empresas transnacionales y el comercio exterior de México: Un estudio empírico del comportamiento de las empresas," p. 1160.

15. Ibid., p. 1161.

ten or more employees, the foreign share of the value of production (based on sales data) in industry in Mexico was about 45 percent, ranging up to 100 percent in some sectors such as rubber, nonelectrical machinery, electrical machinery, and transportation.[16]

These figures can be interpreted in many ways. One can argue that if not for foreign companies, Mexico's trade picture would be extremely dismal. This interpretation, of course, would not lessen the Mexican sense of foreign domination. Another interpretation is that the commanding presence of foreign companies in dynamic sectors of the Mexican economy is what has led to the U.S. trade dominance. The thesis behind this reasoning is that trade follows foreign investment by multinational companies. Official U.S. data showing that 45 percent of U.S. imports from Mexico in 1979 were from exchange between affiliated companies in the two countries support the contention that trade and investment domination are part of the same phenomenon.[17]

Obviously Mexico's sense of economic dependency is based on facts, even though foreign investment has presumably enhanced Mexican welfare. (The improbable assumption could be made that Mexican investment would have increased to replace foreign investment to maintain the same level of total investment.) Canada feels the same vulnerability in relation to the United States, and an agency was established to review foreign investment on a case-by-case basis to determine the beneficial effect on Canada.[18] The United States established a mechanism to monitor foreign investment in 1975 because of concern about international control of segments of the U.S. economy.[19] The Mexican concern must be much greater than in either Canada or the United States because it follows U.S. territorial annexation and inter-

16. The figures in this paragraph come from Richard S. Newfarmer and Willard F. Mueller, *Multinational Corporations in Brazil and Mexico: Structural Sources of Economic and Noneconomic Power*, Committee Print, pp. 53–57.

17. U.S. International Trade Commission, *Background Study of the Economies and International Trade Patterns of the Countries of North America, Central America and the Caribbean*, p. 163.

18. The Foreign Investment Review Agency, or FIRA.

19. The *Annual Report of the Secretary of Commerce for the Fiscal Year Ended June 30, 1975*, p. 58, contains the following passage: "During fiscal 1975, public and congressional interest in foreign investment was heightened in the United States. Concern was expressed over an anticipated spurt in the rate of such investment, over the control of U.S. raw material resources, and over the new Arab investment potential. Although the actual inflow of funds was not great, it was recognized that the Executive Branch needed more information about the character and scope of such investment."

vention in Mexican affairs. U.S. economic dominance is often portrayed in Mexican literature as a continuation of these earlier U.S. actions.

U.S. condescension toward Mexico may have abated since President Polk distorted facts to justify the U.S. invasion of Mexico, since U.S. Ambassador Henry Lane Wilson intervened in plotting against a Mexican president, and since U.S. diplomatic recognition was withheld to further the interests of U.S. oil companies. But such condescension has not disappeared entirely. During the negotiations in 1977 for the purchase by U.S. pipeline companies of natural gas from Mexico, legislation was introduced in the U.S. Congress making Export-Import Bank financing for Mexico contingent on the price negotiations for the natural gas. The gas purchase was not completed at that time for what may or may not have been valid reasons in the United States. However, the publicly reported assertion of James Schlesinger, the U.S. secretary of energy, that Mexico had no place else to sell its gas anyhow was clearly patronizing.[20] After Mexico decided in March 1980 not to enter the General Agreement on Tariffs and Trade, the U.S. ambassador to Mexico spoke publicly about the error Mexico made.[21] Both incidents aroused a storm of protests in the Mexican press. When it became clear in the late 1970s that Mexican oil discoveries were indeed vast, the first reaction of many prominent Americans was to call for a North American energy common market. The motive may or may not have been benign, but the impression left in Mexico was that this was merely a U.S. tactic to gain a measure of control over Mexico's oil policy.

The current style of U.S. official conduct toward Mexico tends to drift into the older pattern of a superior dealing with an inferior. That this rankles in Mexico is clear. Over and over again in his sixth and final state-of-the-nation report on September 1, 1982, President López Portillo alluded to his success in making dealings with the United States more equal. After citing various global and bilateral negotiations, he said: "Mexico has diverged, converged and, above all, negotiated with the United States along lines of dignity, respect and friendship. This had

20. These events are recounted in Richard R. Fagen and Henry R. Nau, "Mexican Gas: The Northern Connection."
21. In May 1980 U.S. Ambassador Julian Nava stated in a press conference that sooner or later Mexico would have to join the GATT. Mexican press commentary was vitriolic, was critical of "Mister" Nava, and listed Mexican grievances as far back as the nineteenth century. Nava's statement was seen as one more example of unacceptable U.S. pressure on Mexico.

never occurred before."[22] After noting that "continuation of good relations with the United States constitutes a cornerstone" in Mexico's foreign relations, he added: "But there can be no good relations with the United States if they are not primarily based on respect."[23] One of Mexico's most distinguished historians, Daniel Cosío-Villegas, after noting Mexico's hostility toward the United States, which he said could lead to irrational reactions, added the following: "Of course the North American, on his part, has preconceived ideas about the Mexican. There is not the slightest doubt, for example, that the Mexican is considered to be inferior, physically, intellectually, and morally."[24]

Different histories do not preclude cooperation. The very purpose of the essay by Cosío-Villegas just cited was to argue for more cooperation between Mexico and the United States despite what he called the "extreme complexity" of the relationship.[25] Another distinguished Mexican, Octavio Paz, has also commented on the differences separating the two countries and the need to overcome these in cooperative interaction: "What separates us is the very thing that unites us. We are two distinct versions of Western civilization." He referred to the "inclusive" nature of Hispanic Catholicism and the "exclusive" attitude of English Protestantism:

A society is essentially defined by its position as regards time. Because of its origin and its intellectual and political history, the United States is a society oriented towards the future. . . . The country's foundations are in the future, not the past . . . Mexico's orientation . . . was just the opposite . . . Mexico has to find her own road to modernity. Our past must not be an obstacle but a starting point. This is extremely difficult, given the nature of our tradition; difficult, but not impossible.[26]

The issue of dependence is what gives Mexican intellectuals most difficulty when considering closer integration with the United States. In a representative essay, Rico stresses that Mexican acceptance of interdependence with the United States would result in U.S. domination. He describes interdependence as an attractive instrument or slogan for those

22. López Portillo, "Sixth State of the Nation Report to the Mexican Congress," p. 261.
23. Ibid., p. 260.
24. Daniel Cosío-Villegas, "México y Estados Unidos," p. 186.
25. Ibid., p. 183.
26. Octavio Paz, "Mexico and the United States: Positions and Counterpositions," from a talk in Washington, D.C., during the Mexico Today Symposium, September 29, 1978. See also Octavio Paz, "Reflections: Mexico and the United States," pp. 136–53.

who defend the methods and needs of transnational capitalism. Interdependence, in this view, refers to relations among developed capitalist countries.[27] The difference between dependence and interdependence is not an abstraction to many Mexican intellectuals.

Another distinguished Mexican social scientist, Olga Pellicer de Brody, expressed doubt about the "sympathy" shown in various sectors of the United States for greater economic integration within North America. She concludes: "The perspective of a commercial relationship that deepens even more the Mexican dependency on the United States cannot be regarded as the best option; it necessarily assumes the exacerbation of social inequalities in Mexico and a de facto loss of national sovereignty."[28]

There is much looking to the past in Mexican writings on dependency. As Paz stated, this is hard to overcome. Ojeda's book on Mexican foreign relations compiles every conceivable post–World War II event that could be cited to show the U.S. exercise of hegemony over Mexico. Ojeda argues that to reduce this dependency, Mexico should have much broader international relations, particularly with other developing countries.[29] This was in fact the policy under Presidents Echeverría and López Portillo.

Much of Mexico's economic and foreign policy in the past fifty years can be interpreted as an effort to reduce its dependence on the United States. Mexico's trade policy and its emphasis on import substitution were designed to promote industrialization and lessen excessive dependence on exports of primary products. Mexico's unwillingness to accept

27. Carlos Rico F., "Las relaciones mexicano-norteamericanas y los significados de la 'interdependencia,' " pp. 256–91. Rico also has used strong language in opposing what he calls a North American common market in "Prospects for Economic Cooperation," in Susan Kaufman Purcell, ed., *Mexico–United States Relations*, pp. 190–91. He asserts: "For Mexico, openly accepting the principle of integration in a common market would be equivalent to recognizing the failure of the aims of independence and sovereignty that are central to the ideology of the Mexican Revolution." Further, such integration would "constitute the first step toward Mexico's becoming a part of rather than a partner of the United States."

28. Olga Pellicer de Brody, "Consideraciones acerca de la política comercial de Estados Unidos hacia México," p. 1120.

29. Mario Ojeda, *Alcances y límites de la política exterior de México*. The book examines the cold war and how the United States involved Latin America in its anticommunist policy. It stresses the extent of Mexico's trade, investment, and cultural dependence on the United States and argues that Mexico was correct in rejecting concessional aid from the United States under the Alliance for Progress, since Mexico thereby avoided becoming a U.S. satellite. The book's theme is nationalism and its thesis is that Mexico must affirm its national sovereignty.

bilateral concessional aid from the United States or a contingent of Peace Corps volunteers was part of this policy. Most of the press commentary during the Echeverría administration supported the president's efforts to expand Mexico's diplomatic relations with other countries of the third world, including, for example, Mexico's cosponsorship with Venezuela of the Sistema Económico Latinoamericano (SELA), designed to encourage a united Latin American front in bargaining with the United States.[30]

Those who supported the Echeverría foreign policy would probably be alarmed at even a hint that Mexico might, over time, move toward general free trade with the United States. They fear this would damage any leadership Mexico might otherwise enjoy among developing countries.[31] There probably would be such damage, but it is hard to know its significance for the welfare of individual Mexicans. Is the symbolism of "leadership" more important than economic growth? If Mexico grew stronger as a result of movement toward trade integration with the United States, its influence in the third world might be enhanced. In any event, this hardly seems to be an issue of lasting importance for Mexico since influence, even if it could be defined, is transitory when compared with economic development.

To the dispassionate non-Mexican observer, the crucial political issue is the nature and extent of Mexico's internal development. This, obviously, is not wholly independent of Mexico's external environment. The openness of the U.S. market to Mexican goods and the willingness of the United States to absorb hundreds of thousands, perhaps millions, of Mexican workers each year inevitably affect Mexico's internal political climate.[32] In this sense Mexico is dependent on the United States.

30. A selection of press and periodical commentary on these issues is contained in Javier Marquez, ed., *Pensamiento de México en los periódicos: Páginas editoriales, 1976.* See especially pp. 541–82 on foreign relations commentary.

31. President Echeverría proposed the Charter of Economic Rights and Duties of States at the Third United Nations Conference on Trade and Development in Santiago, Chile, in 1972, and Mexico provided the leadership in getting the resolution adopted at the United Nations General Assembly. The resolution is 3281 (XXIX) of December 12, 1974. It is interesting that the principal Mexican negotiator, Jorge Castañeda, had written much earlier about a suggestion Mexico made in 1949 that there be an annex to the U.N. Charter to be called a "Declaration on Rights and Duties of States." See Castañeda. *Mexico and the United Nations,* pp. 24–36.

32. Based on data from the Immigration and Naturalization Service (*Annual Reports* for the years in question), an annual average of 868,000 persons were deported or

However, the conditions in Mexico that for the last several years have led to unemployment, underemployment, and high rates of population growth—among the factors encouraging emigration—are the consequence mainly of internal policy. Mexico's import substitution development model, for example, explains more about the general noncompetitiveness of Mexican manufactured goods in export markets than do import restrictions in the United States and other countries. The relative capital intensity of Mexican industry stems primarily from Mexican development policy, abetted to some extent by how foreign investors have mixed capital and labor in their production processes.[33] Inequality in income distribution and in the distribution of economic activity among Mexico's states also flows from internal power relationships and decisions in Mexico. In short, Mexico is responsible for the politics of its development; scapegoating the United States (because of annexation, intervention, or condescension) is only a diversion.

Mexico's attempts to avoid dependence on the United States have met with some success. A Mexican industrial structure does exist. Overall growth rates were high for twenty-five years, although with some pauses and a severe setback starting in 1982. Mexico's main failures have been the general noncompetitiveness of Mexican industry and the inability to provide employment for a large part of Mexico's economically active population. This is Mexico's enduring political problem. A country that must export up to 10 percent of its potential work force cannot easily escape dependence regardless of other actions it takes.[34]

The critical political issue, therefore, assuming that Mexico can

---

required to depart from the United States to Mexico from 1975 to 1977. The current deportation and departure figures exceed 1 million annually. Some of these represent repeat offenders, which tends to inflate the numbers, and many Mexicans who cross the border without documents are never caught, which gives a downward bias to the number of undocumented Mexican workers. It is not known how many Mexicans come to the United States each year without documents and how many stay.

33. The industrial development plan document developed during the López Portillo administration recognized these problems but did not emphasize the labor-intensity of industry. See chapter 5 for a discussion of this plan.

34. In round numbers, Mexico's economically active population totals 20 million. If the number of Mexicans permanently living in the United States without documents is 3 million and if the annual flow adds another million who come to work and then return to Mexico, these 4 million represent about 20 percent of Mexico's economically active population. In my view, this is dependency, and no rhetoric about broader international relations can alter this.

overcome its historical aversion to the United States, is whether a move toward free trade will help or hinder Mexico in creating sufficient jobs for its young and growing population. Other issues such as political dependency and unity with the third world have political implications and may therefore obscure objective economic analysis. It would be naive to expect these issues to go away, but they are more obstacles than aids to looking ahead.

In addition to the conceptual opposition to a movement toward bilateral free trade, there would be practical opposition on economic grounds. These issues will be taken up in later chapters. The economic considerations would be reflected in any national political debate in Mexico. Because many small manufacturing plants would be threatened if their protection disappeared, their owners would oppose greater trade integration just as their trade organization opposed Mexico's entry into GATT. (This will be discussed further in chapter 4.) Producers of competing agriculture products, particularly grains, would oppose free trade unless their sector of agriculture were excluded. It is hard to predict how labor would react. Organized labor would be concerned about a possible limitation of wage increases to make Mexican industry more competitive. Many workers, like small industrialists, would fear the loss of jobs. On the other hand, if trade integration succeeded, wages would become more equal with those in the United States. Many Mexicans in the work force are not part of organized labor, so they should have no strong feeling against greater trade integration, which would not threaten them.

The debate in Mexico on bilateral free trade would thus be a combination of the conceptual concern about dependency and its political and economic ramifications, compounded by a historically based animosity toward the United States, and the practical concern of who loses from free trade and who might gain. The conceptual and the practical would merge in the actual political process. This hostile and exploitive yet cooperative attitude toward the United States already exists among Mexicans. Attitude surveys show substantial animosity toward the United States for its treatment of Mexico but simultaneously a belief that the United States is the country with which Mexico should work most closely, both politically and economically.[35]

35. USICA, "Mexico, Reluctant Friend of the U.S.," p. 45; USICA, "Better-Educated Mexicans Have Serious Misperceptions of U.S."

An analysis of the economics of trade integration occupies most of the remainder of this book, but the practical assessment of these economics would take political form in Mexico, as it would in the United States.

U.S. Political Concerns

The asymmetry in power between the United States and Mexico has been reflected in asymmetry of attention paid by policymakers of each country to the other. No matter how much Mexico has broadened its formal relations in Latin America and elsewhere, the United States has been the center of Mexico's international relations. This has been dictated by the economics and politics of foreign trade and investment and the extensive social interaction between the two countries. Mexico's foreign investment laws have been directed primarily at curbing U.S. control of vital areas of Mexico's economy. The logical market for Mexican natural gas exports is the United States. Tourism earnings and the contracting of foreign debt that helped finance Mexico's trade and current account deficits came primarily from the United States or U.S. banks in the Eurodollar market. The escape valve for unemployed and underemployed Mexicans is emigration to the United States.

On the other hand, U.S. sales of goods to Mexico, although substantial, have represented only 5 to 7 percent of total U.S. merchandise exports in recent years. U.S. investment in Mexico, also significant, was only 2.4 percent of the total book value of U.S. foreign direct investment at the end of 1979. Mexico tends to capture the attention of most Americans only at times of crisis. Some examples of such crises are the program introduced in 1942 to compensate for manpower shortages in the United States during World War II, and the effort made in 1969 to control entry of drugs into the United States from Mexico.[36] U.S. attention on Mexico in the late 1970s was stimulated by U.S. concern about oil shortages and Mexico's discovery of potentially huge oil and natural gas reserves. U.S. attention focused on Mexico in 1976, when the peso was devalued and short-term lending was granted to Mexico,

---

36. Known as Operation Intercept. Ojeda, *Alcances y límites de la política exterior de México*, pp. 154–55, cites this unilateral U.S. action as the clearest proof of Mexican vulnerability to decisions made by other countries.

and again in 1982–83, when the peso was devalued still more and Mexico was unable to meet its scheduled debt obligations. In short, the United States has dealt with Mexico mostly in terms of an actual or perceived crisis and in a generally unilateral or unequal fashion. A U.S. approach to a progressive move to general or selective free trade with Mexico from this standpoint would obviously be unacceptable to Mexico and would intensify Mexican fears of dependency.

However, one big difference between the present and past U.S. attitude is the existence of Mexican oil, which already has aroused emotions of U.S. dependence on Mexico. Mutual dependencies—the United States over time on Mexican oil and on the growing Mexican market for goods, and Mexico on the U.S. market for its goods and services and for the export of its labor—are among the bases for interdependence. But the Mexicans have not yet learned how to deal with U.S. demand for Mexican oil and tend to interpret this as U.S. exploitation.[37] It is equally true that the United States has not learned how to deal with Mexico on a more equal basis. President Jimmy Carter's unilateral introduction of legislation on illegal immigration, which if enacted could have had a more profound effect in Mexico than in the United States, was a vivid example of old patterns of thought. There was more consultation with Mexico when President Ronald Reagan submitted immigration legislation, but policymakers only superficially considered its potential effect on Mexico.[38]

Many businesses and agricultural producers in the United States would undoubtedly greet the proposal of free trade with Mexico as an opportunity to penetrate and exploit a market that is now highly protected. (Much of this exploitation presumably would come from production in the United States.) However, this would not be the only U.S.

37. One example of this was the speech President López Portillo gave at the dinner given for President Carter on February 14, 1979, at the Ministry of Foreign Relations in Mexico City, in which he referred to "deceit and sudden abuse" in an obvious allusion to U.S. behavior toward Mexico. Another was the article by Carlos Fuentes, "Listen, Yankee! Mexico Is a Nation, Not an Oil Well," *Washington Post*, February 11, 1979.

38. U.S. government officials told the author that there was prior consultation with Mexican authorities before the Carter administration submitted its immigration legislation but that the Mexicans did not respond. In any event, the consultations were not extensive for an issue of such great importance to Mexico. The Reagan administration seems to have been more meticulous in its consultations with Mexico on immigration policy, although this does not imply Mexican agreement with the proposed legislation as submitted or as it was altered in Congress.

reaction. U.S. labor would probably oppose free trade, no matter how long the transition period, out of fear of a mass exodus of production facilities from the United States to low-wage areas in Mexico. Free trade would be perceived as diminishing protection for such sensitive U.S. industries as textiles, clothing, and shoes and as an eventual threat, therefore, to many other types of consumer-goods production. With free trade, special arrangements under the U.S. tariff schedule, in which U.S. import duties are paid only on the value of the goods added outside the United States, would lose relevance even if 100 percent of the value originated in Mexico. If free trade were general, restrictions on imports of textiles and apparel from Mexico under the umbrella of the international textile arrangement would eventually cease to apply. The U.S. industries involved and their workers almost certainly would oppose complete freedom of trade for these products. Agricultural producers now protected from Mexican competition would oppose free trade of agricultural products. The heaviest protection is the seasonal duties, ranging in some cases to almost 50 percent, on a variety of fruits and vegetables.[39] Many agricultural products also are subject to federal marketing orders regulating product grade, size, and quality, whether domestically produced or imported. Mexico has complained from time to time about the protective effect of these orders, particularly on tomatoes.

These examples of tariff and other import restrictions on goods from Mexico illustrate one aspect of the political problem facing the United States if a movement to free trade between the two countries were launched. In each case cited, the protection exists in the United States because Mexico has a comparative advantage in the production of the restricted products; under free trade, this advantage would be given full rein over time.

To improve its efficiency, the United States should presumably allow its protected industries to survive or founder on their own. Given long enough lead times, it may be possible to overcome the political opposition to trade liberalization for these labor-intensive activities. Perhaps most

39. An interesting analysis of the cost of these restrictions for Mexico is in Carlos Pomareda, "Evaluación de la política comercial de Estados Unidos sobre importaciones de hortalizas," pp. 1244–62. David R. Mares, "Agricultural Trade: Domestic Interests and Transnational Relations," in Jorge I. Dominguez, ed., *Mexico's Political Economy: Challenges at Home and Abroad,* pp. 79–132, discusses Mexican politics and the U.S. and Mexican interests in the tomato trade.

of the current restrictions on textiles and clothing, for example, could eventually be reduced or eliminated even without a special arrangement with Mexico. The main difference between a general freeing of imports of these items and doing it in the context of an agreement with Mexico is that in the latter case, Mexico would be the beneficiary. In the former, other producers more efficient than Mexico would probably be the main beneficiaries.[40] U.S. producers of these products are more likely to survive loss of protection if free entry is confined to Mexican products and not expanded to Asian products as well. More persistent problems than any resulting from the lifting of import restrictions might occur in industries in which Mexican competitive ability would come into play only gradually. What these industries might be is speculation, but considering Mexican priorities, capital goods and consumer industries would most likely be affected.[41]

Free trade in any of the industries Mexico plans to encourage might stimulate production in Mexico, the United States, or both through greater specialization. The last possibility would have to predominate if free trade were to benefit both countries. In any event, many U.S. industries will have trouble accepting the possibility that they have anything to gain in a movement toward free trade between Mexico and the United States.[42]

Many persons and organizations in the United States would also fear that free trade with Mexico would lead to legalized movement of Mexican labor into the country. This concern would be job related, on the same grounds that the AFL-CIO now opposes the entry of temporary workers from Mexico.[43] There might also be concern that the entry of Mexicans would change the ethnic composition and political power structure of many cities and states, particularly in the Southwest.[44]

40. Susumu Watanabe, "Constraints on Labour-Intensive Export Industries in Mexico," p. 39.

41. Secretaría de Patrimonio y Fomento Industrial, *Plan nacional de desarrollo industrial, 1979–1982.*

42. Gunnar Myrdal, *Economic Theory and Under-Developed Regions.* R. L. Birmingham, "Interterritorial Imbalance in Customs Unions among Developing Economies: Adjustment Mechanisms," compiles on pp. 276–79 citations on imbalance or polarization of development between more- and less-developed regions or economies.

43. For example, see statement by the AFL-CIO executive council of August 29, 1977. The statement argues that "illegal alien workers . . . take jobs from Americans and undermine U.S. wages and working conditions." Some variant of this statement has appeared annually ever since.

44. A good summary of the racist content of past and current U.S. immigration policy can be found in the U.S. Select Commission on Immigration and Refugee Policy, *U.S. Immigration Policy and the National Interest,* pp. 161–220.

However, as already noted, free movement of goods does not necessarily imply free movement of labor. In fact, most intercountry economic integration schemes have not included legal free movement of labor.

Fears in the United States about an influx of Mexican labor are emotional and so would be just as hard to dispel as Mexico's fears of dependency. A large number of Mexicans now enter the country regardless of legalities, and it is unlikely that the United States will be able to stanch this entry in the foreseeable future. The United States may not even want to curtail the entry of Mexican workers because, first, they may be needed to fill jobs in the secondary (lower-paying) labor market,[45] and second, because an abrupt halt of emigration from Mexico could lead to social and political instability there. This is a particularly delicate matter at a time of economic crisis in Mexico, such as in 1983. A primary U.S. foreign policy goal with respect to Mexico is that the latter be stable. If a choice had to be made, curtailment of emigration would be sacrificed for political stability.

U.S. opposition to movement toward free trade with Mexico would be based on traditional protectionist and predictable emotional grounds, mirroring the conceptual and practical political opposition that would emerge in Mexico. The emotion in Mexico would be historically based, whereas the emotion in the United States would be based primarily on fear of the future.[46] In both cases, the emotional reaction would have to be addressed by showing that free trade would mutually benefit both countries.

Possible Political Effects of Free Trade

One practical argument made by early advocates of a common market in Western Europe was that steps toward economic integration would lead to greater political cohesion. This was the vision of Jean Monnet, the man who has been called the father of European integration. To some degree, political cohesion has taken place in Europe. Free trade

45. There have been several studies on the age structure of the U.S. population that predict labor-supply shortages of persons in lower-paying occupations in the United States in the 1990s. For example, see Clark W. Reynolds, "Labor Market Projections for the United States and Mexico and Their Relevance to Current Migration Controversies," pp. 121–55.

46. This conforms with the comments of Octavio Paz, cited earlier, that the United States is a society oriented to the future, whereas Mexico looks more to the past.

evolved into a common commercial policy, and a common agricultural policy also exists. Both policies have considerable political implications for the member countries of the European Community. For example, labor is freer to move across borders than it was before the EC's formation. There have been attempts to construct a common monetary policy, but this has been difficult to achieve because of disparate economic tendencies in the member countries. There is no unified capital market. Above all, there is no political federation in Western Europe and no current expectation that this will be achieved, although political cooperation has been enhanced and EC countries sometimes take common positions. Most did so in 1982, declaring a trade boycott against Argentina following the invasion of the Falkland Islands, but then other countries, such as the United States, took similar action without the stimulus of EC membership. In fact, the EC is more than a customs union but far from an economic or political union. In trade integration schemes that were never intended to have political spillovers, there were none.[47] It was difficult enough in these cases to achieve free trade among the members, let alone labor, monetary, or capital market integration or political cohesion.

There are many examples of the lack of political spillovers from trade integration. The Latin American Free Trade Association (LAFTA) never managed to achieve even free trade. The Central American Common Market, which was more successful than the LAFTA in its trade measures, foundered in part because of the military conflict between El Salvador and Honduras. There were no political effects in the East African Common Market (Kenya, Tanzania, and Uganda) and none in the Andean Pact in South America. The United States and Canada reached agreement on substantial bilateral free trade in the automotive sector, and that is as far as free trade went. There was no progression from one sector to another and certainly no political results.

The historical evidence is that political results of moves toward free trade are rare. They may occur if they are wanted, as in the German *Zollverein* (customs union), but even then circumstances have to make the political outcomes propitious. Political outcomes are so improbable if they are not wanted that they can be dismissed as an argument for or against a free-trade agreement. The examination in this book of the costs

47. Hansen has called the spillover effect from the economic to the political a weakness of earlier integration models of industrial countries when applied to developing countries. Roger D. Hansen, "Regional Integration: Reflections on a Decade of Theoretical Efforts," pp. 242-71.

and benefits of a movement toward free trade between the United States and Mexico assumes that no further steps toward economic integration need ensue and that political outcomes will be negligible. For political cohesion to occur, the two countries would have to make additional decisions to bring this about. It is hard to conceive that free trade could lead to anything approaching political union.[48]

This is not to say that there will be no political outcomes of any kind from a movement toward bilateral free trade. The rationale for trade integration must be that it would help each country solve some of its economic problems. One would expect, therefore, that there would be ramifications for the industrial structure of each country. Habits of consultation between officials and businessmen of the two countries would develop, as they have in other countries with free-trade agreements. This could affect not only mutual trade but also related areas such as the flow of technology and even the educational systems, which could contribute to more efficient trade cooperation and industrial specialization. Movement of capital and labor could become freer between two countries in which there is already substantial movement of these factors due to free trade. Also, although a common commercial policy need not follow bilateral free trade any more than free movement of capital and labor, each country would at least have to consult the other before it adopted new commercial policy measures that would affect the other.

These outcomes of free trade would, in a limited way, detract from national sovereignty, especially in the commercial policy area. However, the constraints on sovereignty would be modest and need not affect vital national interests, such as oil policy in Mexico or oil and natural gas pricing policy in the United States. That an actual loss of Mexican sovereignty would result from a move to free trade with the United States is unsupported by historical experience.

Political Arguments Favoring Free Trade

For Mexico trade integration would have to accelerate the creation of jobs, and for the United States it would have to increase productivity,

48. In writing about European economic integration, Lawrence B. Krause commented: "What is certain is that political integration will occur only as a result of a positive political decision to bring it about, not as a result of economic pressures alone." Krause, *European Economic Integration and the United States*, p. 24.

presumably in capital- or skill-intensive activities. These are economic but also central political objectives in each country.

The discussion in this chapter has focused on the political concerns that would have to be overcome if movement toward free trade made sense otherwise. However, there are some arguments that support the idea of trade integration, which might help each country look to the dynamics of its comparative advantages in a bilateral free-trade area. Reductions of trade barriers could take place in small increments so that there would be ample time for adjustment. Markets that are becoming increasingly integrated (apparently partly through smuggling goods into Mexico to evade quantitative restrictions and tariff barriers[49]) could become so legally, which would benefit consumers in both countries. If each country were able to improve its competitive position as a result of greater efficiencies, their mutual dependencies could be reduced, since the worldwide competitive positions of each would simultaneously be improved.[50] A trading arrangement with the United States need not tie Mexico's trade exclusively to the United States any more than German or French trade is exclusively tied to the EC countries. The free-trade arrangement would be a failure if such exclusivity resulted. Both countries would have to be convinced of mutual and relatively equal benefits resulting from greater trade integration.

49. An article by Marlise Simons, "Mexico Seeks Carter's Aid to Cut Smuggling from U.S.," *Washington Post*, February 13, 1979, stated that Mexican sources estimated contraband imports into Mexico from the United States at $1 billion a year.

50. In an analysis of the Andean common market, Diaz-Alejandro made the following comment: "The new competitive climate may also induce entrepreneurs . . . who often have been lulled into a fat oligopolistic tranquility by excessive protection, to become truly modern managers on the lookout for cost reducing innovations, and who will be able to operate successfully not only in large Latin-American markets, but also in new export markets in the rest of the world." Carlos F. Diaz-Alejandro, "The Andean Common Market: Gestation and Outlook," in R. S. Eckaus and P. N. Rosenstein-Rodan, eds., *Analysis of Development Problems: Studies of the Chilean Economy*, p. 308.

CHAPTER THREE

U.S.-Mexican Trade

WHEN Mexicans allude to the lingering aspects of dependency, they generally focus on two economic themes: the extent and industry composition of U.S. direct investment in Mexico and the dominance of the United States in Mexico's foreign trade. When the two heads of state get together, one item on the agenda usually deals with U.S. protection-ism—both actual restrictions, such as on textiles and apparel, and the threat of restrictions, such as on fresh tomatoes and other vegetables. This chapter will examine the current bilateral trade structure and analyze the justification for Mexico's trade complaints. If there were a movement toward free trade between the two countries, U.S. trade restrictions against Mexico would disappear gradually. But so would Mexico's restrictions against imports from the United States, which are more extensive; that, of course is the core of Mexico's resistance.

Current Bilateral Trade

Trade between Mexico and the United States grew substantially in recent years (tables 3-1 and 3-2) until 1982, when Mexico was forced to limit imports in order to meet a balance-of-payments crisis. U.S. imports from Mexico increased by an average of 36.5 percent a year in current dollars, or by 24.4 percent in 1976 dollars, from 1976 through 1980. U.S. exports to Mexico during the same period grew by an average of 32 percent a year in current dollars and by 20.3 percent in constant 1976 dollars. In 1976 Mexico was the third largest market for U.S. merchandise exports, after Canada and Japan, and remained third in 1980. Mexico grew from being the sixth largest supplier to the United States of merchandise imports in 1976 to the third in 1980, after Canada and Japan.

Table 3-1. *U.S. Merchandise Imports from Mexico, 1976–80*a

Product	1976	1977	1978	1979	1980
	Millions of dollars				
Food, beverages, and tobacco	884	1,235	1,315	1,566	1,414
Industrial supplies	615	1,071	1,676	3,267	6,805
Petroleum and petroleum products	447	890	1,517	3,068	6,041
Manufactures	1,944	2,170	2,859	3,694	3,955
Other	163	218	243	287	345
Total	3,606	4,694	6,093	8,813	12,519
	Percent				
Food, beverages, and tobacco	24.5	26.3	21.6	17.8	11.3
Industrial supplies	17.1	22.8	27.5	37.1	54.4
Petroleum and petroleum products	12.4	19.0	24.9	34.8	48.3
Manufactures	53.9	46.2	46.9	41.9	31.6
Other	4.5	4.6	4.0	3.3	2.8
Total	100.0	100.0	100.0	100.0	100.0

Source: U.S. Bureau of the Census, *U.S. General Imports: World Area by Commodity Groupings,* FT 155, annual reports for respective years. Figures are rounded.
a. Data differ from Mexican trade data.

Table 3-2. *U.S. Merchandise Exports to Mexico, 1976–80*

Product	1976	1977	1978	1979	1980
	Millions of dollars				
Food, beverages, and tobacco	249	484	537	760	1,911
Industrial supplies	497	520	798	912	1,510
Manufactures	3,972	3,544	4,892	7,555	10,925
Other	185	174	314	436	536
Total	4,904	4,723	6,542	9,667	14,885
	Percent				
Food, beverages, and tobacco	5.1	10.2	8.2	7.9	12.8
Industrial supplies	10.1	11.0	12.2	9.4	10.1
Manufactures	81.0	75.0	74.8	78.2	73.4
Other	3.8	3.7	4.8	4.5	3.6
Total	100.0	100.0	100.0	100.0	100.0

Source: U.S. Bureau of the Census, *U.S. Exports: World Area by Commodity Groupings,* FT 455, annual reports for respective years. Figures are rounded.

In total bilateral trade, counting both U.S. exports and imports, Mexico was the third most important U.S. trading partner in 1980, after Canada and Japan. Another way to look at this growth is to note the significant increase in the proportion of imports from Mexico as a percentage of total U.S. imports. This proportion grew from 3 percent in 1976 to 5.2 percent in 1980. U.S. exports to Mexico in 1976 were 4.3 percent of total U.S. exports. The pattern was irregular in the subsequent years but the trend was definitely upward, reaching 6.9 percent in 1980.

The United States has been México's dominant trade partner for the same period, and the relative importance of the United States in México's trade has remained stable. At the same time, the relative importance of Mexico in U.S. trade has grown.[1] Mexico has deliberately tried to diversify its trade to reduce its dependence, but there has been precious little diversification away from the United States—except to some extent for oil, but this is really a superficial spreading of one category of exports for which there is a world market. The biggest increase in U.S. imports has been in petroleum and petroleum products, which in 1980 amounted to almost half of the value of U.S. imports from Mexico. Since petroleum and petroleum products accounted for about two-thirds of Mexico's exports to all destinations in 1980,[2] it would seem that Mexico's exports to the United States are at least more diversified than they are to other countries.

The most substantial proportionate increase in U.S. exports to Mexico has been for food, feed, and related products, from 5.1 percent of total U.S. exports to Mexico in 1976 to 12.8 percent in 1980. The magnitude of Mexico's agricultural imports in 1980 became a domestic political issue—some argued that Mexico was exporting its oil mainly to feed itself—and stimulated the López Portillo administration to create a plan for allocating more resources to agriculture. The lagging growth in agricultural production (since 1965 lower than population growth) has been one of the acknowledged failures of Mexico's development.

Omitting petroleum, the category breakdown of trade in both directions is superficially similar (tables 3-3 and 3-4). Manufactures dominate the nonpetroleum trade in both directions, but the content of the manufactures is quite different. U.S. manufactured exports to Mexico are about 90 percent capital and other nonconsumer goods, but about two-thirds of Mexico's manufactured exports are consumer goods.[3] Mexico deliberately seeks to limit consumer imports, including food, when it can.

1. The figures on U.S. trade come from the U.S. Bureau of the Census and those on Mexican trade from the Banco de México. The bilateral trade data are taken from U.S. sources, and these differ from data taken from Mexican sources. Both sets of sources, however, yield the same conclusions.
2. Banco de México, *Informe Anual, 1980*, pp. 177–83.
3. Schedule A (U.S. imports) and Schedule E (U.S. exports), codes 5 through 7, were categorized as nonconsumer goods and code 8 as consumer goods. This general assumption was modified for particular items not fitting either category to obtain percentages cited.

Table 3-3. *Main U.S. Imports from Mexico, 1980*
Millions of dollars

Product	Amount
Food and live animals	1,316.2
Beverages and tobacco	98.2
Crude materials, inedible, except fuel	208.9
Mineral fuels, lubricants, and related materials	6,592.6
Animal and vegetable oils and fats	3.8
Chemicals and related products	275.1
Manufactured goods	762.6
Machinery and transport equipment	2,047.0
Miscellaneous manufactured articles	870.3
Articles not classified elsewhere	344.8
All imports from Mexico	12,519.5

Source: U.S. Bureau of the Census, *U.S. General Imports*, FT 155, Annual 1980, pp. 3-14 and 3-17 through 3-23.

Table 3-4. *Main U.S. Exports to Mexico, 1980*
Millions of dollars

Product	Amount
Food and live animals	1,908.3
Beverages and tobacco	2.6
Crude materials, inedible, except fuel	1,078.7
Mineral fuels, lubricants, and related materials	340.9
Animal and vegetable oils, fats, and waxes	90.3
Chemicals and related products	1,441.5
Manufactured goods	2,063.4
Machinery and transport equipment	6,563.5
Miscellaneous manufactured articles	856.6
Commerce and transactions not classified elsewhere	535.8
All exports to Mexico	14,884.8

Source: U.S. Bureau of the Census, *U.S. Exports*, FT 455, Annual 1980, pp. 3-14 and 3-17 through 3-25.

The sheer volume of bilateral trade dictates that there will be an inevitable mutual attraction of export markets. For now and the foreseeable future, growing sales to the United States do and will make a vital contribution to Mexico's economic health. In 1980 merchandise exports were an estimated 9.2 percent of Mexico's gross domestic product (GDP) and exports of goods and services were 14.9 percent. Exports of merchandise to the United States alone made up 6 percent of Mexico's GDP in 1980, and of goods and services about 10 percent. There is no current substitute for the U.S. market if Mexico is to meet its growth and development objectives. Mexico is justifiably concerned about signs of U.S. protectionism. Mexico also obviously has a clear stake in the health of the U.S. economy and was adversely affected by the U.S. recession in 1982.

The United States is not as dependent on the Mexican market as Mexico is on the U.S. market. Merchandise sales to Mexico in 1980, while significant, made up only about half of 1 percent of the U.S. gross national product (GNP). If U.S. sales of services to Mexico are added—especially investment income—the proportion would increase slightly but probably not by more than a tenth of 1 percent. Mexico is not a crucial source of vital raw materials for the United States, except for oil, but even in this case the most important U.S. interest is served when Mexico makes crude oil available in the world market.

This difference in dependency inevitably colors the thinking of economic actors and policymakers in the two countries. U.S. economic actors focus mainly on the opportunities that exist for them in both direct investment in and exports to Mexico. Mexican actors also focus on opportunities, but they and the government concentrate more on U.S. protectionism than the United States does on Mexican protectionism. The daily press in the United States does not dwell constantly on Mexico's investment and trade restrictions; the daily press in Mexico does keep its readers informed about U.S. trade policy actions.[4] U.S. presidents, even U.S. secretaries of state, do not normally inform themselves of the minutiae of even U.S. trade policy, let alone of Mexico's policy; Mexican presidents and foreign ministers must be informed in detail about both U.S. and domestic trade policy. Trade policy is at the heart of Mexican politics. Mexican presidents often try to resolve trade issues at summit meetings with U.S. presidents. U.S. presidents, on the other hand, generally delegate this responsibility to subordinates, and then these senior subordinates redelegate the responsibility further downward in the bureaucracy.

What finally made U.S. senior officials aware of Mexico's economic importance was the fact that Mexico, from which lines of transportation

4. This attention on U.S. trade actions must contribute to the perceptions of persons surveyed in Mexico City in August 1979, a majority of whom (59 percent) believed it was easier for the United States to export its products to Mexico. A minority (12 percent) felt it was easier for Mexico to export its products to the United States. USICA, "Mexico, Reluctant Friend of the U.S.: Mexico City Opinion on Bilateral and International Issues," Research Memorandum, prepared by William J. Millard (USICA, September 12, 1979), p. 28.

were reasonably secure, was becoming a major supplier of oil to the world. This stimulated the idea of a North American common market for energy. This was a visceral U.S. reaction; Mexico's reaction was just as instinctive and predictably negative. Despite all the rhetoric surrounding the U.S. suggestion for a common market just for energy, the motive was evident: the United States wanted preferred access over all other countries to Mexican oil. When this idea did not prosper, it became apparent that the revenue from oil exports created market opportunities in Mexico for many types of U.S. goods and services. Mexico's optimistic plans for GDP growth of about 8 to 10 percent a year through the 1980s whetted this appetite for the Mexican market. U.S. suppliers are well positioned to take advantage of Mexican import growth because of the U.S. dominance in trade relations, the familiarity between buyers and suppliers, and the transportation cost advantages over competitors in Europe and Asia. This opportunity, not vague mutterings about a common market for energy, dominates the thinking of economic actors in the United States.

Official U.S. attention on Mexico grew when the extent of Mexico's financial and economic crisis became evident in 1982. Mexico's inability to service its debt on schedule raised fears about the solvency of some U.S. banks because of their loan exposure in Mexico.[5] The decline in Mexico's economic growth and the consequent increase in unemployment caused concern about political and social instability and a quantum increase in illegal Mexican migration to the United States.

If Mexico recovers from its economic crisis, the estimate made by Mexico's National Industrial Development Plan in 1979 that merchandise imports would increase in current dollars from $17 billion in 1982 to $90 billion in 1990 is probably conservative.[6] The estimate was even conservative when it was issued, since imports in 1980 were already $18.5 billion. Part of the conservatism was due to the underestimation of petroleum production and exports and of export revenue from petroleum. U.S. exports to Mexico, which tripled between 1976 and 1980, will probably at least triple by 1990, assuming that Mexico recovers rapidly from its economic crisis. This would make U.S. exports to Mexico, in

5. This concern was discussed in the statement by Paul A. Volcker, chairman, Board of Governors of the Federal Reserve System, in *International Financial Markets and Related Problems*, House Hearings, pp. 41–89.

6. Secretaría de Patrimonio y Fomento Industrial, *Plan nacional de desarrollo industrial, 1979–1982*, p. 115.

current dollars, about $45 billion in 1990. This is a conservative projection based on experience before the 1982 economic crisis and assumes that economic stabilization in Mexico will be achieved by 1984 or 1985.

Another way to look at this potential growth is to compare U.S. exports to Mexico with those to Canada. U.S. exports to Canada in 1980 were $34 billion compared with exports to Mexico of $15 billion. Since Canada has a population of 24 million, this represents $1,420 worth of U.S. exports for each Canadian. Mexico's population is about 70 million, so the value of U.S. exports in 1980 for each Mexican was $213. The disparity is a reflection of per capita income differences between Mexico and Canada.[7] If Mexico is able to restore its economic growth, the market growth potential in Mexico is substantially greater than that in Canada because so many more imports are required to sustain that growth, despite the far richer and therefore more important current market in Canada.

This potential exists regardless of whether or not free trade is established between the United States and Mexico. Expanding U.S. opportunity depends on restored economic growth in Mexico and the avoidance of Mexican actions that would discriminate against the United States as a source of imports. If free trade stimulated Mexican growth, it would also, therefore, enhance the market potential for the United States and secure it even more, since the discrimination in that case would favor the United States over other external suppliers.

Bilateral Trade Complaints

Although bilateral trade thrived until 1982, the trade relationship between the United States and Mexico has not been without friction. There have been some constants in the mutual recriminations about each other's trading practices and other specific complaints that alter as circumstances change. Before examining mutual trade complaints, it may be useful to summarize the essential elements of trade policy. This is done in the next section for U.S. trade policy and to some extent for Mexican trade policy. Mexican policy is analyzed in greater detail in chapter 4.

7. Population and GNP data are from World Bank, *1981 World Bank Atlas*, p. 20.

Key Elements of U.S. Trade Policy

Except in relations with communist countries—that is, countries with centrally planned economies in which trading is controlled by the state—the United States practices multilateralism in its external trade. Ever since its establishment shortly after World War II, the General Agreement on Tariffs and Trade has been the principal forum where major trade initiatives to reduce trade barriers have been launched and where trade disagreements have been discussed. The GATT articles of agreement, as amended from time to time, contain a reasonably accurate summary of the philosophy that guides U.S. trade policy. Two features of these articles merit special attention: the most-favored-nation (MFN) principle and the exchange of rights and obligations inherent in this international agreement. Mexico is not a contracting party to the GATT and so has no obligation under it, but Mexico does benefit from the GATT's MFN principle.

The MFN principle is one of nondiscrimination. No foreign country to which MFN treatment is extended is treated less favorably than the most favored foreign country. In the absence of a specific bilateral agreement or treaty, the United States is under no legal obligation to extend MFN treatment to any country that is not a contracting party to the GATT. One of the major accomplishments of nations acting under the aegis of the GATT has been to reduce tariffs, and under the MFN principle these reductions apply to imports from Mexico as well as to imports from GATT members. However, the United States would not violate its international commitments if it nullified these tariff reductions for Mexico, although Mexico would undoubtedly retaliate by increasing its tariffs as well.

As a general rule, the United States has not wished to make bilateral agreements outside the GATT calling for MFN trade treatment. Any such bilateral agreement would have to deal with more than the MFN principle and cover other matters dealt with in the GATT articles, such as procedures for settling disputes, handling of dumping and subsidies, reciprocity, the nature of tariff and other trade negotiations, and a host of other technical matters. But the United States has in recent decades made bilateral trade agreements with communist countries, for example, since most of them are not contracting parties to the GATT, which is not well designed to deal with their state trading system. The GATT does have provisions dealing with state trading, but it is dealt with as an exception to the general philosophy of market-oriented exchange underlying the GATT.[8] The use of tariffs as the main protective device, which is built into the GATT articles, presupposes a trading system under which the price of a good is a major determinant in its exchange. Under state trading, other considerations generally play the dominant role in the direction of trade, and the tariff, therefore, has different implications for a state-trading country than for a market-oriented country. This is why the United States has made an exception for communist countries and used bilateral agreements rather than the provisions of the GATT as a basis for trading relations.

Despite public ownership of many large companies, Mexico is predominantly a market-directed international trader. In theory, Mexico treats traders from all foreign countries alike; that is, it offers them MFN treatment. There are exceptions to this, such as the preferences offered within Latin American economic integration schemes, but even the GATT articles contain such exceptions.[9] Mexico's use of nontariff measures such as import licenses to protect its domestic industry and agriculture means, however, that the dominant philosophy of Mexico's industrial and trade policy is different from that which permeates the articles of the GATT. Mexican economists occasionally recommend to the Mexican government that it expose Mexican industry more fully to price competition by shifting from absolute protection of domestic industry—inherent in import licensing—to more modest price protection. Moderate tariffs varying according to the degree of protection the country wished to offer different industries would accomplish this. Mexican economists do not as a rule prescribe for Mexico a uniform tariff for all imports to eliminate the favoring of some industries over others, a policy many economists support.

Mexican authorities might or might not support the idea of a bilateral trade agreement with the United States to make legally explicit what is now embedded in practice, but a bilateral trade agreement with Mexico has never found favor in the U.S. government. A bilateral agreement with a trading partner as significant for the United States as Mexico is would raise questions about U.S. support of the GATT. Mexico is not the only developing country that relies heavily on nontariff measures in its industrial and trade policy. An exception for Mexico would probably

8. State trading is dealt with in article 17 of the GATT.
9. The customs-union and free-trade area exception to the MFN principle is contained in article 24 of the GATT.

lead to a clamor from other developing countries for similar bilateral agreements with them, even if they were GATT contracting parties. Such bilateral agreements might only replicate the GATT, and in doing so possibly undermine its future. Bilateral agreements could, of course, specify what and how much trade countries might want with each other under the provisions of the GATT, but the United States has seen no valid purpose in concluding such agreements.[10] In any event, this type of agreement would not apply to U.S. trade relations with Mexico since the latter's objection to adhering to the GATT is based on its provisions and philosophy.

One area in which the United States and Mexico have been negotiating a possible bilateral agreement concerns the granting of trade subsidies by the Mexican government and the treatment of such subsidized exports by the United States. Mexico's failure to adhere to the code on subsidies and countervailing duties agreed to in the Tokyo round of multilateral trade negotiations has meant that the mere existence of an export subsidy by the Mexican government subjects the product in question to a possible countervailing duty by the United States. For signatories to the code, the United States cannot impose a countervailing duty to compensate for foreign subsidies without showing that the subsidy caused injury to a domestic industry.[11] As of late 1983, it had not been possible to conclude the agreement with Mexico.[12] The issue is a difficult one for

10. Other countries have used bilateral trade agreements to supplement their GATT rights and obligations. Mexico, using the leverage of its oil exports, reached bilateral trade agreements with various GATT contracting parties, such as Canada, Japan, and countries of the European Community.

11. In accepting the protocol of provisional application of the GATT of 1947, the United States was obligated to accept part 2 of the agreement "to the fullest extent not inconsistent with existing legislation." The existing U.S. legislation did not require an injury test, whereas article 6:6(a) provided that "no contracting party shall levy any . . . countervailing duty . . . unless it determines that the effect of the . . . subsidization . . . is such as to cause or threaten material injury to an established domestic industry, or is such as to retard materially the establishment of a domestic industry." GATT, *Basic Instruments and Selected Documents*, vol. 1 (revised), article 6:6(a), p. 17. In signing the agreement of April 12, 1979, on the interpretation and application of articles 6, 16, and 23 of the GATT, the United States committed itself to "take all necessary steps to ensure that the imposition of a countervailing duty on any product . . . is in accordance with the provisions of Article VI of the General Agreement and the terms of this Agreement." Explicit reference is made to the injury provision of article 6 in the 1979 agreement. See U.S. State Department, *United States Treaties and Other International Agreements*, p. 519.

12. See United States–Mexico Chamber of Commerce, "Countervailing Duty Cases," p. 4.

Mexico, since it deals with a central element of its industrial development policy—the use of domestic and export subsidies. It is a difficult one for the United States, since it raises the question of why Mexico should be granted special treatment only because it refuses to adhere to the GATT or its codes. In this case, however, both countries have decided to seek a bilateral agreement.

Besides the most-favored-nation tenet, reciprocity is basic to U.S. trade policy and highly relevant to U.S. trade treatment of Mexico. As now defined in the articles of the GATT, reciprocity does not mean that developing countries must provide trade treatment or trade concessions equivalent to those it receives from developed countries, nor does it mean that developing countries do not have to provide concessions in exchange for benefits received.[13] One can assume that in practice the concessions granted by a developing country in exchange for benefits obtained are graduated by degree of development. The United States expects more reciprocity from Mexico than it would from, say, Costa Rica or Bolivia, but not as much as it would from the countries of the European Community.

In the negotiations for its possible accession to the GATT, Mexico made it abundantly clear that it wished to be treated as a developing country. Such treatment has several implications. One is that Mexico would be entitled to receive benefits from developed countries without being expected to provide equivalent benefits. Other concessions to developing countries embodied in GATT provisions and practice include allowing them to use export subsidies more freely than developed countries, reducing contention with other contracting parties when nontariff techniques are used to develop domestic industry, and the granting of nonreciprocal preferential treatment from industrial countries. Mexico now enjoys each of these benefits without GATT membership and would have continued to enjoy them for a time even if it had adhered to the GATT. However, in perhaps ten or twenty years, GATT

13. Article 36:8 of the GATT reads: "The developed contracting parties do not expect reciprocity for commitments made by them in trade negotiations to reduce or remove tariffs and other barriers to the trade of less-developed contracting parties." The note attached to this paragraph explains that the phrase *do not expect reciprocity* means that "the less-developed contracting parties should not be expected, in the course of trade negotiations, to make contributions which are inconsistent with their individual development, financial and trade needs, taking into consideration past trade developments." General Agreement on Tariffs and Trade, *Basic Instruments and Selected Documents*, vol. 4, article 36:8, p. 54, and supplementary note, p. 76.

membership would have opened Mexico to challenge about its trade practices, whereas nonmembership precludes legal challenges to these practices.

In addition, trade policy positions of developed countries tend to promote "graduation." This means that as a country progresses economically, expectations and benefits granted would graduate accordingly. The degree of special treatment for developing countries more advanced economically, such as Mexico, would be less than that for less-advanced countries, such as Haiti and Honduras. The United States has been a principal proponent of graduation, and no country has been more vociferously opposed to it than Mexico.

Each of these basic principles of U.S. trade policy has changed somewhat since the end of World War II. The United States, despite misgivings, agreed to grant tariff preferences to beneficiary developing countries, as have other industrial countries.[14] These preferences, however, were always considered an exception to the general MFN principle and were encumbered with severe restrictions on the duration of the preferences and the volume of trade for any given product that could enjoy them. The U.S. general system of preferences contains "competitive need" provisions to remove the preferences from products exported by particular countries no longer deemed to need these benefits.[15] President Ronald Reagan proposed an additional system of special preferences—the Caribbean Basin Initiative—limited to designated beneficiary countries in the Caribbean Basin. This was accepted by the Congress and represents a departure from past U.S. trade policy.[16] Mexico is not a beneficiary of tariff preferences under this proposal; it is considered to be too developed for this.

14. The relevant U.S. legislation authorizing a general system of preferences is Title V of the Trade Act of 1974, P.L. 93-618, enacted by the Senate and House of Representatives, January 3, 1975 (H.R. 10710). The U.S. authority to grant those preferences expires on January 3, 1985.

15. The operation of the U.S. GSP system is discussed in *Report to the Congress on the First Five Years' Operation of the U.S. Generalized System of Preferences (GSP)*, House Committee Print.

16. As President Reagan put it: "The centerpiece of the program that I am sending to the Congress is free trade for Caribbean Basin products exported to the United States." He added later in the speech: "This economic proposal is as unprecedented as today's crisis in the Caribbean. Never before has the United States offered a preferential trading arrangement to any region." See "Transcript of President's Address on Caribbean Aid Program," *New York Times*, February 25, 1982.

The United States agreed to dilute the reciprocity provisions of the GATT in favor of developing countries but has not been prepared to give up the principle of reciprocity altogether. In negotiations with Mexico, such as those that took place during Mexico's application for accession to the GATT, the United States has always sought some concessions from Mexico in return for those granted. The United States has also criticized Mexico's use of performance requirements in its industrial policy despite Mexico's explanation that these are necessary because Mexico is a developing country. Performance requirements refer to provisions in Mexican law and regulations specifying that foreign investors must procure a minimum percentage of their inputs in Mexico or that they must guarantee that imports in a given sector be matched by an equivalent amount of exports in that sector.

Each of these issues would arise in any discussions about a movement toward bilateral free trade. The United States has been reasonably consistent in its trade policy since World War II in that it has not completely forsaken original principles. At the same time, actual practice has been flexible: departures from such basic concepts as MFN and reciprocity have been made and, in U.S. consideration of a bilateral agreement with Mexico outside the GATT, policy on subsidies and countervailing duties may be bent. Mexico's trade policy also has been consistent in the protection of domestic industry and agriculture and in the insistence that Mexico be treated as a developing country. But Mexico has also shifted position from time to time on basic issues. Mexico did entertain the idea of acceding to the GATT and steps were taken early in the López Portillo administration to shift from relying on import licensing to using tariffs as the principal protective device. The latter would have shifted Mexican industrial policy from development behind walls of absolute protection to development based primarily on competitive pricing, assuming that the tariff levels were not prohibitive. However, in neither case was the Mexican shift carried to its logical conclusion. Mexico did not enter the GATT, and it reverted to licensing to protect itself against imports when its balance of payments began to deteriorate in 1980.

The point that deserves emphasis is that although each country has shown continuity in trade policy, neither has been rigid in pursuit of its policy. Negotiation concerning bilateral free trade would require a willingness to look beyond past policy to a future that is mostly uncharted.

Mexican Complaints about U.S. Policy

The most persistent Mexican complaint about U.S. trade policy has been that the U.S. tariff structure deters Mexican exports because the more value added to a product abroad, the more U.S. duties escalate. As the American press emphasized when President López Portillo visited President Reagan in June 1981, Mexico wanted trade concessions on labor-intensive products.[17] The bias against labor-intensive products in the tariff structures of industrial countries has been a general complaint of developing countries. The charge clearly is accurate. Although Mexico's tariff structure is constructed the same way (see chapter 4), Mexico and other developing countries with similar tariff structures justify them on the grounds that an equitable international division of labor requires deployment of certain industries from the more to the less developed countries and that less developed countries need protection more than developed countries.[18]

The joint communiqué issued after President Carter visited Mexico in February 1979 referred to the need, in President López Portillo's view, to reduce the historic trade deficit of Mexico in relation to the United States by permitting an increase in the export of Mexican goods, "particularly those of higher value added."[19] This communiqué linked U.S. trade restrictions with the problem of undocumented workers migrating to the United States. It stated that "Mexico does not wish to export workers but goods" and that a solution to the migrant issue is impeded by "restrictive measures in other areas."[20]

For Mexico, the issue of tariff escalation is real but becoming less important. Mexico benefits from the U.S. general system of preferences, and those goods allowed preferential entry into the United States are not subject to any duty. More significantly, neither the United States nor other major industrial countries and areas, such as Japan and the EC, will have many tariffs on industrial goods above 10 percent and even

17. See "Mexico: Can We Become Partners?" *Newsweek* (June 15, 1981), p. 49.
18. Anticipatory redeployment of potentially noncompetitive industries from industrial countries to developing countries has been a principal objective of developing countries since the Second Conference of the United Nations Industrial Development Organization in Lima, Peru, in March 1975. Redeployment need not be anticipatory, however. It can take place by allowing competitive forces to work without government interference to prevent change.
19. "U.S.-Mexico Joint Communiqué," p. 60.
20. Ibid., p. 62.

fewer tariffs above 15 percent once the results of the most recent multilateral trade negotiations take effect in the late 1980s. The average U.S. tariff level at that time, weighted by most-favored-nation imports, will be 4.4 percent.[21] Industrial-country tariffs are by no means inconsequential, but they do not impede trade the way they have in the past.[22] This is true even when tariffs are measured on the basis of the effective protection (on value added abroad rather than on the total value of an imported good) as opposed to nominal rates offered to most favored nations.

Mexico's other constant concern about U.S. trade policy is its alleged uncertainty. This is typified by a statement attributed to the president of the Mexico Coordinating Committee of the United States–Mexico Chamber of Commerce: "Mexican exporters worry every time the U.S. Congress meets."[23] This may be hyperbole, but Mexico fears that success in exporting to the United States brings U.S. restrictions in its wake. This has not happened frequently to Mexico, but it has happened enough to lend credence to the apprehension. The principal U.S. import restrictions that either affect Mexican trade or threaten it are for those products in which Mexico is competitive.

The only substantial nontariff barriers affecting Mexican exports to the United States are for yarns, textiles, and apparel. These barriers take the form of quotas. The quotas are defined in a bilateral agreement similar to the roughly eighteen other agreements the United States made following the multilateral Arrangement Regarding International Trade in Textiles, designed to regulate trade in cotton, wool, and manmade fibers, textiles, and products. The U.S.-Mexico agreement is a complex document.[24] It contains firm quotas on some categories of products but

21. Thomas R. Graham, *The Impact of the Tokyo Round Agreements on U.S. Export Competitiveness*, p. 22. An "average" tariff level obviously is an arbitrary figure, and weighting tariffs by trade to reach this average obscures the trade-limiting effect on imports of products with high tariff rates.

22. According to a calculation by the U.S. International Trade Commission, the average duty on imports from Mexico was 3.36 percent in 1979. The average duty on dutiable imports was 7.28 percent. U.S. International Trade Commission, *Background Study of the Economies and International Trade Patterns of the Countries of North America, Central America and the Caribbean*, p. 153. This is not negligible, but it is far less than the recent yearly differences between the U.S. and Mexican inflation.

23. Miguel Blasquez, "Mexico-U.S. Trade," p. 5.

24. U.S. Department of State, Press Release 61 (March 9, 1979), contains the text of the agreement. The exchange of letters of December 23–24, 1981, amending and extending the agreement is reported in U.S. Department of State, Press Release 42 (February 2, 1982).

more generally establishes a means by which the United States can call for consultations regarding this trade. For fibers and nonapparel items, minimum consultation levels are established, and in other categories the triggering mechanism for the consultation is more fluid. The intent of the agreement is to limit the increase of Mexican exports of clothing to 6 to 7 percent a year. Most of this clothing is made of fabrics cut in the United States. Mexico has contended that the U.S. component of these items should be excluded from the quotas under the bilateral agreement, but the United States has not agreed, primarily because of pressure from U.S. labor unions.[25]

Free trade would probably influence textile and apparel trade significantly. There is little doubt that Mexico could expand these exports to the United States if there were no agreement limiting expansion. Temporary export limitations might exist even under a free-trade agreement, but not restrictions that have been as durable as those under various textile agreements. In free trade, not only would more textile and apparel imports be allowed into the United States, but they would enter free of duty. One would expect that a gradual adjustment to free trade would have to take place in this sector in the United States for the benefit of producers in Mexico—some of whom are Americans. If the United States were to eliminate quota restrictions and tariffs on textile and apparel imports from all countries, Mexico probably would not be the principal beneficiary since there are other more efficient supplying countries. However, in bilateral free trade, the United States would be obligated to eliminate tariffs and quantitative restrictions only for Mexico.

Other U.S. nontariff measures affecting Mexican exports are most problematic for agricultural trade. Under a voluntary restraint agreement program, there is a maximum allocation to Mexico for annual meat imports into the United States in years when import restrictions are in effect. There were no restrictions in either 1980 or 1981. But in recent years Mexico has been unable to ship amounts up to its allocation even

25. It is not clear whether the size of the quotas granted Mexico for these sensitive apparel items was adjusted to take account of the fact that only part of the imports registered in the United States actually came from value added in Mexico and the rest from value added in the United States. The only evidence is assertions to the author by both countries. U.S. officials state that the size of the quotas reflects the fact that a portion of the imports represent original U.S. exports, while Mexican officials argue that there is no evidence that such an allowance is made in the bilateral agreement establishing quotas.

when restrictions were in effect.[26] There are no U.S. ceilings on imports of live cattle from Mexico, although Mexico occasionally limits these exports to ensure an adequate domestic supply. Livestock and meat imports are subject to U.S. health and sanitary controls. Hoof-and-mouth disease was eliminated in Mexico in the 1950s following a cooperative binational program, and a joint program exists to control the screw worm. Meat consumed in the United States must meet permissible levels of pesticide residues set by the Environmental Protection Agency for imported and domestic meats alike. In 1978 there was an increase in Mexican meat shipments that did not meet U.S. sanitary standards, and the U.S. Department of Agriculture withdrew certifications from some Mexican meat-packing plants. The problem is a potentially long-lasting one because its correction requires curtailing the use of pesticides in Mexico.

Mexican fruits and vegetables are also occasionally excluded from the United States because they exceed U.S. pesticide tolerance levels or contain insects and diseases absent from the United States. The tolerance levels are set by the U.S. Food and Drug Adminstration for both domestically produced and imported foods. The restrictions have affected Mexican shipments of peppers, beans, strawberries, cabbage, and squash. The most important Mexican product restricted because imports may introduce pests hazardous to the U.S. product is the avocado, whose pulp is subject to weevil infestation. In joint programs the U.S. Department of Agriculture helps Mexico eliminate certain insects and plant diseases involving citrus, mangoes, and avocados. Although these sanitary restrictions constitute nontariff barriers against Mexican products, there is no convincing evidence that they are used as a camouflage for protectionism, and both countries are trying to eliminate the causes of the restrictions.

Mexico is more concerned about two other actual or potential types of U.S. restrictions affecting fruits and vegetables: the use of marketing orders and the threat to invoke U.S. antidumping laws. The main target

---

26. Mexico shipped 60.1 million pounds of meat in 1977, about 3 percent under its allocation. In 1978 Mexican shipments of 62.7 million pounds were about 14 percent under the allocation. The allocation for 1979 was 76.1 million pounds and imports were 5.3 million pounds. Imports from Mexico in 1980 were only 242,000 pounds, some of which may have been transshipments from other meat-exporting countries. Data from U.S. Department of Agriculture, Foreign Agricultural Service, Dairy Livestock and Poultry Division.

of these protective efforts has been the Mexican tomato, and the instigators of the protective techniques have been tomato growers and their representatives in Congress. Mexico does have a legitimate grievance about harassment from U.S. officials and importers.

Marketing orders are issued to establish and maintain orderly marketing conditions for certain agricultural products. These orders permit producers, in consultation with the U.S. secretary of agriculture, to limit the quantity or regulate the quality (grade, size, and maturity) of domestically grown fruits, vegetables, and nuts. Orders may be revised seasonally or even within a season as marketing conditions change. But what is most significant is that when a specified commodity is regulated by a marketing order, imports of that commodity are prohibited if they do not also comply.

Before the 1970–71 season, the United States maintained two marketing programs for tomatoes, one applicable to mature green tomatoes, grown mostly in southern Florida, and the other to vine-ripened tomatoes, grown throughout the United States and the type exported by Mexico. The mature green tomato is picked and shipped to market at an earlier stage of growth than the vine-ripened tomato and therefore tends to be smaller. The marketing order required larger minimum sizes for vine-ripened than for mature green tomatoes. Since the 1970–71 season, however, there has been only one marketing order under which minimum size is based on the mature green. The use of marketing orders to restrict trade is too new and too persistent for the Mexicans to ignore the protective potential inherent in this program.[27] This protectionist concern was renewed when both Florida senators introduced legislation in 1977 to include the regulation of packaged tomatoes in the existing marketing order. If made into law, this legislation would have forced an increase in costs on the Mexicans, since the Mexican growers and the government maintain their own system of minimum grade standards to ensure the quality of exported tomatoes.

The much more dramatic example supporting Mexico's concern that its export success breeds protectionist pressure was the petition submitted in September 1978 by Florida winter-vegetable growers, under the Anti-Dumping Act of 1921, alleging Mexican dumping of tomatoes in the

27. Technical material on Mexican and U.S. winter vegetables can be found in Richard L. Simmons, James L. Pearson, and Ernest B. Smith, *Mexican Competition for the U.S. Fresh Winter Vegetable Market.*

U.S. market. The allegation was that five varieties of fresh produce, particularly tomatoes, were being sold in the United States at less than "fair value," and that this was damaging the U.S. industry. The U.S. Department of Commerce usually examines the charges of petitions to determine whether sales at less than fair value are taking place. If such is the case, the International Trade Commission determines the extent of injury, if any, for the purpose of imposing an antidumping duty. If the U.S. Department of Commerce determines that dumping is taking place, appraisement for customs purposes is withheld until there is a determination on injury. If an antidumping duty then is assessed, it is applied retroactively from the time appraisement was withheld. In short, if dumping is taking place, U.S. importers are uncertain about how to price the product in the U.S. market. The 1978 petition was significant because it triggered the first antidumping investigation involving a fresh-market, perishable agricultural commodity.[28] The legal argument of the Florida growers was that the fresh winter vegetables imported into the United States often are sold at less than the cost of production. The response was that there is nothing inherently unfair or unusual in making some sales of perishable produce at less than the full cost of production, since, if unsold, the product perishes and nothing is recovered. The Mexican argument was that profit should be looked at not for each sale but over the course of a single or several seasons.

The petition eventually was rejected in March 1980, but only after months of uncertainty. For Mexico, the stakes in this case were high. Table 3–5 shows Mexican exports of the five products involved in the antidumping investigation. According to the brief submitted on behalf of the Mexican producers and the U.S. importers, the Mexican industry consists of about 2,100 growers concentrated near Culiacan in the state of Sinaloa, employing about 100,000 agricultural workers. The products are sold mostly in Canada and the United States from November through June of each year and then sold to customers by fifty distributors, all American companies and virtually all located in Nogales, Arizona. In

28. The brief of June 5, 1979, submitted on behalf of the Union Nacional de Productores de Hortalizas and the West Mexico Vegetable Distributors Association in response to the petition by the Florida growers emphasized this point and went through the legislative history of the Anti-Dumping Act in an attempt to show that the legislation was not intended to apply to such products. This brief noted that an antidumping case of Concord grapes from Canada (1969) concerned agricultural produce, but produce destined mostly for processing rather than the market.

Table 3-5. *U.S. Imports of Selected Fresh, Chilled, or Frozen Fruits and Vegetables from Mexico, 1973–80*

Year	Tomatoes	Peppers	Cucumbers	Eggplant	Squash
		Thousands of dollars			
1973	115,138	16,132	14,468	4,176	4,838
1974	64,071	9,124	8,059	1,332	2,130
1975	64,132	7,928	5,869	1,306	1,893
1976	72,429	10,485	11,487	1,594	3,006
1977	149,406	21,450	17,893	3,278	6,049
1978	161,097	32,530	42,405	7,537	17,561
1979	153,184	35,837	42,785	6,912	17,748
1980	130,956	52,579	40,940	5,924	13,823
		Thousands of pounds			
1973	749,121	88,363	166,484	39,156	38,700
1974	590,601	86,583	167,864	26,201	41,925
1975	559,095	62,397	122,316	25,806	36,711
1976	648,584	88,416	196,218	29,719	51,032
1977	785,386	112,873	236,154	31,871	66,863
1978	814,116	144,617	284,884	41,759	81,561
1979	710,250	135,319	296,941	39,702	93,439
1980	649,483	166,691	299,352	36,251	86,384

Sources: U.S. Department of Agriculture, Foreign Agricultural Service, *Mexico: United States Imports, Fruits and Vegetables* (USDA, 1980), for data up to 1979; U.S. Department of Agriculture, "Seven-Years Import Trade," December 31, 1980, for 1980.

other words, the Mexican producers and exporters do have many U.S. allies. For the last decade, Mexico has supplied about half the winter vegetables consumed in the United States; most of the remainder comes from Florida.

The winter industry in Florida is concentrated mainly but not exclusively in Dade County, the location of about thirty operating farms.[29] The petition submitted by the Florida growers contained a letter from

29. Data on the concentration of the industry in Dade County for sales from January through March of each year are contained in *Inspection Standards of Vegetable Imports*, pt. 3, Senate Hearings, pp. 71–73. On the number of farms in Dade County, see pt. 1 of the same hearings, p. 123. These hearings are an excellent example of Mexican concern about U.S. congressional procedures, since the chairman of the subcommittee and the person who convened the hearings was Senator Richard B. Stone of Florida, who had been in the forefront of the effort to protect the Florida tomato growers. The hearings extended beyond issues of inspection standards of vegetable imports into protection of U.S. industry. Senator Lawton M. Chiles, for example, raised the allegation of Mexican dumping of tomatoes. So did Congressmen Dante B. Fascell and Louis A. Bafalis, both from Florida (pt. 1, pp. 2–9). Dr. Elmer Close, assistant director of marketing, Florida Department of Agriculture and Consumer Services, raised issues of import quotas, market sharing, and increased tariffs (pt. 1, pp. 10–12).

the Florida Department of Commerce estimating that the south Florida winter vegetable industry employed 16,000 persons in 1978. The U.S. Bureau of Labor Statistics gave a lower estimate, saying that employment ranged between 12,700 and 13,800 persons in 1978.[30] Comparisons in market shares between Mexico and Florida can be distorted in any one year because of weather (such as freeze damage in Florida in the 1969–70 season) or by the threat of U.S. restrictions. The Florida share of the winter tomato market was 42 percent in 1969–70 (November to May) but has been larger—between 50 and 70 percent—since then. It reached 76 percent in 1979–80.[31]

The purpose of this discussion is not to argue the legal merits of the antidumping petition or even the competition between the two industries, but rather to note the legitimacy in this case of Mexico's concern that success in penetrating the U.S. market does lead to protectionist pressure in the United States. The independent evidence is that production costs in Mexico are substantially lower than in Florida because of lower wage rates, an advantage that is diminishing because of rising Mexican wages and greater mechanization in Florida. Also, Florida costs become competitive only after the additions of a "complex and expensive set of border-crossing inspection and handling charges, and higher sales commissions than are charged in Florida," plus the U.S. tariff, which changes seasonally for tomatoes, eggplant, and cucumbers.[32]

Two other Mexican concerns about U.S. trade policy deserve mention. The first relates to the growth in countervailing duty cases against Mexico (a countervailing duty is imposed by an importing country to compensate for a subsidy provided by the government of an exporting country), and the second to the discrimination that some Mexican products might face in the U.S. market once the preferential trade aspects of the Caribbean Basin Initiative go into effect. U.S. law requires the imposition of a countervailing duty on any dutiable imported product when there is proof of an export subsidy for that product. However, under the subsidies and countervailing duties code to which the United

30. Ibid., pt. 2, p. 67.

31. U.S. Department of Agriculture, Agricultural Marketing Service, Fruit and Vegetable Branch.

32. Simmons and others, *Mexican Competition for the U.S. Fresh Winter Vegetable Market*, p. 42. On the question of costs and competition, see G. A. Zepp and R. L. Simmons, *Producing Fresh Winter Vegetables in Florida and Mexico: Costs and Competition*.

States agreed in 1979 in the Tokyo round of multilateral trade negotiations, the countervailing duty can be imposed on products exported from other signatories to the code only if injury from the subsidy can be shown to have adversely affected a U.S. industry. Mexico did not sign the code, so the injury test does not apply to subsidized exports from that country. Only the simpler test applies before a U.S. countervail against Mexican exports can be made—that is, the existence of an export subsidy.

As of January 1983, eleven countervailing duty cases had been brought against Mexican products. Actual countervailing duties were imposed in six cases, three were still pending as of this writing, and Mexican exporters agreed not to accept export subsidies for the remaining two, under penalty of countervail if they are found to have accepted such subsidies. The number of cases involving complaints against Mexican subsidies began to proliferate in mid-1982; all but one of the eleven complaints have been made since then.[33] The subsidy and countervailing duty problem became the main irritant in U.S.-Mexican trade relations in 1983, so some solution to the problem will probably be found.

Mexico's concern about the Caribbean Basin Initiative is potential rather than actual. President Reagan proposed granting one-way free-trade benefits to beneficiary countries and territories in what he called the Caribbean Basin.[34] These are island countries in the Caribbean itself and countries on the mainland of Central America and the northern coast of South America. Mexico, Venezuela, and Colombia—the more developed countries in the Caribbean Basin—will not be granted tariff preferences under the initiative. This means that once the preferences go into effect, dutiable competitive Mexican products will face discrimination in the U.S. market compared with the same products manufactured in beneficiary countries. Certain sensitive products, such as textiles

33. A listing of the cases can be found in United States–Mexico Chamber of Commerce, "Countervailing Duty Cases," pp. 4, 8. The six products on which countervailing duties have been imposed are leather apparel, ceramic tiles, toy balloons, litharge, polypropylene fibers, and nonmetal castings; the three pending cases concern anhydrous and aqueous ammonia, fresh asparagus, and carbon black; and the two products exporters agreed not to accept subsidies for are pectin and polypropylene film.

34. There are various technical requirements for eligibility for these preferences, the most important of which is that at least 25 percent of the product value must be added in the beneficiary country. According to the Office of the U.S. Trade Representative, about 15 percent of U.S. imports in 1980 from beneficiary countries were dutiable in the United States. The relevance of this percentage is that tariff preferences are not germane for goods that already can be imported free of duty.

and apparel, will be excluded from these tariff preferences.[35] The trade and tax aspects of the Caribbean Basin Initiative were approved by the Congress, and the procedures for carrying out the law are being worked out at this writing. If the incentives lead to increased investment in and exports from beneficiary countries, comparable Mexican exports to the United States might suffer. The likely candidates for preferences are labor-intensive manufactures produced in assembly plants and ones that benefit from the U.S. tariff code provisions under which U.S. duty is paid only on the value added abroad. The Caribbean Basin Initiative may entice the owners of such plants, which now exist in Mexico (and other nonbeneficiary countries), to move them to beneficiary countries. This is only speculation, since the preferences may not stimulate movement of assembly plants from Mexico to beneficiary countries. But this could become a serious issue in U.S.-Mexican trade relations.

U.S. Complaints about Mexican Policy

A recurring theme in U.S. complaints about Mexico's trade policy is that Mexico is a free rider, and seeks to remain so, in the international trading system. Mexico is the only main trading country, other than communist countries, that is not a member of the GATT. The free-rider theme arises in many guises. In the negotiations on tropical products which preceded the multilateral trade negotiations in the GATT and in which Mexico participated as part of its accession negotiations, the United States insisted on some degree of reciprocity in the agreement signed in December 1977. In the multilateral trade negotiations themselves, the U.S. negotiators were frustrated because the Mexican negotiators were prepared to offer few concessions but demanded many. The complaint was not that Mexico should grant equivalent concessions but rather that it should show some reasonable token of reciprocity to reflect its stage of development.

Disagreement on the degree of reciprocity that developing countries in different stages of development should provide in return for trade concessions granted is general in international trade negotiations. U.S.

---

35. When enacting the measure into law, Congress added more product exclusions, including petroleum products, tuna, watches and parts, footwear, handbags, flat goods (such as wallets and eyeglass cases), work gloves, and leather apparel. Other conditions were imposed to exclude communist countries and those not cooperating to control drug traffic. *Congressional Quarterly Weekly Report*, vol. 4 (July 30, 1983), p. 1542.

trade officials tend to view Mexico as a relatively advanced country with a reasonably well-developed industrial structure and a country that, therefore, should make some reciprocal contributions. In Mexico, on the other hand, the issue of accession to the GATT became controversial precisely because it seemed to involve giving away too much for concessions received, which many Mexicans felt was inappropriate for a country at Mexico's stage of development. A precisely articulated expression of this view was contained in the letter and analysis sent to President López Portillo on May 23, 1979, following the Third National Congress of Economists held in Mexico City.[36] Mexico eventually decided not to accede to the GATT both for the foregoing and other reasons discussed in chapter 4.

Another U.S. complaint is the unpredictability of Mexican trade policy. For many years U.S. policy was to urge Mexico to join the GATT, thinking GATT accession might impose some predictability in Mexico's trade policy. Now, for example, import licenses can be imposed or lifted following internal bargaining in Mexico. GATT membership would also imply the use of tariffs rather than quantitative restrictions (import licenses) as the main instrument of trade policy. To some degree, the urging by U.S. officials has made Mexicans wary about acceding to the GATT.[37]

Besides the complaint that Mexico continuously seeks but rarely grants concessions, many product-specific complaints about Mexican import restrictions, both in agriculture and industry, arise periodically. The main complaints, however, focus on the absolute nature of Mexican protection and the performance requirements, particularly in the automotive industry, that restrict imports from the United States. Mexico has decreed that import increases, at least in theory, must be matched exactly by export increases. These performance requirements imposed on automotive producers in Mexico amount in theory—but not in practice—to zero-net-import quotas and have been the subject of many U.S. policy statements.[38]

---

36. Colegio Nacional de Economistas, A. C., "Política alternativa al proteccionismo y a la adhesión de México al GATT." This letter appeared widely as an advertisement in Mexican newspapers and journals and formed the basis of many internal debates.

37. See chapter 4.

38. For example, see speech of C. Fred Bergsten, former assistant secretary of the treasury, on "The Need for International Cooperation in the International Investment Area," delivered before the conference on International Trade and Investment Policy of the National Journal, May 11, 1979. Speech reprinted in the *Department of the Treasury News*, May 11, 1979.

Table 3-6. *U.S. Imports under the General System of Preferences, 1976–80*

Millions of dollars unless otherwise specified

Year	GSP imports from Mexico	GSP imports from all countries	GSP imports from Mexico (percent of total)
1976	253	3,160	8.0
1977	368	3,878	9.5
1978	458	5,204	8.8
1979	551	6,280	8.8
1980	509	7,328	6.9

Sources: *Report to the Congress on the First Five Years' Operation of the U.S. Generalized System of Preferences (GSP)*, Committee Print, transmitted by the President of the United States to the House Committee on Ways and Means, WMCP: 96-58, 96 Cong. 2 sess. (GPO, 1980), pp. 150–63, for 1976–78; Office of the U.S. Trade Representative, for 1979–80.

The Balance of U.S. Concessions and Restrictions

There are two sides to the story of U.S. treatment of merchandise imports from Mexico. One side is the actual import restrictions, or quotas, that affect textiles and apparel almost exclusively. It is an open question whether the U.S. restriction of textile and apparel imports hurts Mexico because of the quotas or benefits Mexico because of comparable quotas for more competitive suppliers. Mexico does indeed benefit from particular aspects of U.S. trade policy, namely the U.S. general system of preferences and the provisions of the U.S. tariff schedule that impose import duty only on value added outside the United States.

The general system of preferences does not require duty to be paid on specified imports from certain developing countries, including Mexico. Table 3-6 shows the value of these imports from Mexico from 1976 through 1980. Mexico ranked fourth in 1980 in U.S. imports under these preferences, after Taiwan, Hong Kong, and South Korea. U.S. legislation limits the import of any eligible item by "competitive need" ceilings. Imports from a single beneficiary country may not exceed 50 percent of imports of any specific product under the preference system from all countries in any calendar year or may not exceed a specific dollar value that rises each year with the increase in the U.S. GNP. For 1979 the specific dollar ceiling was $41.9 million, and for 1981 it was $45.8 million. The 50 percent rule can be waived if U.S. imports of an item did not exceed $1 million in the base year 1979, also adjusted upward for increases in the U.S. GNP. The 1980 exception was $1,081,021.

To take advantage of U.S. tariff provisions that allow producers to add value outside the United States to U.S. exports and then return the product to the United States and pay tariff only on the value added abroad, Mexico enacted in 1965 legislation permitting in-bond plants to be established to finish goods—made of imported components—for subsequent export. These plants, or *maquiladora*, could at first be established only near the U.S.-Mexican border, but since 1972 they can be located anywhere in Mexico. At the end of 1980, there were about 575 such plants, 90 percent located in border cities. These plants provided employment then for approximately 100,000 Mexicans. Although Mexico's foreign investment law stipulates that new foreign equity investment should not normally exceed 49 percent of a firm's total equity, a regulation of the Foreign Investment Commission permits 100 percent ownership of an in-bond plant.[39]

The operation of the *maquiladora* is controversial in both countries. U.S. labor unions argue that the U.S. tariff provisions encourage investors to "run away" to Mexico and other low-wage countries to acquire cheap labor for operations that otherwise would use U.S. labor. But the producers contend that without these tariff provisions the entire product and not just the assembly or value added would be produced outside the United States. Mexican opponents of the system argue that it merely encourages simple assembly operations, involving mainly women who perform rote work, thus providing little to Mexico in new technology or skills. Those who work in *maquiladora* in border cities spend much of their income on the U.S. side of the border, which has led to the contention that the in-bond system adds only modestly to Mexico's net balance-of-payments receipts.

The purpose of this discussion is not to argue whether the *maquiladora* system is good or bad or a mixture of both for either country. The point, rather, is that it clearly permits exports from Mexico to be larger than they would be without the benefit of the U.S. tariff provisions (table 3-7). In 1980 Mexico was by far the leading developing country supplying goods under these tariff provisions and ranked third, after Japan and Germany, among all suppliers of these items.

It seems clear that U.S. trade policy helps generate more trade from Mexico than it restricts. Table 3-8 shows just how much of Mexico's exports to the United States must meet normal competitive conditions.

39. U.S. Department of Commerce, "Marketing in Mexico," pp. 5, 16.

Table 3-7. *U.S. Imports from Mexico under Tariff Items*
806.30 and 807.00, 1976–80

Millions of dollars

	806.30			807.00		
Year	Total value	Duty-free value	Dutiable value	Total value	Duty-free value	Dutiable value
1976	77	55	22	1,058	545	513
1977	49	35	14	1,107	596	511
1978	50	35	15	1,490	791	699
1979	63	44	19	2,002	1,005	997
1980	65	45	20	2,276	1,141	1,135

Sources: U.S. International Trade Commission, *Import Trends in TSUS Items 806.30 and 807.00*, USITC 1029 (USITC, 1980), pp. B-3, B-7, for imports through 1978; USITC, *Imports Under Items 806.30 and 807.00 of the Tariff Schedules of the United States, 1977–80*, USITC 1170 (USITC, 1981), pp. B-5, B-12, for subsequent years.

Table 3-8. *U.S. Merchandise Imports from Mexico, 1979*

Millions of dollars

Import category	Item
Petroleum and petroleum products	3,068
Duty-free imports under regular most-favored-nation provisions	1,669
Imports under general system of preferences	551
Imports under U.S. tariff items 806.30 and 807.00	2,065
Subtotal	7,353
Other	1,460
Total	8,813

Sources: U.S. Bureau of the Census, *U.S. General Imports*, FT 155, Annual 1979, p. 3-49, for total and petroleum imports; most-favored-nation duty-free import figure from U.S. International Trade Commission, *Background Study of the Economies and International Trade Patterns of the Countries of North America, Central America and the Caribbean*, p. 152; tables 3-6 and 3-7 for preferential imports and for tariff items 806.30 and 807.00.

Only 16.6 percent of U.S. imports from Mexico in 1979 either had to surmount a tariff in the United States or were nonpetroleum imports. Thirty percent of U.S. imports from Mexico benefited from the nonreciprocal benefits of the U.S. system of preferences or the special tariff provisions. The significance of this 30 percent is that much of it is in manufactured goods, the sector in which job creation is greatest in relation to value added in the Mexican economy.

Table 3-8 both overstates and understates the importance of U.S. nonreciprocal trade concessions to Mexico. It overstates it because the total level of imports could be higher if there were no import quotas on Mexican textiles and apparel and no threats of restrictions against fresh vegetable imports from Mexico. It also overstates it because 50 percent of the imports dutiable only for value added outside the United States are goods that originated in the United States. The table understates the importance of U.S. trade concessions because some of the remaining imports are duty free under other rate provisions such as in-bond processing, government use, and temporary duty suspension. It is an understatement also because several hundred million dollars worth of the remainder of U.S. imports—those not in the four categories listed in the table—is made up of automotive products, and some of these imports result from the pressure exerted on automotive producers in Mexico to comply with the Mexican no-net-import requirement in this field. Some of the remaining trade is between affiliates of the same multinational corporation.

Whatever the precise balance is between U.S. trade concessions to Mexico and restrictions on imports from Mexico, the data all suggest the general noncompetitiveness of Mexican industry. That the U.S. market is more open to nonpetroleum exports from Mexico than is the world market generally implies that Mexican industrial noncompetitiveness is not the result of U.S. protectionism. The reasons for Mexican noncompetitiveness are many, including Mexico's development model, the excessive protection under which Mexico's industry developed, and the perennially overvalued exchange rate. In this context, the protectionism Mexico must overcome in foreign markets, although real, is of secondary importance.

National trade policies of industrial countries do not normally conform to the economist's ideal, that in a mature economy imports are not necessarily a burden but rather represent the ability to command resources at a lower price than the country would without trade. Nations negotiate with each other on the basis of concessions granted, a concession being the lowering or freezing at a maximum level of an import duty. This negotiating technique assumes that imports are a burden and exports a benefit. But the actual economic world is not that simplistic, and most of the so-called concessions granted to Mexico by the United States are of mutual benefit. Developed nations negotiate with each other on the basis of reciprocal concessions, and the granting of nonreciprocity to developing nations is considered a favor that need not be returned. As the bilateral U.S.-Mexican trade data show, the question of formal reciprocity is of secondary importance in determining the total level of trade. Mexico, which receives nonreciprocal trade concessions from the United States, normally imports more goods from the United States than it exports in return. U.S. exporters of individual products—particularly producers of consumer manufactures—may suffer from Mexico's import restrictions, but most generally do not. The U.S. trade interest in Mexico is best served by growth in the Mexican economy rather than by particular trade concessions. A move to bilateral free trade must rest on this central point. For the United States, the economic issue in a movement to free trade is not Mexico's dependence, as many Mexicans assume, but growth; the faster Mexico grows, the more the United States will export to Mexico.

Looking Ahead

The U.S. market is currently more open to Mexican and other imports than the Mexican market is to U.S. imports. This is best explained by the two countries' different levels of development. The United States went through an ultraprotectionist phase, and Mexico has not yet passed through its own. Mexico's policy to liberalize restrictions on imports beginning in late 1976 aroused the opposition of those groups with a vested interest in protection as well as those concerned that trade liberalization would result in greater integration of the Mexican economy with that of the United States—which probably will happen. The two groups have different motives, but they can join forces to frustrate or delay the trade liberalization policy. Mexico's refusal to accede to the GATT showed this. The 1976 start on trade liberalization was halted a few years later as Mexico's balance-of-payments deficits grew in the López Portillo administration. The liberalization ceased completely and even was reversed—that is, import restrictions increased—when Mexico had to confront its economic crisis in 1982 and 1983. Any move toward renewed trade liberalization will have to await recovery from this economic crisis. In the United States, protectionism in early 1983 is for the most part narrowly focused on labor-intensive and a few large noncompetitive industries, such as steel and automobiles. However, where it exists, it can be just as intense as protectionism in Mexico. The recession of 1982 encouraged strong protectionist efforts in the United States, with an uncertain outcome.

Both Mexico and the United States complain about the uncertainty of each other's trade policy. The main U.S. complaint is that import restrictions not based on product prices make Mexican protectionism both arbitrary and absolute. The Mexican complaint is that when competitive exports such as textiles, apparel, and winter vegetables are developed, a variety of pressures build up in the United States seeking to frustrate the further development of these products.[40]

An agreement leading to free trade would provide some assurance, but not a guarantee, that export success in both markets would not be followed by import protection. The purpose of a gradual movement to free trade is to allow time for adjustment and to give producers some leeway in the form of temporary exemptions from the steady move toward free trade of their products. However, if the exemptions were to multiply, the move to free trade would obviously be frustrated. There will probably be political pressure in each country for specific exemptions. In Mexico, these pressures will most likely come from small industrialists and others who have thrived because of the protection they are receiving now. In the United States, producers of labor-intensive goods, such as apparel and shoes, and in industries losing competitiveness, such as steel and perhaps automotive vehicles, are apt to seek exemptions from a steady movement to free trade.

These political pressures to prevent free trade existed in other free-trade agreements. Indeed, the pressures were so successful in the Latin American Free Trade Association that free trade never was achieved. The pressures were less numerous and less successful in the European Community. One reason for the disparity was that the ground rules in the two movements were different from the outset. There were automatic across-the-board tariff reductions in the EC, and any exception to the general rule needed specific approval. Many of the tariff reductions in LAFTA were not automatic, and specific approval was needed for the reduction. It turned out to be easier to prevent a nonscheduled tariff reduction than a scheduled one. The Central American Common Market was fashioned along the lines of the EC, and its process of internal tariff elimination was also reasonably complete.

To counter political pressures, a precise and comprehensive schedule for tariff and nontariff barrier reductions is needed for free trade to be possible between Mexico and the United States. Provision for temporary

---

40. Tomás Peñaloza, "Mecanismos de la dependencia: El caso de México (1970–75)," pp. 10–36, is a polemical article listing every conceivable type of U.S. protection against Mexico, some real and many fancied (such as the allegation that U.S. law permits imposition of antidumping duties even if there is no injury to a U.S. industry). Carlos Rangel, "Mexico and Other Dominoes," pp. 27–33, discusses this type of visceral anti-Americanism in analyses by many Mexican intellectuals.

exemptions may be necessary, but the procedures for granting these must be open and onerous—open in the sense that all parties to the decision, from both countries, must be heard, and onerous in the sense that an exemption for one product should require compensation with another product. If safeguards, including a lengthy transition, a definite schedule for across-the-board reduction in trade barriers, a requirement to justify specific exceptions from this schedule, an open procedure for hearing requests for exceptions, and a compensatory provision each time an exception is granted, fail to contain the number and importance of exemptions from the free-trade process, then any agreement will almost certainly founder. It is crucial that there be demonstrated techniques to counter the inevitable political pressures to prevent free trade for specific products.

Looking ahead, Mexico has three main options in developing its trade policy. It can opt for selective protection, making the protection as absolute as necessary in any particular case, as was advocated by the Colegio Nacional de Economistas in its opposition to Mexico's entry into the GATT. Second, Mexico could move toward substantial liberalization, that is, convert practically all its quantitative import restrictions into tariffs and gradually reduce these to modest levels, as was advocated by a World Bank group that studied Mexican industrialization.[41] Finally, Mexico could opt for substantial liberalization but in the context of a gradual movement toward sectoral or total free trade with the United States and perhaps even Canada. In theory, Mexico could follow a fourth option—one which already has been tried—of seeking to organize free trade with countries other than the United States, such as in Latin America and the Caribbean. However, past experience shows that this would probably not be successful.

The outcome of Mexico's trade policy obviously will affect the nature of Mexico's internal development as well as its relations with the United States. The shortcomings of past industrialization policy, particularly in creating jobs and in developing Mexican industries that can compete abroad without special concessions, make a case for a shift from absolute to modest tariff protection, that is, from option one to option two. The political and vested pressures against trade liberalization make the most likely outcome some combination of these first two options—general

41. A. Nowicki and others, *Mexico: Manufacturing Sector: Situation, Prospects and Policies.*

import liberalization coupled with heavy protection of particular industrial and agricultural activities. Liberalization of Mexico's import structure, whether or not in the context of a gradual movement toward free trade with the United States, implies the growing competitiveness of Mexican industry. In addition, given the proximity of the two countries and the ample economic interaction between them, one would expect the two economies to become even more intertwined as Mexican development proceeds. Mexican trade liberalization thus implies even greater interdependence with the United States than exists now.

Assuming that Mexico intends to liberalize its import regime, there is much political advantage in doing so gradually on a most-favored-nation basis. This could be done unilaterally or through some negotiating process, within or outside the GATT, in which Mexico sought some reciprocity. In a sense, Mexico already has received reciprocity for trade liberalization from others through the workings of the MFN principle. The economic outcome of multilateral MFN trade liberalization, in fact, might not be much different, in terms of the proportion of Mexican trade with the United States, from the results of a bilateral free-trade agreement because of the existing integration between the two economies. However, the process of reaching the two outcomes would differ greatly.

The disadvantage of an MFN approach is its uncertainty. A stated intention by Mexico to liberalize its import regime on an MFN basis would not be taken at face value, since the record of the López Portillo administration, which began to liberalize but then went backward, would reinforce doubts about the staying power of Mexico's trade liberalization. When trade liberalization is discretionary, that is, when there is no compulsion to act, political pressures against acting become stronger. Under such a discretionary program opposition must be overcome each time liberalization is proposed to reduce protection for any single product. In Mexico, this is an almost sure-fire formula for inaction. It is instructive that in the EC the action taken was not to eliminate tariff barriers for all countries but only for the countries of the community itself. The same was true for the European Free Trade Association. Markets were opened, but not broadly opened. Over time, as the EC took hold, external tariffs were also reduced, but only in reciprocal negotiations. Discrimination against outsiders still exists.

The choice between lowering trade barriers on an MFN basis and doing so in the context of a movement to bilateral free trade is essentially a choice between vast uncertainty over liberalization and a reasonable degree of certainty. Bilateral free trade need not result in permanently large margins of discrimination against outsiders but can be viewed as a way to increase the trade negotiating power of the free-trade area. This happened for the EC. Free trade with the United States, or perhaps in North America generally, could be good for Mexico because Mexican industry must become more competitive in any event as its import structure is liberalized. A larger, barrier-free trading area would provide more predictability to investors in industries in both countries. The advantage for both countries is that, since each country would be obliged to reduce protectionism within a specified time, fears that export success would spawn protectionism would be less intense.

CHAPTER FOUR

Mexican Trade Policy

MEXICAN trade policy is not constant in that efforts to reduce import restrictions with the goal of improving industrial competitiveness have given way to renewed protectionism at times of balance-of-payments crisis. The years 1982 and 1983 were times of such financial crisis and, hence, of restrictive import policy.

Patterns of Imports and Exports

As a result of Mexico's past policy of industrialization and the heavy emphasis placed on import substitution, Mexican merchandise imports are composed mainly of industrial inputs and capital goods (table 4-1). These two categories normally make up between 80 and 90 percent of the value of total Mexican imports.[1] This industrialization policy was made effective by Mexico's system of protection against imports. Since 1947 import licenses have supplemented tariffs to shield domestic production against competition from outside, and by the 1970s, import

1. For data on Mexico's foreign trade with countries other than the United States or with the world as a whole, the sources generally used are the Banco de México or the International Monetary Fund, which obtains its data from Mexican authorities. However, the IMF and the Banco de México differ in their presentation of trade data. The merchandise trade account in the IMF data includes nonmonetary gold and silver trade, whereas the Banco de México's publication, *Indicadores Económicos*, shows this separately. The IMF data are on a free-on-board basis both for imports and exports since 1971, whereas *Indicadores* showed imports including cost, insurance, and freight until recently. The IMF merchandise trade deficit figures tend to be larger than those in the *Indicadores*. My source for U.S. data on bilateral U.S.-Mexican trade is the U.S. Bureau of the Census, and these figures differ from those reported by the Banco de México. However, although precise trade figures differ according to the source used, the conclusions would not.

Table 4-1. *Mexico's Merchandise Imports, by Type of Product, 1976–80*

Item	1976	1977	1978	1979[a]	1980[a]
	Millions of dollars				
Consumer goods	311	417	427	1,002	2,426
Intermediate goods	2,706	2,537	5,316	7,406	11,028
Capital goods	2,510	2,087	1,981	3,577	5,119
Other	503	849	[b]	[b]	[b]
Freight and insurance	[c]	[c]	419	[c]	[c]
Total	6,030	5,890	8,144	12,097	n.a.
Commercial value	[c]	[c]	7,725	11,985	18,572
	Percent				
Consumer goods	5.1	7.1	5.2	8.4	13.1
Intermediate goods	44.9	43.1	65.3	61.8	59.4
Capital goods	41.6	35.4	24.3	29.8	27.5
Other	8.3	14.4	[b]	[b]	...
Freight and insurance	[c]	[c]	5.1	[c]	...
Total	100.0	100.0	100.0	100.0	100.0

Sources: Banco de México, *Indicadores Económicos,* December 1977 and 1978, pp. 76–79 in each, and December 1979, pp. 68–71; Banco de México, *Informe Anual, 1980,* pp. 191–208. Figures are rounded.
a. Preliminary figures.
b. Not separately listed in official statistics.
c. Subsumed under different categories.

licensing was the main instrument of import policy.[2] Failure to grant an import license gives complete protection, whereas a tariff must be prohibitively high to be an absolute protective device. As table 4-1 shows, the level of consumer goods imports is relatively low, but a large proportion of consumer imports, such as corn and other foodstuffs, is necessary to sustain the economy. In the past, food has been the major variable in consumer imports. Like many other countries that practiced extreme import substitution policies, Mexico cannot easily cope with a balance-of-payments crisis by sharp restrictions of so-called unnecessary imports, since these are already severely curtailed.

Before the oil price increases of the 1970s, Mexico's merchandise exports had been reasonably diverse, by category of goods if not by destination. Until the past few years, exports consisted roughly of one third each of agricultural goods, products from extractive industries, and manufactures (table 4-2). Mexico's discovery of substantial oil and

2. Gerardo Bueno, "The Structure of Protection in Mexico," in Bela Balassa, ed., *The Structure of Protection in Developing Countries,* pp. 169–202; and Bernard S. Katz, "Mexico's Import Licensing Strategy for Protecting Import Replacements: An Aspect of Trade Policy and Planning for Industrial Development," pp. 381–92.

Table 4-2. *Mexico's Merchandise Exports, by Type of Product,*
1976–80

Item	1976	1977	1978	1979[a]	1980[a]
	Millions of dollars				
Agriculture and livestock	1,186	1,439	1,503	1,779	1,545
Extractive industries	835	1,288	1,988	4,082	10,382
Manufactures	1,191	1,611	2,726	2,936	3,380
Unclassified	104	80	[b]	[b]	[b]
Total	3,316	4,418	6,217	8,798	15,307
	Percent				
Agriculture and livestock	35.8	32.6	24.2	20.2	10.1
Extractive industries	25.2	29.2	32.0	46.4	67.8
Manufactures	36.0	36.5	43.8	33.4	22.1
Unclassified	3.0	1.8	[b]	[b]	[b]
Total	100.0	100.0	100.0	100.0	100.0

Sources: Banco de México, *Indicadores Económicos,* December 1977 and December 1978, pp. 70–75 in each, and December 1979, pp. 72–77; Banco de México, *Informe Anual, 1980,* pp. 177–90. Figures are rounded.
a. Preliminary figures.
b. Subsumed under other categories.

natural gas resources increased the relative importance of exports from extractive industries. This can be seen in the data since 1978.[3] In 1980 oil and natural gas made up 67 percent of Mexico's exports.

Mexico, until the past two years, generally has had a deficit in its merchandise trade balance. The deficit was substantial in 1975, then diminished for two successive years because of slow economic growth in 1976 and 1977, and in 1977 because of the substantial devaluation of the Mexican peso on August 31, 1976. The deficit grew again in 1978, 1979, and 1980 as economic growth recovered and as the trade effect of the 1976 devaluation was eroded by Mexico's inflation. The slowdown of the Mexican economy in 1982, coupled with policy measures to restrict imports for balance-of-payments reasons, led to a shift in the trade balance from a deficit of about $4.5 billion in 1981 to a surplus of $6.6 billion in 1982.[4] Table 4-3 shows how these trade data fit into the total structure of the Mexican balance of payments. In normal times, there is a regular pattern of deficits on merchandise trade and on current account,

3. Petroleum and petroleum derivative exports, in millions of dollars, were: 1975, $460; 1976, $557; 1977, $1,033; 1978, $1,803; 1979, $3,861; and 1980, $10,306. See chapter 5 for more detail on Mexico's oil production and exports.
4. "Comercio exterior en el primer semestre de 1983," *El Mercado de Valores,* vol. 43 (September 19, 1983), p. 973.

Table 4-3. *Summary of Mexico's Balance of Payments, 1976–80*[a]

Millions of dollars

Item	1976	1977	1978	1979[b]	1980[b]
Trade balance	− 2,716	− 1,471	− 1,926	− 3,190	− 3,266
Balance on goods and services	− 3,069	− 1,623	− 2,342	− 4,856	− 6,597
Capital balance	5,202	2,229	3,224	4,332	8,541
Errors and omissions	− 2,452	− 101	− 659	− 873	− 867
Changes in reserves	− 321	504	223	419	1,151

Sources: Banco de México, *Indicadores Económicos,* December 1978 and 1979, pp. 64–65 in each, and April 1981, p. 56.

a. Different institutions use different techniques for calculating the elements of the balance of payments. Data in the International Monetary Fund's *International Financial Statistics* indicate smaller merchandise deficits and sometimes either smaller or larger other balances. Both sets of data show the same trends, however.

b. Preliminary figures.

financed by capital inflows, largely debt.[5] The extraordinarily large figure for errors and omissions in 1976 reflects withdrawal of capital caused by loss of confidence in Mexico and in the economic policies of the regime of President Luis Echeverría. The slowdown of this withdrawal in 1977 followed Mexico's commitment in late 1976 to a stabilization agreement with the International Monetary Fund (IMF). Mexico's balance-of-payments pattern will almost certainly change as the result of Mexican oil and, potentially, natural gas exports and the success or failure of Mexican development efforts generally. Imports for industrialization were augmented during the López Portillo administration by financing from energy exports, but the debt financing also grew excessively, as was evident from the need for refinancing coupled with assistance from the IMF in 1982 and 1983.

The United States is overwhelmingly Mexico's dominant trading partner (tables 4-4 and 4-5). In 1979 the United States provided 63 percent of Mexico's imports and took 69 percent of its exports. Mexico's percentage of imports from the United States was slightly higher for the first nine months of 1980, but the percentage of exports to the United States declined. The decline was due to diversification of petroleum exports. In contrast, according to U.S. trade data and despite the fact that Mexico was the fifth largest trade partner of the United States in 1979, Mexico provided only 4.3 percent of U.S. imports and took 5.4 percent of the value of U.S. exports. In 1980, 5.2 percent of U.S. imports came from Mexico and 6.9 percent of exports were sent to Mexico. In 1981 Mexico was the third largest market for U.S. exports.

5. This was not the pattern in 1982, when there was a trade surplus. But 1982 and 1983 were years of economic crisis and cannot be considered normal.

Table 4-4. *Mexico's Merchandise Imports, by Country and Area, 1976–80*

Item	1976	1977	1978	1979ᵃ	1980ᵃ
	Millions of dollars				
United States	3,765	3,485	5,023	7,637	8,638
Canada	141	166	162	197	262
Europeᵇ	1,275	1,131	1,768	2,508	2,461
South America	245	244	346	576	483
Caribbean and Central America	163	73	64	123	170
Other	441	390	780	1,056	1,161
Israel	0.5	0.5	1	4	4
Japan	306	295	590	787	693
People's Republic of China	9	9	24	43	48
Total	6,030	5,489	8,143	12,097	13,175
	Percent				
United States	62.4	63.5	61.7	63.1	65.6
Canada	2.3	3.0	2.0	1.6	2.0
Europeᵇ	21.1	20.6	21.7	20.7	18.7
South America	4.1	4.4	4.2	4.8	3.7
Caribbean and Central America	2.7	1.3	0.8	1.0	1.3
Otherᶜ	7.3	7.1	9.6	8.7	8.8
Israel	*	*	*	*	*
Japan	5.0	5.3	7.2	6.5	5.2
People's Republic of China	*	*	*	*	*
Total	100.0	100.0	100.0	100.0	100.0

Sources: Banco de México, *Indicadores Económicos*, December 1978, pp. 66–69; February 1980, p. 66; and December 1980, p. 59. Figures are rounded.
* Less than 0.5 percent.
a. Preliminary figures. Figures for 1980 are for January through September.
b. Predominantly Western Europe.
c. In the years shown, Japan generally has accounted for 75 percent of the "other" category.

In recent years, Mexico has imported more from developed countries than it has exported and has exported more to developing countries than it has imported. Since the bulk of Mexico's trade is with developed countries, the global result generally has been a merchandise trade deficit. However, like the past pattern of Mexico's balance of payments, a merchandise trade surplus or deficit, particularly when measured bilaterally or regionally, is not a central economic issue. Oil and natural gas exports will change many of these balances. So will the health of the Mexican and the world economies. Mexico believes the dominance of the United States in its international trade accentuates Mexico's dependency and hence sees trade diversification as a political rather than an economic issue. Oil may permit Mexico to diversify its export markets, although by itself this is a superficial diversification. The central elements

Table 4-5. *Mexico's Merchandise Exports, by Country and Area, 1976–80*

Item	1976	1977	1978	1979[a]	1980[a]
	Millions of dollars				
United States	1,854	2,399	4,411	6,147	7,028
Canada	48	44	61	74	96
Europe[b]	367	397	572	1,098	1,716
South America	315	371	381	419	444
Caribbean and Central America	191	215	240	271	466
Other	214	224	552	905	1,203
Israel	65	70	106	299	432
Japan	100	82	171	248	333
People's Republic of China	9	17	123	129	58
Total	2,989	3,650	6,217	8,914	10,954
	Percent				
United States	62.0	65.7	70.9	68.9	64.2
Canada	1.6	1.2	1.0	0.8	0.9
Europe[b]	12.3	10.9	9.2	12.3	15.7
South America	10.5	10.2	6.1	4.7	4.0
Caribbean and Central America	6.4	5.9	3.9	3.0	4.2
Other	7.2	6.1	8.9	10.2	11.0
Israel	2.2	1.9	1.7	3.3	3.9
Japan	3.3	2.2	2.8	2.8	3.0
People's Republic of China	0.3	0.4	2.0	1.4	0.5
Total	100.0	100.0	100.0	100.0	100.0

Sources: Banco de México, *Indicadores Económicos*, December 1978, pp. 66–69; February 1980, p. 67; and December 1980, p. 58. Figures are rounded.
a. Preliminary figures. Figures for 1980 are for January through September.
b. Predominantly Western Europe.

of uncertainty will be oil prices and the composition of Mexico's trade other than oil. These factors are related to Mexico's industrial program, its development program generally, its ability to create productive employment, its trade policy, and its exchange-rate policy.

Table 4-6 shows Mexico's foreign trade in relation to its total economy—that is, its exports in relation to its gross domestic product (GDP)—and compares Mexico with the United States in these terms. For both countries, merchandise exports have played a secondary but growing role in the total economy. In 1977 the relationship between merchandise exports and GDP or gross national product (GNP) was practically identical in Mexico and the United States at 6.2 or 6.3 percent.[6] However,

6. Table 4-6 shows the relationship between merchandise exports and GNP for the United States at 6.3 percent for 1977. The relationship would be identical if GDP were used as the denominator instead of GNP.

Table 4-6. *Mexican and U.S. Merchandise and Service Exports as a Percent of Gross National or Gross Domestic Product, 1974–80*

Year	Mexico		United States	
	Merchandise exports/GDP	Merchandise and service exports/GDP	Merchandise exports/GNP[a]	Merchandise and service exports/GNP[a]
1974	4.6	9.8	6.9	10.2
1975	3.8	8.0	6.9	10.1
1976	4.4	9.0	6.7	10.0
1977	6.2	10.1	6.3	9.6
1978	6.9	12.5	6.6	10.3
1979	7.8	13.3	7.5	11.9
1980	9.2[b]	14.9[b]	8.4	13.0

Sources: International Monetary Fund, *International Financial Statistics* (IMF, June 1981), pp. 268–69, 408–09; Banco de México, *Informe Anual, 1980*, pp. 145, 169.

a. GNP rather than GDP data were used for the United States because they are more familiar. The percentages are virtually identical if GDP data are used.

b. Estimated.

from 1978 to 1980 merchandise exports in relation to total output grew faster for Mexico than for the United States. Those were years of high oil prices, and the increasing oil exports altered earlier relationships. Mexico's foreign trade picture changed again in 1981, as oil prices declined. A picture of reasonably similar external dependencies in both the United States and Mexico emerges if exports of goods and services are compared rather than just the export of goods. Both countries are important exporters of services, although of different types,[7] and the importance of the foreign sector in the total economy of each country shows up more clearly if these are included than if one looks at merchandise exports alone. Merchandise exports would also be more important in both economies if the denominator were only goods production rather than total production, which includes services that are not traded.

Each country has tended to neglect foreign trade, particularly exports. This conclusion is based on the perception that since merchandise exports amounted to only about 4 to 7 percent of total GNP, the appropriate priority targets of economic policy were domestic and that stimulation of foreign trade required no special effort. Indeed, key policy

7. For example, the United States earns substantial net sums from capital remittances by U.S. corporations operating overseas. Mexico, on the other hand, receives net balance-of-payments inflows from worker remittances and generally from tourists visiting the country.

measures have often impeded foreign trade. In the United States, this was reflected in the maintenance of an overvalued exchange rate until August 1971, and some corrective actions concerning balance of payments that restricted capital account movements rather than encouraged merchandise exports.[8] This tendency has persisted even longer in Mexico. The nominal value of a clearly overvalued peso was maintained until August 1976, despite the serious damage it was doing to Mexico's competitiveness in international markets and to service exports, such as tourism. The pattern of the peso's gradually becoming overvalued and then being abruptly devalued was repeated between 1976 and 1982. By 1976, when service and merchandise exports amounted to 9 percent of Mexico's GDP, the overvalued peso became increasingly less tenable, just as it had earlier in the United States. It was even less tenable by 1982, when Mexico was again forced to devalue the peso.

Instruments of Mexican Trade Policy

Several aspects of Mexico's trade policy would need to be changed if there were a movement toward free trade between Mexico and the United States.[9] The most important one is the absolute protection given to most domestic production, almost regardless of the industry's level of efficiency. This protection would have to give way to trade with the United States if the two countries moved toward free trade. In theory,

8. Penelope Hartland-Thunberg, *The Political and Strategic Importance of Exports.*

9. The following studies are useful for those interested in more detailed analyses of Mexican foreign trade policy. Some are in Spanish: Rafael Izquierdo, "El proteccionismo en México," in Leopoldo Solís M., ed., *La economía mexicana: Análisis por sectores y distribución*, pp. 228–69; Bela Balassa, "La política comercial de México: Análisis y proposiciones," also in Solís, *La economía mexicana*, pp. 416–38; Gerardo M. Bueno, "Políticas en relación con el sector externo," in Gerardo M. Bueno, ed., *Opciones de política económica en México despues de la devaluación*, pp. 53–66; Ruth Rama and Robert Bruce Wallace, "La política proteccionista mexicana: Un análisis para 1960–1970," pp. 167–214; René Villarreal, *El desequilibrio externo en la industrialización de México, 1929–1975: Un enfoque estructuralista*; statement by Roberto Dávila Gómez Palacio, technical secretary of the cabinet on foreign trade, entitled "Estrategía para el comercio exterior de México," pp. 668–72. Others are in English: Bueno, "The Structure of Protection in Mexico"; Clark W. Reynolds, *The Mexican Economy: Twentieth-Century Structure and Growth*, especially pp. 197–254; A. Nowicki and others, *Mexico: Manufacturing Sector: Situation, Prospects and Policies*; Rafael Izquierdo, "Protectionism in Mexico," in Raymond Vernon, ed., *Public Policy and Private Enterprise in Mexico*, pp. 241–89.

Mexico could maintain whatever protection it wished against imports of goods from other countries even as it moved toward free trade bilaterally, but this would not be practical. The purpose of moving toward free trade with the United States would be to make Mexican industry competitive, and a competitive industry does not need the kind of absolute protection Mexico has provided. Important changes in Mexico's protection occurred in the first few years of the López Portillo administration, but these did not go far before they were reversed for balance-of-payments reasons. Protection has been provided in a variety of ways; following is a description of these instruments of Mexico's trade policy.[10]

The Tariff Structure

Mexico's tariff structure is similar to that of most countries in that rates applicable to imports escalate as value is added to products and become prohibitively high for goods considered luxury items. Raw materials and necessary foodstuffs generally carry import duties between 0 and 15 percent, and intermediate products have rates of 20 to 35 percent if not produced in Mexico and from 40 to 60 percent if produced in Mexico. Luxury goods are subject to customs duties of 60 to 100 percent. Machinery imports are subject to low rates, 10 percent when the product is not or cannot soon be manufactured domestically, rising to 60 percent when local production is available.

Additional levies are imposed on certain imports. There is a 2 percent duty for most imports, except for those whose general duty is 5 percent or less or if the item was given preferential treatment by the now defunct Latin American Free Trade Association (LAFTA). Imports are also exempt from the 2 percent duty if the item is imported into a free zone or for incorporation into Mexican products destined for later export. Goods destined for municipalities pay a 3 percent duty, and a 10 percent duty is imposed on imports by post.

The base to which the duty used to be applied was something Mexico called the official price. This price was usually higher than the invoice price, and if it was not, the duty was applied to the invoice price. In theory, the official price was an adjustment of the invoice price to the wholesale price level in the main exporting country of the item in

10. The material that follows comes mainly from official Mexican documents augmented by conversations with Mexican authorities.

question, as determined by the Mexican Ministry of Commerce. This was a sore point in U.S.-Mexican trade relations, since any official determination or raising of price must be arbitrary. This practice was stopped in 1980 but later resumed.

Nontariff Barriers

The tariff structure has been a secondary line of protective defense. In late 1976, when Mexico began negotiations with the IMF for assistance under what was then Mexico's stabilization program, and then more systematically for a few years starting in 1977, Mexico began gradually to replace prior permits with customs duties. The intent was to make the tariff the main instrument of protection. By December 1979 about 80 percent of Mexico's 7,946 tariff items had been freed from the prior import-licensing requirement (or, stated in reverse, import licenses remained on 1,729 tariff items). However, in terms of import value the liberalization was much less extensive in that about 60 percent of Mexican imports, as determined by value, still required licenses.[11] Mexico's move to rely primarily on tariffs could have augured a significant change in the direction of its trade policy, but it turned out to be a passing phase. A new effort to liberalize imports will have to wait until Mexico recovers from its economic crisis.[12] A World Bank study in 1979 suggested that an appropriate tariff structure to be achieved "in several years" would be to have import duties averaging 10 to 15 percent for manufactures, ranging upward to 20 to 25 percent for infant industries with undeveloped potential. This recommendation was coupled with one calling for greater reliance on the exchange rate to maintain the real peso cost of imports.[13]

There are many reasons to be skeptical about Mexico's resolve to liberalize its import structure. The decision in 1980 not to enter the General Agreement on Tariffs and Trade, discussed later in this chapter, was one indication that Mexico would not easily abandon actual import restrictions and replace them with tariffs, even when the economy was not in a state of crisis. In June 1981, faced with an increasing trade

11. Rocío de Villarreal and René Villarreal, "El comercio exterior y la industrialización de México a la luz del nuevo GATT," pp. 145–46.

12. The recommendation that Mexico should reduce excess import protection and gradually liberalize import quotas is not new. It is the main recommendation in Bueno, "The Structure of Protection in Mexico," p. 202, published in 1971.

13. Nowicki and others, *Mexico: Manufacturing Sector*, p. 23.

deficit, Mexico imposed prior import permit requirements on 865 products, to remain in effect at least until June 30, 1982.[14] The requirements still exist as this is written and now cover almost all imports because of the balance-of-payments crisis.[15] In other words, when its debt became overwhelming in mid-1981, Mexico resorted to the familiar practice of restricting imports through licensing rather than change its exchange rate. The peso was devalued only in 1982, by which time devaluation had become inevitable. In a speech in June 1981, the finance minister referred to the slowdown in manufactured exports and the increase in imports and asserted that these developments called for "a more adequate trade policy and also for steps to avoid a too drastic and unjustified abandonment of the protection due to Mexican producers."[16]

One can argue whether Mexico's policy of protectionism, designed to promote industrialization, was a correct policy in its time. Most analysts have asserted that the level of protection used and perhaps even its duration were indispensable in achieving the degree of industrialization that was reached. Others have argued that the policy forced Mexico to look inward because it created an industry unable to compete internationally or even at home without excessive support.[17] But no matter how much Mexico may have needed a protectionist policy at an earlier stage of development, it is obviously not effective now for promoting manufactured exports or for helping to create enough jobs to meet Mexico's needs. Mexican industry is not generally competitive,

14. American Chamber of Commerce of Mexico, "Prior Import Licenses List Increased Sharply," p.12.

15. The dual exchange-rate system instituted in late 1982 also made prior permission necessary for granting the preferential rate. The regulations on prior licensing can be found in *El Mercado de Valores*, vol. 42 (September 27, 1982), pp. 992–94. These regulations are subject to frequent change as the administration of President Miguel de la Madrid proceeds with Mexico's economic stabilization program.

16. Condensation of speech by David Ibarra Muñoz, "The Annual Convention of the Mexican Bankers' Association," pp. 224–25.

17. Izquierdo, "El proteccionismo en México," is categorical about the need for protection in the early stages of industrialization. "Despite its limitations, there is no doubt that protectionism has been beneficial, even indispensable" (p. 269). Balassa has made a similar point, that the previous import licensing system was useful in the first stages of Mexico's industrialization. See "La política comercial de México," p. 433. On the other hand, Gustav Ranis has stressed the lack of competitiveness fostered by the policy of excessive protectionism, in "¿Se esta tornando amargo el milagro mexicano?" pp. 22–33. Rama and Wallace, "La política proteccionista mexicana," stressed the price paid by Mexico's agricultural and mining sectors in subsidizing industry.

and most of Mexico's manufactured exports find a market only because of special incentives. About one-third of Mexico's manufactured exports to all destinations in 1980 were from plants that assemble products for the U.S. market and benefit from provisions in the U.S. tariff that limit import duties to the value added in Mexico.[18] An additional 15 percent of Mexico's manufactured exports in 1980 benefited from U.S. tariff preferences, that is, from special privileges.[19] Exports from the automotive industry, which in 1980 amounted to more than $400 million,[20] are made possible not necessarily because Mexico is competitive but because Mexican legislation and regulations impose a zero net-import requirement—that is, automobile producers must in theory match each dollar of imports above a base level by exports. The World Bank study cited earlier notes these and other special incentives that have made possible even the relatively low level of manufactured exports that Mexico has achieved to date.[21]

The reasons for the lack of competitiveness of highly protected industry are familiar from the literature and from the experiences of countries that have followed this path to industrialization since World War II.[22] This does not mean that countries with highly protected industry have never succeeded in developing a manufacturing sector competitive in world markets. Japan developed through protection of its industry and then reduced overt import barriers as they became superfluous. But it did so with a large internal market and an educated population base, neither of which Mexico has. The developing countries that have been most competitive have deliberately promoted exports of manufactured goods.[23] These countries include Hong Kong, Taiwan, South Korea, Yugoslavia, Greece, Israel, Portugal, Singapore, Spain, and most recently, Brazil. Mexico, on the other hand, at least until recently, actually burdened its exports of manufactures. More than a decade ago, Bueno calculated biases against exports by industry categories and found them

18. The one-third figure is based only on the value added in Mexico, not the reexport of components originally imported. Data from Banco de México, *Informe Anual, 1980*, p. 178, and table 3-4.
19. See table 3-3.
20. Banco de México, *Informe Anual, 1980*, p. 182.
21. Nowicki and others, *Mexico: Manufacturing Sector*, pp. 11–13.
22. A thorough relatively recent study is Anne O. Krueger, *Liberalization Attempts and Consequences.*
23. Hollis B. Chenery and Donald B. Keesing, *The Changing Composition of Developing Country Exports,* contains data on these developments.

to be substantial.[24] The biases came from tariffs or actual prohibitions on imported inputs, from the high cost of protected domestic production, and from an exchange rate that was overvalued for most of the 1960s and 1970s. It is possible to provide absolute protection against imports, but it is more complex to compensate for this by encouraging exports, as Mexico has learned. One reason for the success of Mexico's border industry program is that the imports for further assembly are not burdened with duties.

The Exchange Rate

One major impediment Mexico has imposed on its exports for long periods has been an overvalued exchange rate. World Bank economists developed a "free trade equilibrium" exchange rate, the rate at which Mexico's balance of payments on current account (not trade account) would have been at or near equilibrium if all protection and export incentives and disincentives were removed. They concluded that overvaluation, using this benchmark, was 2.8 percent in 1970 and 18.4 percent in 1975.[25] From 1954, when the peso was valued at 12.50 to the U.S. dollar, until September 1, 1976, when the rate was devalued, policy was rigid in maintaining the nominal peso-dollar relationship. There were periodic small devaluations between 1976 and February 1982, when the peso was again devalued, but these did not compensate for the inflation difference between Mexico and the United States. Because of the dominance of the United States in Mexican trade, it is the relationship of the two countries' inflation rates that is the crucial one for Mexico. Beginning in the 1960s, the peso became increasingly overvalued. Table 4-7 compares the evolution of wholesale prices in the two countries from the year the 12.50 rate was set until the year it was changed.

Mexico's reasons for maintaining a virtually fixed nominal rate

24. Bueno, "The Structure of Protection in Mexico."
25. Nowicki and others, *Mexico: Manufacturing Sector*, pp. 18–20, annex II, pp. 83–91. They admit that their methodology shows less overvaluation than other approaches. The extent that the peso was overvalued lowers the level of effective protection. The authors estimated effective protection for manufactures at 18.8 percent in 1970 and 40.9 percent in 1975. After netting out overvaluation, these figures fell to 15.6 percent in 1970 and 19 percent in 1975. They estimated that net export incentives for manufactures were negative in both years, − 14.4 percent in 1970 and − 9.5 percent in 1975.

Table 4-7. *Wholesale Price Indexes for the United States and Mexico City, 1970 and 1976*[a]

1954 = 100

Year	United States[b]	Mexico City
1970	126	174
1976	209	356

Sources: For the United States, *Economic Report of the President, January 1978*, p. 319; for Mexico City, Nacional Financiera, *Statistics on the Mexican Economy, 1977*, pp. 218–19.

a. The wholesale price index for Mexico City is used because a national wholesale price index is not available.

b. Data converted from 1967 = 100 to 1954 = 100.

between the peso and the dollar rather than adjusting the rate periodically to compensate fully for inflation differentials, as other Latin American countries were doing, were partly rooted in the times when devaluation was a sign of some national failure. Another reason was the fear that nominal devaluation might trigger capital flight because of Mexico's proximity to the United States. (Mexico was not the only country that resisted devaluation in the 1960s. The United States did the same.) It is unclear whether maintaining a real fixed relationship with the dollar by regular peso rate changes, as opposed to fixing the nominal rate, would actually have stimulated capital flight.[26] This did not happen in Brazil, Chile, and Colombia. At any rate, in 1976 overvaluation of the peso coupled with diminishing confidence in the economic policies of the Mexican government did bring on massive capital flight. The value of the peso fell from 12.50 to more than 25 to the dollar in October 1976 but eventually settled at between 22 and 23 to the dollar, a devaluation of about 85 percent. The exchange rate at the end of June 1982 was 48 pesos to the dollar, a devaluation of 57 percent compared with the market rate of 30.5 pesos to the dollar during January 1982. Since then, the Mexican exchange-rate structure has changed radically. Exchange controls were imposed in August and September 1982, and there have been several alterations in the controls since then. A structure of multiple exchange rates was instituted, which also underwent rapid modification month by month. In December 1982, the controlled peso selling rate for documents was 96.53 pesos to the dollar, compared with 70 the previous month and 26.26 in December 1981. At the end of October 1983, the controlled rate

26. Norris Clement and Louis Green, in "The Political Economy of Devaluation in Mexico," p. 72, state: "In the short run the peso exchange rate and its stability will play an important role in determining whether private funds will remain lodged in U.S. banks and whether domestic demand and employment will remain at low levels."

was 132 pesos to the dollar and the free-market rate for nontrade transactions was 156 pesos to the dollar.[27]

It is unclear what Mexico's future exchange-rate policy will be. The unsuccessful experiment with exchange controls introduced in August and September 1982 only added to this uncertainty. From 1977 through 1980, Mexico's exchange rate remained between 22 and 23 pesos to the dollar even though inflation in Mexico exceeded that in the United States for that period. Before the 1982 devaluation one heard references in Mexico to its exchange-rate policy of "fixed floating." Mexico's exchange-rate policy is crucial, especially in the context of a possible free-trade arrangement with the United States. An overvalued exchange rate precludes maximum benefit from free trade as well as trade generally, since it requires import protection and export subsidies to overcome the trade effects of overvaluation. Such measures would not be consistent with free trade.

The problem of an overvalued exchange rate may become more complicated in the future, depending on the evolution of Mexico's oil exports and the current account in its balance of payments. A current account surplus—a possibility in the late 1980s—and subsequent real oil price increases would tend to strengthen the peso and could, consequently, prejudice non-oil exports. President López Portillo's industrial development plan posited a current account deficit not to exceed 2 percent of GDP during any year of the 1980s, predicated on import growth of 15 percent a year in real terms.[28] Even as proposed, the plan required maintaining a difficult balance between permitting burgeoning imports without excessive waste and avoiding strengthening of the peso following large receipts from petroleum exports. Obviously, a strengthened peso has not been the problem so far. Mexico's economic fortunes, however, are captive to the state of world markets for oil and other products.

There is no single form the exchange-rate relationship with the dollar must take under a free-trade arrangement. The peso could be allowed to float freely. Under a free float, the peso would probably not be overvalued

27. American Chamber of Commerce of Mexico, "Key Economic Indicators," p. 10, for the 1981 and 1982 official peso selling rate. The later free-market rate observations are based on personal experience in changing dollars for pesos and on reporting in the press. See *Washington Post*, October 21, 1983.

28. Secretaría de Patrimonio y Fomento Industrial, *Plan nacional de desarrollo industrial, 1979–1982*.

for long periods, but undershooting and overshooting of the optimal rate could occur because of political developments that either bolstered or weakened confidence in the peso (or the dollar). Mexican authorities might prefer a managed float, which could provide for regular small devaluations to compensate for the differences in inflation between Mexico and the United States. It is possible, of course, that inflation in the United States could exceed that in Mexico, in which case the dollar would have to depreciate. In any case, a fixed peso-dollar rate, which has led to periodic overvaluation of the peso, would not be compatible with bilateral free trade.

Factors Encouraging Exports

Despite impediments, Banco de México data show that the volume of Mexico's manufactured exports grew by 9 percent a year in the 1960s and 6.2 percent a year from 1970 to 1975, the last year before the 1976 devaluation. Much of Mexico's manufactured exports benefit from special privileges unilaterally given by the United States, negotiated preferences included in agreements within LAFTA or the Latin American Integration Association, forced exports by the automotive industry, and low-interest financing for many exporters given by FOMEX (Fondo para el Fomento de las Exportaciones de Productos Manufacturados). In addition to these incentives, Mexico has a system of tax refund certificates, or CEDIs (Certificados de Devolución de Impuestos Indirectos). The CEDI system was in force from 1971 to 1976, was suspended temporarily after the 1976 peso devaluation, and was reinstituted in modified form in April 1977.

The reconstituted CEDI system allows refunds of up to the full amount of net federal indirect taxes charged on the product and its inputs. The CEDI, or refund certificate, can be used exclusively for payment of nonearmarked federal taxes. The CEDI is not transferable and is valid for five years. Refunds are not granted for products that carry export duties. In 1978, about 87 percent of the items in the export tariff were eligible for CEDIs. The amount of refundable tax varies from 25 to 100 percent, depending on gross value added, domestic content of the product, and whether the exporter has increased exports over the past year. To be eligible, a product must normally have at least 30 percent domestic content measured against the free-on-board export price. The gross-value-added requirement was relaxed in January 1980 for products requiring imported inputs.

Mexico also issues what are called EXTRA-CEDIs, for refunds of indirect taxes, to consortia of manufacturers that have formed capital stock companies for the purpose of increasing exports. These foreign trade undertakings accounted for about 25 percent of Mexico's exports of manufactures in 1978. When Mexico instituted a value-added tax system in 1980, exporters became entitled to a further entitlement of up to 10 percent devolution of the value of exports to compensate for the value-added tax.[29]

Tax Incentives under Free Trade

The Mexican system is designed to encourage domestic content of manufactures, which might be acceptable during a movement to free trade but would not be compatible with a full-fledged free-trade area. In the latter case, production in one member country should be deemed tantamount to production in other member countries. The CEDI system is unsuitable because the percentage refund varies according to an interplay of criteria and hence is arbitrary rather than automatic. Arbitrariness promotes uncertainty and permits covert bargaining between government officials and exporters. Using the criterion of greater refunds for greater increases in export performance is similar to the incentive under the U.S. Domestic International Sales Corporation legislation that gives tax deferrals based on incremental exports. This would also be suspect in a full-fledged free-trade area.

In a move toward free trade with the United States, Mexico would simultaneously have to alter the central elements of its trade policy. A free-trade area is not compatible with a comprehensive system of import licensing under which Mexico could exclude more competitive production from the United States, nor with a system under which export subsidies are used as incentives to encourage domestic content. For Mexico a move toward free trade would be difficult because it would mean changing a pattern of development that has prevailed for thirty years. However, some change in policy has long been advocated by

29. "Decreto que dispone el otorgamiento de estímulos a las exportaciones de productos manufacturados en el país," *Diario Oficial*, January 7, 1980. Reprinted in *El Mercado de Valores*, vol. 40 (January 14, 1980), pp. 23–24.

Mexican economists, and there were halting steps in the first years of the López Portillo administration away from reliance on import licensing and toward using tariffs as the main instrument of industry protection. Also, required changes would be gradual, therefore lessening any potential trauma. If Mexico developed a competitive industrial structure, domestic content provisions, for example, would not be necessary. If it is accepted that Mexico must develop a more competitive industrial structure in any event, whether it moves to free trade with the United States or not, the additional steps toward free trade, while they would be significant, would not be revolutionary.

What may be more dificult to deal with in a prospective free-trade area are the subsidies inherent in Mexico's industrial development plan. Border adjustments involving the rebate of indirect taxes when goods are exported are familiar in international trade and consistent with the trade doctrines embodied in the GATT (although the arbitrariness of the Mexican rebate system would be of questionable legality if Mexico were a member of the GATT). But direct incentives are another story. In Mexico these include tax credits ranging from 10 to 25 percent for new investment, increases in employment, additional work shifts, and purchases of new machinery and equipment made in Mexico. Energy and petrochemical prices are also subsidized at varying levels. Such domestic subsidies are not unusual. They were not really addressed internationally until the negotiation under GATT auspices of the nontariff codes in the Tokyo round of trade negotiations, and even then there was no resolution of how to deal with domestic subsidies that might affect international trade. However, it is precisely these internal industrial subsidies that are likely to create serious trade conflicts because of their possible effect on international competition.[30] Mexico makes no secret of the fact that one purpose of the subsidies is to develop industries capable of expanding exports and substituting for imports.

During some part of a transition to free trade and in some cases even after the transition, many of these subsidies would presumably be acceptable. The United States also has investment tax credits, and many states offer their own versions of tax relief to new and expanding industrial enterprises. However, differential pricing in Mexico and the

30. The effect of domestic subsidies on international trade is discussed in Robert E. Baldwin, *Nontariff Distortions of International Trade*, pp. 110–32; Steven J. Warnecke, ed., *International Trade and Industrial Policies: Government Intervention and an Open World Economy*.

United States of such vital industrial inputs as energy and primary petrochemicals would not be consistent with a full-fledged free-trade area. U.S. producers and U.S. labor undoubtedly would find this an unfair form of competition. But this need not be an insuperable barrier to reaching a free-trade agreement if Mexico is allowed some flexibility during a transition to free trade. According to Mexico's industrial plan, its domestic subsidies will be temporary anyway, for up to ten years for energy and petrochemicals. The potential problem is that temporary subsidies often are extended indefinitely.

Subsidized exports from Mexico may attract countervailing duties in the United States and elsewhere even in the absence of free trade with the United States. Mexico was not part of the subsidy and countervailing duty code negotiated in the Tokyo GATT negotiations. This may turn out to be significant in the United States, since U.S. law requires that a countervailing duty be imposed when a foreign subsidy or bounty is provided for an imported product, whether or not injury is shown to a domestic U.S. industry. For exports from signatories of the code an injury test is provided. Problems of subsidies and countervailing duties may dominate U.S.-Mexican trade relations in the years ahead regardless of understandings reached in a gradual movement toward free trade.[31] Mexican industrial subsidies might be more acceptable to the United States if they were subsumed under some broader trade agreement rather than left in isolation.

Mexico and the GATT

Although Mexico participated in the Tokyo round of GATT negotiations, on March 18, 1980, President López Portillo announced that Mexico would "delay" its entry into the organization. This decision does not bode well for the even more ambitious step of moving toward free trade with the United States, which is why it is important to understand the factors involved in Mexico's decision. Mexican authorities explicitly stated that it was not based on dissatisfaction with the actual exchange of concessions that had been negotiated between Mexico

31. See Sidney Weintraub, "Mexican Subsidies and U.S. Law: Potential Collision Course."

and other countries.[32] Indeed, Mexico received tariff concessions on 1,329 tariff items with a trade value in 1976 of $2.5 billion.[33] The Mexican decision not to adhere to the GATT was based rather on a combination of political and economic considerations. The alliance against entry into the GATT was made up of the intellectual left, small manufacturers, and others with less apparent vested interests who wanted Mexico to retain complete freedom to determine its own commercial and industrial policy. These groups are precisely the ones that would oppose free trade with the United States.

The viewpoint of the intellectual left was well represented by the Colegio Nacional de Economistas, which campaigned actively against entry into the GATT. The Colegio's position was made public in a letter to President López Portillo dated May 23, 1979, and entitled "Policy Alternative to Protectionism and to Adhesion by Mexico to the GATT." The main points of the letter, published widely in the press, were that Mexico would lose its autonomy if it entered the GATT and that failure to enter did not mean that Mexico had to necessarily continue its overprotectionist policy. The statement argued that Mexico should adopt a policy toward the GATT similar to its oil policy, that is, obtain the benefits of the GATT by way of the most-favored-nation principle just as Mexico enjoyed the benefits of higher oil prices established by the Organization of Petroleum Exporting Countries without joining OPEC. The position of many of the intellectual left went beyond this and made the GATT issue a proxy for relations with the United States. The argument advanced was that the external pressure for Mexico to join the GATT came almost exclusively from the United States and that the U.S. motives must have been ulterior ones. These motives were to open the Mexican market even more to U.S. products by removing protective tariff and nontariff barriers and to prevent Mexico from pursuing independent industrial and oil policies. Such a strong attack on the United States for an issue as technical as GATT membership probably means attacks will be even stronger if a move to a free-trade area with the "hegemonic" power is proposed.[34]

32. This raises the question of why Mexico went through the negotiating process at all. There probably are several reasons for this, including lack of knowledge about the GATT and miscalculation about the extent of opposition to Mexico's joining the GATT.

33. The GATT used 1976 as the base since at the time of the negotiations that was the most recent year for which full Mexican trade data were available.

34. The anti-Americanism involved in the GATT debate erupted again in May 1980, after Mexico made its decision not to join. The U.S. ambassador, Julian Nava, implied

One of the organizations that raised the question of consistency between GATT membership and the independence of Mexican oil policy was the Cámara Nacional de la Industria de Transformación (CANA-CINTRA), whose members are the small manufacturers of Mexico.[35] The CANACINTRA position essentially is that the GATT would not resolve such priority issues as the generation of employment and distribution of wealth and that, since products for which Mexico has received tariff concessions face excess demand at home, there is no immediate question of exporting them. This position is straightforward and protectionist: "Commercial freedom by itself does not stimulate efficiency; what must come first is to determine the parameters of efficiency appropriate to the Mexican situation."[36] The CANACINTRA position is similar to that of producers in other countries who are uncertain about their ability to compete in the world market. Given the current state of Mexican competitiveness for industrial products, the CANACINTRA concern is justified, but only in relation to its own members. Whether this position is justified in terms of the general good of Mexico is more questionable.

CANACINTRA and the intellectual left made strange bedfellows. The Colegio Nacional de Economistas did not try to justify protectionism as such but instead argued that an arbitrary degree of protection could be provided more efficiently in the future than it had been in the past. CANACINTRA is quite openly protectionist, composed primarily of conservative business people, and not political in the sense of being anti-American. Many from the intellectual left, on the other hand, are anti-American, or at least antihegemonic. Those Mexican institutions representing larger industry and international traders tended to be in favor of Mexican entry into the GATT, the traders on self-interest grounds and the industrialists presumably because they felt they could compete

---

in a press interview that the Mexican decision had been a mistake. Newspaper columnists pounced on this as proof of the correctness of the Mexican decision. Nava was severely castigated as an interventionist (which he obviously was) and imperialist. The worst epithet was to refer to Nava, an American of Mexican descent, as "Mister" Nava. See, for example, the column by Arturo Sotomayor, "Las profecías del embajador," *Uno Mas Uno,* May 12, 1980, p. 26.

35. CANACINTRA published a pamphlet (undated) called "GATT, March 18, 1980: A Decisive Moment in Our History." (The date was of the president's announcement of the decision not to enter.) Material on CANACINTRA's position comes from this pamphlet, personal interviews with its officers, and the press.

36. Ibid., p. 51.

on a world scale. The picture is clouded in this sector of industry because of the affiliations that often exist with foreign corporations. Large industry would also be much more inclined to support a movement to free trade with the United States than would small industry.

The opposition to GATT entry finally rallied around the argument that Mexico needed freedom of action to determine its own commercial policy. In the president's words: "We have not gathered the full necessary elements of protection and impulse required by the flexibility of our economic development, under the global plan and the sectoral programs."[37] Mexico obviously feared that eventually its protectionist apparatus might have to be dismantled. The Tokyo negotiations gave Mexico at least fifteen years to deal with its import licensing system and left Mexico ample leeway to maintain high protective tariffs. But the old argument that had been taking place internally about whether the Mexican import-substitution model of industrial development should be altered drastically clearly was not resolved.

Flexibility concerning exports was also an issue. In the GATT working party on the accession of Mexico, much debate centered on the subsidies inherent in Mexico's industrial development plan. The draft protocol of accession contained the following paragraph:

Without prejudice to the rights and benefits accruing to contracting parties under the General Agreement as applied pursuant to the other provisions of this Protocol, the CONTRACTING PARTIES are aware that Mexico intends to implement its National Plan for Industrial Development through the legal instruments and complementary requirements therein and to establish such further legal instruments and industrial policy measures including those of a fiscal and financial character as may be necessary for the effective fulfillment of the objectives and targets of the Plan.[38]

The second part of this paragraph dealing with "fiscal and financial" measures to make the plan effective was the important section for Mexico. The first part, that of reserving their rights under the GATT, was the important section for other GATT members. The issue of the extent to which other GATT members would accept Mexican industrial

37. From remarks on March 18, 1980, in Guadalajara, announcing his decision on GATT entry (unofficial translation). The remarks were made at a meeting commemorating the forty-second anniversary of Mexico's expropriation of the petroleum industry, a bit of symbolism of national freedom that presumably was not accidental. Remarks obtained from CANACINTRA pamphlet and an unofficial translation distributed by the United States–Mexico Chamber of Commerce.

38. General Agreement on Tariffs and Trade, "Draft Protocol for the Accession of Mexico to the General Agreement on Tariffs and Trade," p. 22.

subsidization without imposing countervailing measures was left open; President López Portillo referred to this in his announcement that Mexico would not enter the GATT.[39]

It was not merely the general GATT provisions that concerned Mexicans intent on maintaining commercial and industrial independence but also the provisions relating to subsidies and countervailing duties and hence the code on this subject agreed to in the Tokyo negotiations. Several Mexican analysts cited another code, that on government procurement, as an impediment to Mexican entry into the GATT because under this code, it was argued, Mexico might be forced to open government purchases to foreign competition, which would conflict with Mexico's industrial plan.[40] Mexico could have acceded to the GATT and not subscribed to certain or any of the codes but chose instead complete rejection.

The logic of the Mexican decision in terms of the subsidy and countervailing duty code is not clear-cut. The GATT contracting parties maintain their autonomy in relation to Mexico whether or not Mexico is a member. It is even possible that Mexico would have had greater freedom as a signatory since the code offers greater freedom of action to developing countries than to developed ones. Also, because Mexico does not participate in the code, a U.S. complainant against Mexican subsidies now need show only that a subsidy was granted on an imported product, not that the subsidy caused any injury to U.S. industry.

Mexico's focus on the United States in its decision not to join the GATT is stressed in an interesting way by Villarreal and Villarreal. They argue that Mexico can obtain more from bilateral negotiations with the United States than from negotiations in the multilateral GATT framework because "in the 1980s, and for the first time in this century, the United States will need more from Mexico than the reverse, not only in the energy area, but also in foreign trade and foreign investment."[41] However, there is nothing in the GATT that prevents bilateral negotiation as long as the outcome does not violate the trade interests of third countries. Nor is it evident that the United States would prejudice its global trading interests because it needs Mexico more than Mexico needs

39. Other Mexican commentators have addressed this issue. For example, see Bernardo Sepúlveda Amor, "Las nuevas reglas del GATT y el marco jurídico mexicano," p. 140.
40. Villarreal and Villarreal make this point in "El comercio exterior," p. 144.
41. Ibid., p. 148 (my translation).

the United States, unless it did this in some broader context of U.S.-Mexican relations, such as movement to free trade.

Another seemingly technical but in fact highly relevant issue that concerned Mexican analysts is that of graduation.[42] This refers to changing the status of countries from "developing" to some other category, such as developed, semideveloped, newly industrializing, or transitional, and the consequent loss of special and discriminatory privileges in their favor. The most important benefits the GATT confers on developing countries is the ability to participate in trade negotiations without granting reciprocity and to receive preferential treatment for some exports (mostly of manufactured goods) to developed countries. Mexico did grant some reciprocal concessions in the Tokyo negotiations, but not equivalent to those it received. Mexico was, in fact, treated as a developing country. In addition, Mexico receives tariff preferences from developed countries and has been among the main beneficiaries of the U.S. general system of preferences.[43] These factors render Mexico's decision not to enter the GATT somewhat murky, for if the United States and other industrial countries were to insist on graduation, particularly for preferential treatment of exports (and it is in their power to terminate preferences since these are unilaterally granted), Mexico would not receive special treatment because it is outside the GATT. It could only receive special treatment from the United States under some overall agreement regarding a move to free trade.

In his statement on the GATT on March 18, 1980, President López Portillo also said: "The negotiations for the assurance of basic supplies by the contracting parties is one of the issues that worry us more, because of their terms and in relation to our world energy plan proposed before the United Nations."[44] The president presumably was referring to an issue raised during the debate in Mexico that GATT articles would prevent Mexico from pursuing an independent oil policy. The argument is based on GATT language that requires a country limiting its exports of a product for reasons of shortage to impose these limitations without

42. Ibid. The Villarreals note that Mexico has always opposed the concept of graduation.
43. *Report to the Congress on the First Five Years' Operation of the U.S. Generalized System of Preferences*, House Committee Print. In 1980 Mexico ranked fourth as a supplier to the United States under the GSP after Taiwan, Hong Kong, and South Korea.
44. See note 37.

discriminating among recipients and to limit domestic consumption if exports are limited for conservation purposes. Since Mexico's oil export policy is designed explicitly to meet internal needs, to diversify export markets by limiting exports to any one country—implicitly, the United States—to no more than 50 percent of total exports, and to use oil as a lever in bilateral trade and investment negotiations, it is understandable that Mexico would not want its hands tied on oil policy.[45]

The issue, however, is a red herring. It was pointed out during the GATT debate that even the United States has limited soybean exports in an emergency, that the OPEC countries carried out an embargo against the United States and the Netherlands in 1973, and that large oil-producing OPEC members are also part of the GATT—Indonesia, Kuwait, Nigeria—and have not suffered any loss of freedom to form whatever oil policies they like.[46] In fact, many industrial countries are concerned that GATT articles are defective precisely because they do not deal with the crucial issue of access to vital raw materials.[47]

There were other extraneous issues raised by those who opposed Mexican entry into the GATT, for example, that the legal status of the GATT was so unclear internationally that entry was risky and that Mexico would be at a disadvantage in the organization because Spanish was not used in GATT negotiations and policymaking.[48] The critical issues, however, were the trade and industrial policies Mexico intended to pursue, how much freedom it wished for this purpose, and Mexico's trade and political relationship with the United States. These are the same issues Mexico would have to analyze in a national debate on a slow but steady movement to bilateral free trade with the United States.

The public debate in Mexico about GATT membership reflected a conflict between the ideology of the Mexican elite and the practical considerations of small industrialists trying to keep their businesses afloat. This conflict between ideology and practicality takes place in most countries, and a national style can be adduced from the strength of the dominant group. In Mexico, dominance has shifted back and forth

45. The use of the oil lever in bilateral trade negotiations is well illustrated in the joint communiqué between Mexico and Japan of May 4, 1980. *El Mercado de Valores*, vol. 40 (May 19, 1980), pp. 481–83.

46. Mateo, "Contribución a la polémica sobre el GATT," pp. 115–16.

47. C. Fred Bergsten, "Access to Supplies and the New International Economic Order," in Jagdish N. Bhagwati, ed., *The New International Economic Order: The North-South Debate,* pp. 199–218.

48. See CANACINTRA pamphlet, "GATT, March 18, 1980."

between the ideological (but by no means impractical) position under President Lázaro Cárdenas and to some extent Luis Echeverría and the more practical approach under Presidents Miguel Alemán and Gustavo Díaz Ordaz. President López Portillo's position was conflicted. He considered adhering to the GATT and negotiated hard until the moment of decision but then had doubts and solicited a national debate so that both the practicalities and the ideology of Mexico's stand could emerge in full flower. The current president, Miguel de la Madrid, started his administration emphasizing the practical, saying in his inaugural address: "I will govern with imagination but avoid fantasy."[49] He simplified Mexico's foreign-exchange controls, increased interest rates, and tried to reassure the business community by showing a willingness to confront the country's economic crisis. Only time will tell whether this attitude will last throughout his six-year term or whether he will end his administration as did López Portillo, in a flurry of vituperation, placing blame on others for Mexico's problems.[50]

Summary

Whatever merits Mexico's trade policy may have had earlier as the country was building its industrial structure, current trade policy is not suited to Mexico's future development needs. For the most part Mexican industry is not competitive in world markets and is able to survive at home only because it receives absolute protection from imports. Fear that Mexican industry would not survive was the heart of the CANA-CINTRA opposition to Mexican accession to the GATT. Altering Mexico's trade policy does not require eliminating all import protec-

49. Miguel de la Madrid, "President de la Madrid's Inaugural Address," p. 417.

50. A few examples of this blame-placing from López Portillo's sixth and final state-of-the-nation report on September 1, 1982, illustrate this point. Citations are from López Portillo, "Sixth State of the Nation Report to the Mexican Congress," pp. 248–325. In justifying the nationalization of private banks, he said: "I can state that, in the last few years, it has been a group of Mexicans—whoever they may have been—making use, to be sure, of their rights and liberties, but led, advised, and supported by private banks, who have taken more money out of the country than the empires that have exploited us since the beginning of our history" (pp. 313–14). In explaining Mexico's economic crisis, he said: "Our economic policy has not been erroneous. . . . The external factors I have referred to so often have forced us to make successive adjustments to adapt to fortuitous circumstances which, now that they have combined to create a crisis, can be identified as a major evil requiring a major remedy" (p. 312).

tion—even more economically advanced countries have not done that—but it does require introducing more competition than exists now. In Japan and earlier in the United States, this competition came primarily from domestic sources, but these countries had internal markets considerably more substantial than what exists in Mexico. For the fast-growing middle-income countries of Asia, such as Taiwan, South Korea, and Singapore, one of the main impulses behind their growth has been a competitive export sector, but this is not being developed under current Mexican policy.[51]

Mexico could stimulate growth through a free-trade agreement with the United States that would become effective over an extended period. There are other theoretically viable approaches. These are negotiated reductions of protection on a multilateral basis (the GATT approach), unilateral trade liberalization (which is what occurred for a few years at the outset of the López Portillo administration), or more extensive preferential agreements with other countries in Latin America and the Caribbean. Mexico tried the last two options and found them wanting, and the first generated so much internal opposition that it was abandoned.

A movement to free trade with the United States would require significant though gradual changes in Mexican trade and industrial policy to introduce more competition and efficiency into Mexican industry. Four types of policy changes would be especially important. The most significant and that which defines a free-trade area is that the absolute protection afforded Mexican industry from outside competition would have to disappear gradually but surely, at least for imports from the United States. Protection need not be reduced for imports from other countries, but the current degree of absolute protection would make little sense if the bilateral free-trade arrangement did lead to a more competitive industrial structure in Mexico.

The second policy change relates to the subsidies, on which Mexican trade heavily relies. Although these subsidies are predominantly internal, there are extensive export subsidies as well. The trade policy that has developed in Mexico—a combination of absolute import protection for most industries and a periodically overvalued exchange rate—made subsidies inevitable if most Mexican products were to penetrate export markets. Under a bilateral free-trade agreement many of the domestic subsidies could remain, both in Mexico and the United States, but the

---

51. See Lawrence B. Krause and Sueo Sekiguchi, eds., *Economic Interaction in the Pacific Basin.*

explicit export subsidies affecting exports into the U.S. market would have to disappear gradually. Internal subsidies would presumably be the subject of negotiation on a case-by-case basis as complaints were registered, which is essentially what occurs now without a free-trade area. In return for the elimination of export subsidies, Mexican products would enjoy preferential treatment in the United States, either what it has already been enjoying or greater preferences.

Third, an overvalued exchange rate is not compatible with a durable free-trade arrangement. The Mexican exchange rate would have to serve two foreign-trade objectives under bilateral free trade: it would have to help make Mexican products competitive with imports from the United States without the use of tariffs or nontariff measures, and it would have to provide the right price conditions for exports to the United States and elsewhere without the use of export subsidies. The relevant exchange-rate relationship would be between the peso and the dollar. Mexican policy would have to be redesigned to avoid persistent overvaluation of the real value of the peso in relation to the dollar after taking into account the differential between U.S. and Mexican inflation. Mexican exchange-rate policy in the past has not followed this course, although de la Madrid said that it will in the future. Instead, the peso has been allowed to become overvalued as Mexican inflation exceeded that in the United States. Correctives came only in explosive spurts, in 1954, 1976, and then in 1982 and 1983. The exact form a new exchange-rate policy would take, whether a free float or a managed exchange rate, would be a decision for Mexican policymakers, but renewal of past practice would surely destroy any movement to free trade.

Finally, Mexican performance requirements would have to be altered during a transition to a free-trade area. The performance requirements that would have to be eliminated are those that force a manufacturer in Mexico to add a minimum percentage of value from Mexican sources or to export a given amount of goods to the United States to compensate for an equivalent value of imports from the United States. Such performance requirements could remain for Mexican trade with third countries. However, a bilateral free-trade agreement implies that production in one country is deemed equivalent to production in the other.[52]

Each of these policy areas is now significant in Mexican trade practice,

52. The legislation introduced in the U.S. Congress in 1982 and again in 1983 specifying minimum percentages of production for automobiles sold in the United States would also be incompatible with a bilateral free-trade agreement if they applied to Mexico.

and changing them will not be easy. Even the more modest changes that would have been required had Mexico acceded to the GATT proved unacceptable in the Mexican political milieu of 1980. However, some of these changes are being forced on Mexico by other events. For example, Mexico's debt crisis is forcing the country to modify its exchange rate. Past policy has led to regular crises in Mexico, the most recent in 1982–83 even raising questions about the durability of the country's political structure. Mexicans may argue that Mexican export subsidies should be accepted because Mexico is a developing country, but the country learned during the negotiations about accession to the GATT and from the number of import complaints brought against subsidized Mexican products by U.S. producers that other countries see this issue differently. Whether Mexico seeks bilateral free trade or not, its current trade policy is no longer feasible. The real policy questions for Mexico have to do with the context in which changes are made and the degree of assurance provided to both Mexican and foreign producers that changes are indeed forthcoming and not merely false starts like those of the López Portillo years.[53]

53. Such false starts were the decision to negotiate for accession to the GATT and the subsequent decision against accession despite generous treatment by the contracting parties; the steps toward trade liberalization that were halted at the first signs of balance-of-payments difficulties; and the lapse into use of import controls rather than correction of the peso's overvaluation.

CHAPTER FIVE

Mexico's Development Plans and Strategies

PLANNING was pervasive in Mexico during the López Portillo administration, from 1976 until 1982. Development plans were drawn up for urban affairs, industry, employment, energy, agro-industry, nutrition, water resources, education, and more, all reasonably consistent with each other and with Mexico's global development plan. In addition to these general and sector plans, programs were developed or extended in subsectors, for example, for the automotive and pharmaceutical industries.[1] The crisis that beset the Mexican economy in 1982 and 1983 meant that the plans would not be carried out on schedule, if ever. Indeed, a new national development plan was issued in 1983 during the de la Madrid administration.[2] Nevertheless, the old plans do represent a codification of Mexican aspirations and deserve analysis for this reason as well as for their intrinsic content.

Each plan contains a diagnosis of the problem in that particular area, objectives, and actions needed to achieve the objectives. Taken together, the plans set forth in a coherent framework the intended program of Mexico's government between 1978 and 1980, when the plans were released. The plans were precise for the period until 1982, when the López Portillo administration came to an end, but the intent was to set the policy framework in each area until 1990. Since no administration can commit the one that succeeds it and certainly not the one that succeeds that, the stated objectives and actions are progressively more vague from 1982 onward. But some degree of continuity of aspiration is

1. Calvin P. Blair, *Economic Development Policy in Mexico: A New Penchant for Planning*, contains a summary of the main plans.
2. Poder Ejecutivo Federal, *Plan nacional de desarrollo, 1983–1988.*

likely in the 1982–88 period, since the minister for planning and budget responsible for drawing up the global plan, Miguel de la Madrid, was chosen to succeed López Portillo as president of Mexico. The 1983–88 development plan is mostly consistent with the earlier plans, although more generally phrased. The relevant question is whether the aspirations of Mexico's development plans—particularly the global plan and plans for industry, energy, and agriculture—and the measures set forth to achieve these could be accomplished if there were a gradual movement toward free trade with the United States. It is also worth asking whether Mexico's plans are antithetical to U.S. aspirations for its own development in the 1980s.

A General Diagnosis

There is a consensus analysis in the plans that, although the import substitution industrialization model was an adequate strategy "in its time," its insufficiency eventually showed up in the noncompetitiveness of Mexican industry and in the inadequate growth of agriculture.[3] This theme is repeated in the 1983–88 plan. According to the earlier national industrial development plan, the oligopolistic industrial structure that developed based on past strategy contributed to inequalities in Mexican society "between town and country, between the larger cities and the smaller ones, between wage earners and business owners, and especially between jobholders and the jobless and the underemployed."[4] During the 1960s and 1970s agriculture, for example, experienced low growth despite remarkable growth of Mexico's gross domestic product (table 5-1). Mining nonpetroleum products also suffered from low growth, but this sector is less crucial than agriculture as a source of employment or as a proportion of the total Mexican economy. Mexico is fairly typical of developing economies in that since 1960 industry grew in proportion

3. Secretaría de Programación y Presupuesto, *Plan global de desarrollo, 1980–1982*, p. 34 (hereafter *Plan global*). A short version of this plan is reproduced from the *Diario oficial de la federación* of April 17, 1980, in the weekly publication of Nacional Financiera, S.A., *El Mercado de Valores*, as a supplement to vol. 40 (April 21, 1980). Future references will be to the complete version of the global plan.

4. Secretaría de Patrimonio y Fomento Industrial, *Plan nacional de desarrollo industrial, 1979–1982*, vol. 1, p. 18 (hereafter *Plan industrial*). An English translation was published in London by Graham and Trotman, Ltd., 1979. Future references will be to vol. 1 of the Spanish version.

Table 5-1. *Real Annual Growth of Mexico's Gross Domestic Product, by Sector, 1960–80*[a]

Percent

Sector	1960–76	1977–79	1980[b]
Agriculture	2.9	2.6	5.3[c]
Forestry	2.9	5.9	...
Fishing	3.0	6.1	...
Mining	2.7	2.3	6.5
Petroleum and petrochemicals	9.0	14.9	17.5[d]
Manufactures	7.7	7.0	5.6
Habitual consumer goods	6.2	5.1	3.1
Chemicals	10.4	3.6	n.a.
Capital and durable goods	10.5	11.4	12.8
Construction	7.9	7.5	12.8
Electricity	11.7	8.8	6.5
Commerce	6.1	4.7	n.a.
Communications and transportation	7.5	8.1	n.a.
Tourism	6.8	5.5	n.a.
Other services	6.0	5.5	n.a.
Gross domestic product	6.3	6.1	7.4

Sources: Secretaría de Programación y Presupuesto, *Plan global de desarrollo, 1980–1982*, p. 154, for data through 1979; Banco de México, *Informe Anual, 1980*, pp. 30–31, for 1980.
n.a. Not available.
a. Based on 1960 prices.
b. Preliminary figures.
c. Covers agriculture, forestry, and fishing.
d. Growth rate for petroleum and derivatives. The figure for petrochemicals is 12 percent.

to the GDP while agriculture lagged, but for Mexico the shift was relatively severe (table 5-2). Mexico was among the fortunate developing countries in the 1970s because its petroleum sector grew, although one might question the use to which this fortuitous resource was put.

The unemployment and underemployment to which the industrial plan refers are severe and probably constitute Mexico's most potentially explosive problem. The figures for the jobless and the underemployed are not precise. The U.S. Department of Labor estimated that in 1977 about 9 percent, or 1.5 million people, were unemployed and 40 percent, or about 7 million people, were underemployed.[5] The Mexican government's goal was to reduce open unemployment to 5.5 percent by 1982 and underemployment to 40.8 percent,[6] which thus posited an underemployment figure at the start of the López Portillo administration higher

5. U.S. Department of Labor, *Profile of Labor Conditions: Mexico*, p. 3.
6. "Plan nacional de desarrollo agroindustrial, 1980–82," p. 562.

Table 5-2. *Mexico's Gross Domestic Product, by Sector,*
1960, 1970, and 1979[a]

Percent

Sector	1960	1970	1979[b]
Agriculture, forestry, fishing	15.9	11.6	8.5
Mining	1.5	1.0	0.8
Petroleum and petrochemicals	3.4	4.3	6.4
Manufactures	19.2	22.8	24.0
Construction	4.1	4.6	5.2
Electricity	1.0	1.8	2.4
Commerce	31.2	31.8	29.1
Communications and transportation	3.3	3.2	4.2
Government	4.9	5.8	7.7
Other services	16.5	14.3	12.9
Adjustment for bank services	−1.0	−1.2	−1.2
Total	100.0	100.0	100.0

Source: *Plan global*, p. 136.
a. Based on 1960 prices.
b. Preliminary figures.

than that estimated by the U.S. Labor Department. Employment problems in Mexico are severe because of the youth of the population—close to half are less than fifteen years old—the need to export labor by way of undocumented migration to the United States, and the need to incorporate a large proportion of women into the labor force.[7] The labor force was estimated in 1975 to be between 16 and 17 million, increasing each year by about 3.7 percent, or between 600,000 and 700,000 people.[8] The López Portillo administration claimed great success in creating jobs in its first five years, but many of these gains were lost in that administration's final year.[9]

Evidence of inequality in Mexico is extensive, and the inequality that has been studied most is that of income distribution. What has been most disturbing to those concerned about Mexico's social structure is the persistence of inequality in income distribution despite the consistent high overall Mexican growth rate. According to Felix, income did

7. U.S. Department of Labor, *Profile of Labor Conditions*, p. 2, gives a figure of 3.5 million women in a labor force of 16.5 million in 1975.

8. Ibid., p. 3.

9. In a message to the Congress on December 7, 1982, setting forth the general criteria for his 1983 economic program, Miguel de la Madrid noted that open unemployment had doubled during the previous year. See Miguel de la Madrid, "Documento: Criterios generales de la política económica para 1983," p. 1286.

Table 5-3. *Percentage Distribution of Mexican Disposable Household Income, 1950 and 1975*

	1950 income		1975 income	
Household percentile	*Not adjusted for underdeclaration*	*Adjusted for underdeclaration*	*Not adjusted for underdeclaration*	*Adjusted for underdeclaration*
96–100	29.5	40.2	30.6	35.9
90–95	9.1	8.8	12.9	15.2
81–90	12.6	10.8	16.6	15.0
61–80	18.2	15.6	19.9	16.2
41–60	12.9	10.3	11.8	9.7
21–40	9.9	8.2	6.3	5.4
1–20	7.8	6.1	1.9	2.6

Source: David Felix, "Income Distribution Trends in Mexico and the Kuznets Curves," in Sylvia Ann Hewlett and Richard S. Weinert, eds., *Brazil and Mexico: Patterns in Late Development.*

become more concentrated between 1950 and 1975 (table 5-3).[10] Bergsman uses income adjustment measures different from those used by Felix but reaches the same conclusion. "Mexico," he notes, "has one of the most unequal distributions of income of all less developed countries."[11]

As one would expect, the inequality in Mexico's income distribution is replicated in other areas, such as education and infant mortality. And, as the industrial plan states, there are marked inequalities between town and country. Mexico's urban population increased from 51 percent of the total population in 1960 to 67 percent in 1980,[12] which is typical of the trend in most newly industrializing countries because of greater economic opportunities in urban than in rural areas. In each region of Mexico, the percentage of students completing six years of primary

10. David Felix, "Income Distribution Trends in Mexico and the Kuznets Curves," in Sylvia Ann Hewlett and Richard S. Weinert, eds., *Brazil and Mexico: Patterns in Late Development*, p. 277. Felix theorizes that Mexico's experience—persistent inequality despite robust growth—is probably typical of newly industrializing countries in the twentieth century.

11. Joel Bergsman, *Income Distribution and Poverty in Mexico*, p. 41. Looking at the percentage of disposable income received by the lowest 40 percent of households, Bergsman's figure (p. 15) in 1975 is between 5.4 and 8.9 percent; Felix's is between 8.0 and 8.2 percent. Both authors draw on data compiled by Mexican researchers and use income-adjustment techniques pioneered by Mexican scholars, particularly Ifigenia M. de Navarrete and Oscar Altimir.

12. World Bank, *World Development Report, 1980*, p. 149. The urban-rural dividing line in Mexico is a population of 2,500 inhabitants.

education is substantially higher for urban than for rural areas. For the country as a whole, about 54 percent of urban youngsters completed six years of primary education in 1970 and about 10 percent did so in rural areas. The figures have improved since 1970, but the great disparities remain. Infant mortality is also higher in rural areas.[13]

Essentially, Mexico is trying to address four main problems: (1) an industrial structure that is noncompetitive on a world scale; (2) unsatisfactory growth in agricultural production; (3) an economy unable to generate enough full-time jobs for those in and entering the labor force, despite high levels of overall economic growth; and (4) great inequalities in income and in the availability of essential services such as education, health care, and nutrition.[14]

Other instrumental rather than primary objectives stated throughout Mexico's plans include greater nationalization of Mexican industry, diversification of Mexico's foreign trade, greater balance in regional development, reduced inflation, and more generally, improved cooperation among different sectors of society.

Contents of the Plans

No plan can be followed precisely as written, if only because circumstances change. For example, López Portillo's plans say relatively little about inflation, which rose abruptly in 1982 to about 100 percent.[15] The global plan has a brief, inconclusive section on anti-inflation policy and essentially states the objective of reducing domestic inflation by 1982 to within 4 or 5 percentage points of external inflation. The objective was not achieved.[16] Failure to achieve the inflation objective had repercus-

13. Lyndon B. Johnson School of Public Affairs, *Growth and Equity in Mexico*, pp. 28, 99 (for education data) and p. 105 (for infant mortality data).

14. René Patricio Villarreal Arrambide, "External Disequilibrium and Growth without Development: The Import Substitution Model—the Mexican Experience (1929–1975)," is a careful exposition of why the Mexican growth model resulted in inefficiencies and inequality.

15. The figure is for consumer prices and was cited by President de la Madrid in "Criterios generales de política económica para 1983," p. 1286.

16. *Plan global*, p. 134. The difference turned out to be closer to 55 percentage points for consumer prices. In 1980, when the plan was released, the difference between Mexico's consumer prices and those in the United States was 13.9 percentage points. Mexican data are from Banco de México; U.S. data are from *Economic Indicators* (Government Printing Office, 1981).

sions on government budgets, wages, and foreign trade through the exchange rate, and these nullified, at least for a time, many of the actions contemplated in the plans. The plans themselves recognize that they were setting forth guidelines rather than immutable actions.[17] However, while future actions are uncertain, Mexico's problems will undoubtedly persist.

The Global Plan

This plan was published after the industrial plan began getting publicity and really added little to what already had been stated in other documents.[18] Its main value to analysts was in its tone and insights into the motivations of the Mexican authorities then governing the country. The introduction to the plan stressed that the López Portillo administration intended to use an integrated system of planning "as a style of governing."[19] The plan emphasized nationalism at the outset: "Mexican nationalism is sustained by the permanent struggle for economic, political, and cultural independence of Mexico." This attitude seems to preclude acceptance of a movement toward free trade, no matter how gradual, with the United States, the very country from which Mexico seeks independence.

The plan lists four main objectives: to strengthen Mexico's independence; to provide employment and meet priority needs in feeding, educating, and housing the population; to promote high and sustained economic growth; and to improve distribution of income among persons, factors of production, and regions. It then lists twenty-two general policy measures to accomplish these objectives. These deal with expanding employment, promoting economic growth, strengthening the agricultural sector, improving distribution of income and services to the poor, decentralizing economic activity, and extending cooperation among the public, social, and private groups named in the Alliance for Production,

17. *Plan industrial*, p. 22.
18. George W. Grayson, *The Politics of Mexican Oil*, p. 137, discusses the rivalry between the Ministry of Patrimony and Industrial Development, which prepared the industrial plan, and the Ministry of Planning and Budget, which prepared the global plan.
19. This and subsequent quotations come from the plan itself and were translated by the author.

Table 5-4. *Real Annual Growth Rates in Mexico's Global Plan, 1960–82*
Percent

Item	1960–76[a]	1977–79[a]	1980–82[b]
Global supply	6.3	6.6	9.7
Gross domestic product	6.3	6.1	8.0
Imports	6.4	12.0	20.8
Global demand	6.3	6.6	9.7
Total consumption	6.1	5.2	7.7
Private	5.6	4.7	7.7
Public	9.9	7.4	7.5
Gross fixed investment	8.1	8.7	13.5
Private	7.3	5.1	13.0
Public	11.6	13.2	14.0
Exports	4.6	15.6	14.4

Source: *Plan global*, p. 83.
a. Actual.
b. Projected.

proclaimed earlier in the López Portillo administration.[20] One policy measure was the basis for the other actions, namely to use income from petroleum as the impetus for economic and social development. This point was expanded in the energy plan. The other objectives and policies are not new. They have been stated in some form throughout Mexico's revolutionary period, particularly since the 1930s, and are similar to objectives stated by most governments. The global plan was weak because it mainly listed goals that have been stated endlessly in the past and that continue to need restating because they are never met.

The macroeconomic framework of the plan was more precise than its objectives (table 5-4). The big increases for the three years projected in the plan were for exports and imports, particularly the latter, and for private investment, based on what was until 1982 a climate of renewed confidence in the Mexican government. There was a stated assumption in the plan that the rate of increase in imports would begin to decline after 1980. In terms of current account in the balance of payments, the objective was to limit the deficit in 1982 to 1 percent of the GDP. It was more than 4 percent in 1976, the last year of the Echeverría administration, and between 2 and 3 percent in the first years of the López Portillo

20. The purpose of the Popular and Democratic National Alliance for Production was to stimulate cooperation among the different public and private groups involved in production.

administration.[21] The plan also projected annual growth of 4.1 percent for agriculture and forestry production, 10.8 percent for industry, 13.5 percent for capital goods production within the industrial sector, and 4.2 percent for employment. The last is a high figure and assumed that 2.2 million jobs would be created between 1980 and 1982. Such an increase would have absorbed new entrants into the labor market and cut down the percentage of unemployed and underemployed to 5.5 to 6.0 percent and 40.8 percent, respectively, in 1982—the goal of the national employment plan.

The global plan summarized the key elements of the energy plan: that energy is the driving force behind the global plan, that production of oil will reach about 2.5 million barrels a day, and that the funds generated from hydrocarbon sales will finance other activities. The plan even breaks down the allocation of these revenues: 32 percent for the investment activities of Petróleos Mexicanos (PEMEX) itself; and of the remaining 68 percent, 25 percent for agriculture and rural development, 24 percent for the social sector, 20 percent for transport and communications, 16 percent for industrial activity other than PEMEX, and 15 percent for state and municipal governments. This is the kind of precise advance allocation that creates bureaucratic vested interest and limits flexibility as circumstances change.[22]

After years of evasion, the population issue was finally addressed directly during the Echeverría administration, and Mexico's family planning program may turn out to be the most lasting monument to that administration. Mexico's annual rate of increase in population had been 3.4 percent in the 1960s and apparently fell sharply in the late 1970s.[23] The global plan projected an annual 2.5 percent rate of increase in 1982,

21. Sidney Weintraub, "Case Study of Economic Stabilization: Mexico," in William R. Cline and Sidney Weintraub, eds., *Economic Stabilization in Developing Countries*, p. 285. In evaluating performance during the first year of the plan (1980), the government asserted that the historical average current account deficit in Mexico had been 3.5 percent of GDP. *El Mercado de Valores*, vol. 41 (May 25, 1981), p. 540.

22. The decline in world oil prices in 1981–83 has meant that PEMEX has been unable to finance even its own expansion. See "Why PEMEX Can't Pay Mexico's Bills," *Business Week* (February 28, 1983), pp. 58–62.

23. Nacional Financiera, *Statistics on the Mexican Economy, 1977*, for 1960–70 data. There are no reliable data on current rates of population growth. "Mexico's Birth Rate Seems Off Sharply," *New York Times*, November 5, 1979, cites a study by the U.S. Bureau of the Census to the effect that the birth rate fell from 42 births per 1,000 population in 1975 to 33 to 35 in 1979. This implies a decline in annual population growth from 3.2 to about 2.5 percent.

which would gradually fall to 1 percent by the year 2000. This projection is mostly wishful thinking, but it does show that Mexico no longer believes that a burgeoning population is an asset.

An evaluation of the plan in operation was issued after the first year, that is, for 1980.[24] The conclusion was that most plan objectives, but not all, had been accomplished in 1980. Growth in the GDP in 1980, according to the Banco de México, was 7.4 percent, a preliminary figure and slightly short of the 8 percent figure projected in the plan. Gross fixed investment increased by 15.8 percent, more than the plan's annual target of 13.5 percent. On the other hand, the 1980 current account deficit in the balance of payments was about 2 percent of the GDP, or double the 1 percent objective. Consumer prices increased by 29.8 percent, substantially more than had been projected. These two failures, in the balance of payments and in containing the rise in prices, turned out to be harbingers of the future. They were not corrected in subsequent years and, indeed, got worse. A reasonable case can be made that adherence to other objectives of the plan in the face of these failures, and doing so despite the changed international situation (that is, the worldwide recession and declining real oil prices) was a main contributor to Mexico's external debt buildup and to its 1982 economic crisis. In this case, the effort to carry out the plan after circumstances had changed turned out to be a blueprint for disaster.

The Industrial Plan

The global plan refers to the industrial sector as the most dynamic in Mexico, and the industrial plan was conceived as the centerpiece of the planning process. It is the most germane plan for examining the possibility of free trade. The plan's strategies for meeting its growth and employment objectives are to promote exports, reorient production toward basic consumer goods, improve Mexico's industrial structure, decentralize economic activity geographically, and reduce the oligopolistic tendencies of Mexican industry. Like the other plans, the industrial plan depended on revenues from petroleum production for much of its financing. When income from oil exports fell below expectations, the Mexican authorities resorted to increased external debt to finance the plan. As was true with the global plan, trying to carry out the plan under

24. "Primera evaluación del plan global," pp. 537–50.

conditions radically different from those prevailing when it was conceived contributed substantially to Mexico's economic crisis in 1982 and
1983.

One of the deep concerns of Mexicans, particularly those critical of
Mexico's energy policy, is what is derisively called the "Venezuelani-
zation" of Mexico. The concern is that Mexico will become an exporter
of petroleum and little else. Energy policy critics argue that not only will
the petroleum run out one day, but also that reliance on it will subject
Mexico to booms and busts in foreign-exchange earnings, just as is the
case for other countries that rely on one or a few commodities for the
bulk of their export earnings. Supporters of the energy policy promulgated during the López Portillo administration claimed that, unlike
Venezuela and many other large oil exporters, Mexico does have an
industrial structure and one that is being made more efficient.[25] Certainly
the industrial plan to increase the efficiency of Mexico's industry is
ambitious, indeed so ambitious and so encompassing that it immediately
raised doubts about the rigor of its contents.

The industries listed for priority treatment accounted for 60 percent
of Mexico's gross industrial output.[26] The plan has three interlinked sets
of priorities for industrial groups, regions, and small businesses. The
industrial priorities were given in two categories with subcategories
including about seventy industrial activities. The highest priority was
given to agro-industry, first for those industries that process food
products for human consumption, then for those that process inputs for
agriculture, and finally for those that produce other agro-industrial
products such as chemicals and cellulose derived from agriculture. The
next highest priority in category 1 was capital goods production, particularly machinery and equipment for food production. The capital goods
industry priorities were production of machinery for the oil and petrochemical industry, the electrical industry, mining and the metallurgical
industry, construction, transportation, and then the remainder of capital-
goods-producing industries. The third priority in category 1 was for
capital goods industries producing strategic inputs for the industrial
sector, specifically for the manufacture of iron and steel in integrated
processes and the manufacture of cement. These last two are growing
industries in Mexico. They profited from the high level of GDP growth

25. Samuel Berkstein K., "México: Estrategía petrolera y política exterior," pp.
65–82, contains an example of this argument.
26. Blair, *Economic Development Policy in Mexico*, p. 7.

when the plan was promulgated, without meeting domestic demand. The second category included nondurable consumer goods such as yarns, fabrics, garments, footwear, soaps, cardboard, glass, tinplate containers for food packaging, other paper and cardboard items, and school products. This category also included durable consumer goods such as home appliances, transportation equipment (particularly automotive parts), and various items of service equipment for optical, electronic, computer, and hand tool production. The final group of products in category 2—intermediate products—includes petrochemicals, chemicals for industrial use, basic medicines, inputs for mining and metallurgy, construction materials, and industrial refractories and abrasives.

The plan contained two growth trajectories: the base trajectory to describe probable outcomes without the plan, and the plan trajectory. Separate annual growth rates were projected in the plan trajectory for each major category, one for the period 1979–82 and another for 1982–90. The agro-industrial growth rates ranged from a low of 4 to 6 percent for the processing of foods of vegetable origin to a high of 9 to 11.5 percent for production of cellulose and chemicals derived from agriculture. The projected growth rates for capital goods production were substantially higher across the board, from a low of 13 percent from 1982 to 1990 for machinery for food production to a high of 23 percent during 1979–82 for machinery for the oil and petrochemical industry.[27] The projected plan trajectory growth rates for category 2 were between the two sets of figures of category 1. Nondurable consumer goods production was projected to increase from between 11 and 16 percent a year, depending on the product and the time period. Production of durable consumer goods was expected to increase less, from between 7.5 and 16.0 percent a year; and intermediate goods from between 13 and 20 percent. The growth rates projected obviously were influenced by the growth rates existing when the plan was written for items such as equipment for the petroleum industry and intermediate petrochemical products and by Mexico's emphasis on energy-related industry.

The priorities in the industrial plan seem to have been chosen partly to correct past development failures, particularly the failure to give sufficient attention to agriculture and the processing of agricultural products. Mexican authorities undoubtedly were stung by the criticism

27. Volume growth in this area appears to have been 25 percent in 1980, thus exceeding the plan's target in the first year. "The Mexican Economy in 1980: The Industrial Sector," p. 378. The failures came later.

leveled at past policies that preached the importance of agriculture, particularly of the small farmer, but then in practice focused on large, commercial farmers by giving credit mainly to them and by allocating resources for large irrigation works that hardly benefited the bulk of Mexico's farmers. The growing expenditure of foreign exchange on imported food has also been a sore point and highlights criticism of the energy policy. Critics claim that while Mexico exploits a nonrenewable resource, the proceeds are being used to finance consumption rather than an economic structure that would endure when oil runs out or the demand for it diminishes. Much of the rhetoric accompanying the industrial plan's stress on agriculture was undoubtedly politically motivated, but additional resources were in fact allocated to agriculture and related sectors, although the distribution of these resources was not clear.

The stress on the production of capital goods is not new in Mexico. In 1977 the Nacional Financiera published an extensive study on a strategy to develop a Mexican capital goods industry.[28] That study saw this development as a way to create jobs and make Mexico a more formidable competitor in world markets. In addition to the internal economic merits, the development of a capital goods industry is also seen as a way to increase Mexico's bargaining power in the world. As one analyst put it, the countries that export capital goods, oil, and essential foodstuffs are in a solid bargaining position, while countries that produce "soft" primary products and luxury consumer goods are not.[29] With a capital goods industry, Mexico would have two of the three allegedly strong bargaining elements; and if Mexico could cut back or eliminate the importation of basic foodstuffs, the country would be in an ideal bargaining position.

The second priority category, for durable and nondurable consumer goods, is largely a continuation of the import-substitution program Mexico started after World War II. The idea of the plan was to strengthen the efficiency of these industries, although nothing in the plan ensured this outcome.

The regional priorities were established by zones. Zone 1A's priorities were for industrial port development and zone 1B's priorities for urban industrial port development. The industrial seaports chosen for this

28. *México: Una estrategía para desarrollar la industria de bienes de capital.*
29. Mario Ojeda, "El poder negociador del petróleo: El caso de México," p. 45.

highest priority are Lázaro Cárdenas in the state of Michoacán, including the nearby municipality of La Union; Salina Cruz, in Oaxaca, and eight other municipalities on the Tehuantepec Isthmus; Coatzacoalcos, in Veracruz, and six nearby municipalities; and Tampico, Tamaulipas, and five nearby municipalities near the Gulf of Mexico. Each of these four ports and what the plan calls their "areas of influence" were chosen as the highest priority areas of development because of their importance as seaports in promoting exports and because of the availability of energy, particularly natural gas, for industrial use. Zone 1B is more extensive, made up of ninety-nine municipalities mostly near the coast or in border areas. Twenty-one of Mexico's thirty-one states have one or more urban areas included in this priority listing. The plan states that these municipalities were chosen primarily because of their proximity to the coast or to the border and because of the availability of energy.

Zone 2 is what the plan calls the state priority zone and is composed of areas chosen by state governments for industrial activities. These selections are formalized by agreements with the federal government. It has been noted that this arrangement, although it leaves final decision-making in the hands of federal authorities, allows room for the "push and shove" of state and national politics.[30]

Zone 3 is a mixture of deterrents and reassurance for areas not included in the first two zones. Labeled the *controlled growth area,* zone 3A consists of the federal district and fifty-four nearby municipalities, all but one (Tizayuca in the state of Hidalgo) in the state of Mexico. Zone 3B, labeled the consolidation area, is more extensive, consisting of 144 municipalities in the states of Hidalgo, Mexico, Morelos, Puebla, and Tlaxcala, all not far from Mexico City. The intention, quite explicitly, was to discourage further growth in Mexico City and the surrounding area. The federal district, which includes Mexico City and the state of Mexico, contains more than 25 percent of Mexico's population and is responsible for more than 40 percent of its GDP.[31] The phrase *consolidation area* was intended to reassure the population and authorities in

30. Blair, *Economic Development Policy in Mexico,* p. 8.
31. *El Mercado de Valores,* vol. 41 (August 24, 1981), p. 889, gives population by state in 1980. Data on GDP by state are not available for 1980, but the 1970 figures show that the federal district and the state of Mexico had 21.1 percent of total population and generated 40.4 percent of Mexico's GDP. See Economic Commission for Latin America, *Distribución regional del producto interno bruto sectorial en los países de América Latina,* p. 36.

those areas that discouraging their further industrial concentration would be accomplished without harming the industrial dynamism that existed when the plan was promulgated.[32] This approach provided room for bargaining. Zone 3 does not include Monterrey and Guadalajara, the two most important centers of growth outside the federal district. This, undoubtedly, was part of the political bargain struck between the provincial authorities and local business communities and the López Portillo administration. Inclusion of these cities in zone 3 would have disqualified them from receiving federal subsidies for priority industries and small businesses.

Although the regional priorities did not explicitly call for redistribution of income, the incentives could have accomplished this by favoring industrial development in areas of relatively low per capita income and discouraging further development of regions with relatively high per capita income.

The industrial plan's third priority, for small businesses, was designed to attenuate the oligopolistic structure that developed in the most dynamic industries; to disperse industry throughout Mexico's regions; to take advantage of the relative importance of small business in various segments of priority production, such as agro-industry, basic consumer goods, and the metal-mechanical industry; and to help generate employment, since small industries are usually more labor-intensive than larger firms. A small firm is defined as one whose investment in fixed assets is less than 200 times the annual minimum wage in the federal district, which at the time the plan was written meant fixed assets of about 10 million pesos.[33] Both the product and the regional priorities were designed to promote exports, and the emphasis on production of consumer goods for domestic consumption is also meant to increase exports of these goods. The capital goods industries selected for encouragement were intended not only to replace imports but to increase Mexico's impact on the world trading scene; and the highest regional priorities are given to ports and border areas.

The plan's priorities for products, regions, and small businesses were to be carried out by substantial financial inducements. Export promotion was to be facilitated by both tax benefits and export subsidies. From the viewpoint of trade relations with the United States and, for that matter,

32. Blair, *Economic Development Policy in Mexico,* p. 8.
33. This is not a trivial ceiling. At that time 10 million pesos amounted to $435,000.

with other countries, it is these internal and external subsidies that will be most controversial if they are revived. It was precisely because of the subsidies inherent in Mexico's industrial plan that the contracting parties to the General Agreement on Tariffs and Trade reserved their right to countervail in the draft protocol for Mexico's accession. The reason for this reservation does not lose validity now that Mexico has decided to remain outside the GATT.

The question of subsidies is particularly sensitive in Mexico's trade relations with the United States. It has already been noted that U.S. law contains no provision requiring a demonstration of injury to a U.S. firm when imported goods are shown to have benefited from a subsidy unless the exporting country is a signatory to the GATT subsidy and countervailing duty code. Mexico is not a signatory and, as noted in chapter 3, many subsidy complaints have been brought against Mexico by U.S. companies. Even though it can stall for time the U.S. executive branch may find that it has little choice but to countervail if subsidy complaints are brought against imports from Mexico, thereby frustrating the desire of the Reagan administration to improve U.S.-Mexican relations. One possible escape from this dilemma brought on by Mexico's failure to adhere to the subsidy and countervailing duty code is to enact legislation in the United States that would make it possible to treat Mexico as if it were a signatory. This is not easily accomplished, however, since it creates precedents. If Mexico is to be an exception, why not other countries?

The industrial plan categorized the inducements to be used to achieve its objectives as either direct action tools or indirect action tools. Some of these are unlikely to stimulate subsidy complaints against Mexico because the benefits are similar to those used by many states in the United States and by the federal government, but others could trigger complaints. The use of tax incentives, Mexico's main indirect action tool, is clearly a familiar technique in the United States to promote investment. The Mexican technique is a tax credit, issued by the Treasury in the form of a tax promotion certificate good for five years, the amount dependent on the type of the investment. Table 5-5 summarizes the amounts and allocation of these tax credits. Zone 3A, the municipalities in and around the federal district, receives no investment tax incentives of any kind, except for a credit of 5 percent (of the purchase price) for purchase of machinery and equipment made in Mexico. This credit is given regardless of the geographic zone of the investor and is in addition

Table 5-5. *Tax Credits under Mexico's Industrial Plan*
Percent

Location of investment	Industry sector priority[a]			For all industrial activities	
				Purchase of nationally produced equipment	Employment generated by additional shifts
	Small industry	Category 1	Category 2		
Zone 1, special stimulus	25*I*	20*I* 20*E*	15*I* 20*E*	5	20
Zone 2, state priorities	25*I*	20*I* 20*E*	10*I* 20*E*	5	20
Rest of country	25*I*[b]	20*I* 20*E*	10*I*[b] 20*E*[b]	5	20
Zone 3					
A. Controlled growth	0	0	0	5	0
B. Consolidation	25*I*[b]	20*I*[b] 20*E*[b]	10*I*[b] 20*E*[b]	5	20

Source: Secretaría de Patrimonio y Fomento Industrial, *Plan nacional de desarrollo industrial, 1979–1982*, p. 181.
a. *I* after a percentage figure refers to a tax credit for investment; *E* after a percentage figure refers to a tax credit for employment creation.
b. Applicable only for increases in productive capacity in the same industrial activity.

to any other tax credit to which the firm is entitled. Small businesses receive a credit of 25 percent of the value of new fixed investment in all zones except 3A. In the consolidation zone, 3B, a tax credit is granted only for investment to expand the same industrial activity in which the company is engaged. This is the technique used to discourage investment diversification in this zone without limiting current investment. The investment tax credits are then keyed to the product priority in the plan, higher for category 1 (20 percent) than for category 2 (either 10 or 15 percent).

Despite the employment goal in the global and industrial plans, many of the incentives in the industrial plan operate against employment stimulation. The investment tax credit, the ability to get exemption from the tariff for imported goods for the capital goods industry,[34] and the

34. The conditions for duty exemption can be found in the *Diario oficial de la federación*, January 8, 1981, reprinted in *El Mercado de Valores*, vol. 41 (March 2, 1981). A non-Mexican firm (one whose capital and management are not mostly Mexican) can benefit from import-duty exoneration under this regulation only if the value of imports is matched by exports within one year. As in the automotive industry, this is a no-net-import provision for non-Mexican firms in the capital goods industry.

general emphasis on capital goods production all tend to encourage capital intensity rather than labor intensity in production. In fact, the plan explicitly did not opt for labor intensity in the potentially most dynamic industries, since this would not be the most efficient way to exploit Mexico's natural resources. The projected increase in employment was to come from overall growth, from the encouragement of labor-intensive activities such as the production of many basic consumer goods, and from the benefits granted to small business. Much of the projected increase in employment showed up in the service and government sectors. The plan trajectory showed an increase in the salaried population from about 15 million in 1979 to 27 million in 1990. Of this increase of 12 million, 37 percent was in government and 31 percent in services; that is, more than two-thirds of the projected increase is not expected in goods-producing activities.[35]

The plan does deal with the employment issue directly, however, by providing tax incentives. For each zone except 3A there was a two-year, 20 percent tax credit on the payroll cost of additional employment, calculated on the basis of the minimal annual wage for the zone in which the firm is located. The firm is expected to maintain the additional employment for at least one year after receipt of the subsidy. In zone 3B this credit is available only for increased employment in the same industrial activity in which the company is engaged. In addition, a 20 percent tax credit is granted to firms in all zones except 3A, regardless of the product priority or other incentives, if they increase employment by adding work shifts. The tax incentives do not apply to firms in free zones or border areas, which receive different incentives. The plan stated that the latter incentives will be incorporated into the general scheme in the medium term.

Two other indirect action tools were provided in the plan. The first was more credits for priority products, particularly capital goods, and for small business, and the second was technical assistance for small business. The plan stated that the policy of substituting tariffs for import licenses that was begun in 1977 will continue gradually and on a case-by-case basis, although Mexico's commitment to liberalizing imports clearly was uncertain even in the late 1970s. Apparently the planners were unsure about this liberalization policy, since an important table projecting the expansion of industrial markets up to 1990 and calculating

35. *Plan industrial*, p. 140.

Table 5-6. *Differential Rates for Industrial Energy for New Production under Mexico's Industrial Plan*
Percent discount

	Products to be subsidized			
Geographic location	Natural gas	Residual fuel oil	Electric power	Basic petro-chemicals
Zone 1A, four industrial port areas	30	30	30	30[a]
Zone 1B, only coastal towns[b]				
Townships of Tabasco and Chiapas	30[c]	30[c]	30[c]	30[c]
Townships along pipeline	15	. . .	. . .	. . .
Townships not on natural gas pipeline	. . .	10	. . .	. . .

Source: *Plan industrial*, pp. 179–80.
a. Granted only if a new facility exports at least 25 percent of production for a minimum of four years.
b. Border townships in Zone 1B are not eligible, since they benefit from a separate incentive system.
c. The firm can obtain a discount on only two of the four products.

ratios of imports to total demand by industry was made "on the assumption that there will be no overall liberalization in the area of industrial protection."[36]

For countries that trade with Mexico the more troublesome inducements are the direct action tools, such as internal energy subsidies and export subsidies not listed explicitly in the plan but implicit in its operation. To promote regional dispersion of industry to zone 1, the price of energy in the townships in that zone, particularly in zone 1A, is to be subsidized (table 5-6). The discounts are available to new firms or old firms establishing new plants or expanding existing plants by more than 40 percent of installed capacity. In theory the petrochemical subsidy may last for ten years and the pricing differential for energy until the end of 1988. By then, of course, there will be vested interests in cheap energy. The energy discounts are beyond the differential pricing for energy that will exist in Mexico in any event: "The plan adopts as an explicit policy the principle of maintaining at a lower level than the international one, the domestic price of industrially-used energy sources and basic petrochemicals."[37] The intent of this differential pricing is, of course, to promote the competitiveness of Mexican industry and to some extent to contain inflation. It is debatable whether differential pricing is in Mexico's own interest, regardless of its impact on international trade, just as it is questionable whether the United States economy benefited

36. Ibid., p. 58.
37. From the abridged version of the plan, in English, p. 54.

from keeping oil and natural gas prices below world prices for so long. Pricing energy below the world market level will encourage wasteful use of Mexico's oil and gas resources.[38]

Although the handling of internal subsidies is unclear in international trade practice, energy subsidies have been challenged in the past and triggered demands for countervailing duties when energy prices were an important element in the competitive pricing of a product.[39] This could be significant in the textile industry and in the petrochemical industry generally.

What compounds the trade problem of these internal subsidies is their combination with export subsidies. The plan had explicit export goals: for example, increases in manufactured exports by 12 percent in 1982 and by between 14 and 17 percent a year between 1983 and 1990 (all in real terms). If the exchange rate is permitted to become overvalued periodically, as it did before 1954, before 1976, and again after 1977 until 1982–83, when Mexican inflation surged above U.S. inflation, export subsidies will be needed to meet export goals. Mexican planning assumes that domestic industries will be given whatever protection is necessary to keep them alive, particularly if they produce products considered to be priorities; that internal subsidies will be used to help these industries become more competitive; and that if these measures are insufficient, both performance standards and explicit export subsidies will be used. Whatever the internal justification for such a system, it will not necessarily be accepted with equanimity by non-Mexican competitors in international trade.

Two other direct action tools cited in the plan were increased public outlays for infrastructure to foster industrialization and substantial expansion of government-run industries. Blair has described Mexico's industrial structure as that of an "entrepreneurial state."[40] The plan says that public-sector companies will use their purchasing power to encourage the development of capital goods industries. This is in addition to the subsidized pricing of energy and basic petrochemicals that is facilitated by public ownership of the firms in these fields whose sacrifice makes the subsidies possible. The plan does make a concession to efficiency for public firms in that they now must pay import duties like

38. This has been at least partly recognized. The López Portillo administration found it necessary to raise gasoline prices in 1982.

39. The EC proposed a countervail in 1980 against U.S. imports of synthetic yarns and products.

40. Blair, *Economic Development Policy in Mexico*, p. 3.

other firms. The handling of state trading issues is an area of uncertainty in international trade since criteria for fair competition are not easily established. But Mexico's entrepreneurial state is not new, and state trading is hardly confined to Mexico.

The Mexican economic system is replete with subsidies, for consumption and production, for industry and agriculture, for private firms, and especially for public enterprises. In this sense, the subsidies in the industrial plan were not new. President López Portillo has stated that "monstrous subsidies to stimulate the economy" should be reduced.[41] However, it is the subsidization inherent in the industrial plan and in Mexico's development strategy generally that poses the greatest potential for trade conflict between Mexico and other countries, regardless of any steps toward free trade.

The performance of Mexican industry in 1980 was partly consistent with plan targets and partly not. The volume of manufacturing production increased by less than 6 percent from 1979 to 1980, below the previous year's increase.[42] It increased by 7 percent in 1981 but declined in 1982 by 2 percent.[43] The increase in the volume of production of consumer goods in 1980 was 4.8 percent overall, 3.1 percent for nondurable consumer goods, and 12.7 percent for durable goods.[44] This, too, was less than the increase in 1978 and 1979. Production increased again in 1981 but declined in 1982.[45] Employment in the manufacturing sector increased substantially in 1980, by 6.7 percent. The automobile industry had the largest percentage increase in the number of persons occupied of all main industries,[46] but in 1982 there was an across-the-board decline in the production of motor vehicles.[47]

The plan's export targets were not achieved, not even in the first year.

41. Cited in ibid., from the president's third annual report on the government, in *El Mercado de Valores*, vol. 39 (September 10, 1979), p. 767. In his first major economic message to the Congress, President Miguel de la Madrid referred to the need to modify and reduce Mexico's system of subsidies. See Miguel de la Madrid, "Criterios generales de política económica para 1983," p. 1293.

42. Banco de México, *Informe Anual, 1980*, p. 62. Data are for the first eleven months of the year.

43. "Report on the Economy: The Industrial Sector," p. 428. The 1982 figure is preliminary.

44. American Chamber of Commerce of Mexico, *Quarterly Economic Report* (March 1981), p. 7. Data come from the Banco de México.

45. "Report on the Economy: The Industrial Sector," p. 428.

46. Banco de México, *Informe Anual, 1980*, p. 76.

47. "Report on the Economy: The Industrial Sector," p. 430. See also the summary of a report issued by the Secretaría de Patrimonio y Fomento Industrial on "Expectativas de la industria automotriz," *El Mercado de Valores*, vol. 42 (November 29, 1982), pp. 1230–33.

Non-oil exports declined in real terms in 1980, and exports of manufactures declined in real terms by 8.4 percent.[48] Much but not all of the responsibility for this poor performance was due to the low level of economic growth in the countries to which Mexico ships its goods. In subsequent years, Mexico's export problem was compounded by declining oil prices.

The Energy Plan

For Mexico, energy is a source of hope for overall development, a source of concern that Mexico's wealth of oil and natural gas will arouse expectations that will not be satisfied among less privileged Mexicans and that might lead Mexico to export only one product,[49] and a source of paranoia that the existence of so much oil might tempt the United States or others to invade.[50] The policies set forth in the various plans reflect these concerns. The projected annual GDP growth of 8 percent in the 1980s, the emphasis on the production of basic consumer goods, and the expansion of employment, particularly in the public sector where it is most controllable, were designed with the aroused-expectations theme in mind. Limitations in the energy plan on total hydrocarbon production and exports were intended to lessen the danger of excessive reliance on this nonrenewable resource. As it turned out, this objective was not accomplished. The energy plan is most concrete for the years until 1990 and contains general admonitions for the subsequent decade to the year 2000.[51] The plan deals with oil, natural gas, coal production

48. American Chamber of Commerce of Mexico, *Quarterly Economic Report* (March 1981), p. 34.

49. Alan Riding, "The Mixed Blessings of Mexico's Oil," *New York Times Magazine*, January 11, 1981, discusses these concerns, pp. 22 ff.

50. The fear of invasion is discussed in two articles cited earlier, Berkstein, "México: Estrategía petrolera y política exterior," p. 74; and Ojeda, "El poder negociador del petróleo," p. 51. Berkstein says that the chances of U.S. military invasion are very low, but Ojeda implies otherwise because the inhibitions against invasion in the Middle East—that is, a possible confrontation with the Soviet Union—do not exist in North America.

51. The energy plan was summarized in a supplement to *El Mercado de Valores*, vol. 40 (November 24, 1980); the presidential decree appears in *El Mercado de Valores*, vol. 41 (February 23, 1981). David Ronfeldt, Richard Nehring, and Arturo Gándara, *Mexico's Petroleum and U.S. Policy: Implications for the 1980s*, contains a thorough examination of Mexico's oil resources. Miguel S. Wionczek, "Algunas reflexiones sobre la futura política petrolera de México," pp. 1229–37, discusses some of the developments that disrupted Mexican energy plans in the last few years.

and use, energy generation from hydro-geothermal and solar sources, and increasing rural electrification.

The López Portillo administration originally assumed that oil production would reach 2.25 million barrels a day by 1982 and that natural gas production would reach 3.6 billion cubic feet a day by then.[52] These projected figures were often increased, and oil production actually reached 2.8 million barrels a day in 1982.[53] Export targets also increased from less than 400,000 barrels a day in 1978 to about 1.4 to 1.5 million barrels a day in 1981.[54] In addition, Mexican natural gas production is part of the U.S. gas pipeline system despite the much publicized controversy during the Carter administration over natural gas pricing.[55]

Mexico played a successively increasing role each year in the world oil scene during the López Portillo administration, from the end of 1974 until the end of 1982. In 1974 Mexican crude oil production was 571,000 barrels a day, or 1 percent of world production of 56 million barrels a day. During 1982 Mexican production of crude oil had risen to an average of 2.7 million barrels a day, or about 5 percent of the then estimated world production of 53 million barrels a day.[56] In 1982 Mexico was the leading foreign supplier of crude oil to the United States.[57] In 1974 total proven hydrocarbon reserves of Mexico were 5.8 billion barrels; in 1982 they were estimated to be about 73 billion barrels.[58]

Three conclusions from these summary data deserve emphasis in a discussion of U.S.-Mexican trade. First, the pressure from the ambitious industrialization and growth targets led almost inexorably to the production and export of more oil than was anticipated. Second, this pressure will intensify if Mexico's non-oil exports do not increase as planned.

52. Grayson, *The Politics of Mexican Oil,* p. 62.

53. U.S. Department of Energy, *Monthly Energy Review* (December 1982), p. 95.

54. Jaime Corredor Esnaola, "El significado económico del petróleo en México," p. 1322.

55. Grayson, *The Politics of Mexican Oil,* pp. 183–202. See also Richard R. Fagen and Henry R. Nau, *Mexican Gas: The Northern Connection.*

56. U.S. Department of Energy, *Monthly Energy Review* (July 1983), p. 95.

57. During the period January–October 1982, Mexico supplied a daily average of 685,000 barrels a day of crude oil to the United States, or 23 percent of total daily imports of 2.9 million barrels a day. Ibid, p. 37.

58. Petróleos Mexicanos, *Anuario estadístico, 1980,* p. 29, for 1974 figure, and José López Portillo, "Sixth State of the Nation Report to the Mexican Congress," p. 272, for 1982. These figures include both crude petroleum and the oil equivalent of natural gas. The increases in proven reserves since 1980 are based primarily on revisions of earlier estimates and not on new exploratory strikes.

Third, Mexico's production levels will probably be negatively correlated with oil price changes. The internal political system, which requires meeting the economic needs of many groups, also tends to push up production levels. It is hard to meet political obligations with oil in the ground. There is no assurance, however, that Mexico will be able to substantially increase its crude oil output, especially in the near future, or that the export market will even want more of Mexico's oil in any event.

The plan states that, to avoid Mexican dependency on others, Mexico will try to avoid sending more than half of its hydrocarbon exports to any one country and that, to avoid dependency of others on Mexico, no more than 20 percent of any country's oil and oil product imports should come from Mexico.[59] Both these limitations are directed at the United States. This desire for trade diversification was part of Mexican policy long before the López Portillo administration. Mexico now has achieved its goal of reducing its proportion of crude petroleum exports to the United States. The United States took 84 percent of Mexico's crude oil exports in 1979, the year before the plan was released, and the proportion declined to 49.8 percent in 1981.[60] By 1982, when the essential issue for Mexico was export income rather than export distribution, this issue lost its immediate importance.

The availability of oil was seen during the halcyon years of rising oil prices as a bargaining chip for Mexico. One of the five priority objectives relating energy exports to foreign policy in the energy plan is to exchange oil not just for cash but for technology that might not otherwise be available and to tie oil sales to exports of manufactures and access to foreign financial sources.[61] According to Mexico's foreign minister, Jorge Castañeda, "the oil which Mexico has available as a surplus to sell abroad must be viewed not only as a simple commodity to be sold for the going world price, but as something so much in demand that a premium can be attached to it." He noted that when President López Portillo visited West Germany, France, Sweden, and Canada in mid-

59. The import dependency can reach 50 percent for countries in Central America and the Caribbean.

60. Corredor Esnaola, "El significado económico del petróleo en México," p. 1322.

61. The other four priority objectives are to export hydrocarbons only to the extent that internal needs are not prejudiced and the resources earned can be absorbed productively; increase Mexican value added in these exports; diversify Mexico's foreign trade; and cooperate with others in the search for and exploitation of local energy resources.

1980, the bilateral relationship that he sought was "oil in exchange for partnership in Mexico's economic development," which he defined in terms of "industrial cooperation, financing, the transfer of technology, and joint investment."[62] The joint communiqué issued in May 1980 after Japan's prime minister visited Mexico made this same point.[63]

Mexico expected a good deal from exports of its oil—both the going world price (or higher) and other benefits it believed could not be purchased with money. Whether this was a realistic expectation even when it was promulgated and whether the technology others offer could not be purchased just as readily for cash depends on the bargaining context. Mexico believed it had to be seen as being in a strong bargaining position and able to withhold significant oil sales to extract premium prices. But this was not the case even when oil prices were rising. The price for Mexican oil cannot be above that for non-Mexican oil, a point the Mexican authorities struggled unsuccessfully to deny during the mid-1981 oil glut. Finally, it is not easy for market-economy countries to tie oil purchases with imports of manufactures unless the latter are competitive; otherwise, the governments would have to import for their own account or subsidize the private companies that do the importing.[64]

Energy production in 1980 generally was consistent with the goals of the energy plan. Mexico's proven hydrocarbon reserve figure was 67.8 billion barrels, about 75 percent of which was crude oil. Crude production at the end of 1980 was estimated at 2.75 million barrels, placing Mexico fourth in the world in crude output a day after the Soviet Union, Saudi Arabia, and the United States. Natural gas production in 1980 averaged 3.55 billion cubic feet a day, 21.6 percent higher than the year before. Refinery production increased 19.1 percent in 1980 over 1979. These increases either exceeded or were within plan objectives.[65]

Crude oil exports in 1980 increased in value by 150 percent over 1979. Exports of oil and natural gas together were $9.9 billion in 1980, two-

62. Jorge Castañeda, "Mexico and the United States: The Next Decade," pp. 7–8.

63. *El Mercado de Valores*, vol. 40 (May 19, 1980).

64. Paradoxically, Mexican ability to sell oil on a government-to-government basis to the United States was enhanced in 1982 when Mexico was in the midst of an economic crisis. In August 1982 the U.S. Department of Energy agreed to buy $1 billion of Mexican light Isthmus crude for the U.S. Strategic Petroleum Reserve at a price between $25 and $35 a barrel. See "OGJ Newsletter," *Oil and Gas Journal*, vol. 80 (September 6, 1982).

65. Data are from American Chamber of Commerce of Mexico, *Quarterly Economic Report* (March 1981), pp. 13–16, based on annual report by PEMEX.

thirds of all exports of merchandise and 30 percent of receipts from exports of goods and services.[66] The two-thirds figure is high, indeed well above what Mexico hoped for after the measures taken under the industrial plan bore fruit, and the 30 percent amount is within the 50 percent limitation for these exports stated in the plan.

Since 1980 the oil situation has changed radically. Mexico's dependence on oil exports as a percentage of total export value increased to 75 percent for the first ten months of 1982.[67] At Mexico's current level of oil exports, each sustained $1 drop in the oil export price translates into a drop in foreign-exchange earnings of between $500 million and $600 million a year. The old energy plan is in a shambles and has not really been replaced by a new one. In retrospect, it is evident that Mexico relied too heavily on increasing income from energy exports, and when income did not increase in 1981, corrective measures were not taken. The plan became a straitjacket instead of a flexible guide to policy.

Agriculture and Nutrition

The key document in this area is not any of Mexico's agriculture plans but rather the Sistema Alimentario Mexicano (SAM), roughly translated as the Mexican nutrition system.[68] This was launched in 1980 after an extensive national survey conducted in 1979 to determine food needs in rural and urban areas and in different sections of the country. The main objective of the SAM was to make Mexico self-sufficient in the production of corn and beans by 1982 and wheat, rice, and sorghum by 1985. Another objective was to achieve for Mexicans an average daily diet of at least 2,750 calories and 80 grams of protein.

Mexican history is replete with official pronouncements about how agricultural production and human nutrition are to be improved, but the result has been continued deterioration of the relationship between agriculture and manufacturing and insufficient credit for all but the wealthiest landowners. The latest initiative was more or less on target in that it came after substantial increases in imports of basic foodstuffs and severe criticism of past production and consumption

66. Banco de México, *Informe Anual, 1980*, pp. 177–90.
67. "Report on the Economy: Foreign Trade," p. 435.
68. Reports are issued annually by the Secretaría de Agricultura y Recursos Hidráulicos on the "Plan nacional agropecuario y forestal." The SAM was launched on August 5, 1980, and is summarized in *El Mercado de Valores*, vol. 40 (September 29, 1980), pp. 948–58.

policies. Given the history of bold pronouncements, Mexicans were skeptical about the sincerity of this initiative. There was evidence, however, that the López Portillo government intended to follow up its rhetoric with resources and policy actions, even though its sincerity was compromised as the economic situation deteriorated. In any case, there is a consensus in Mexico that past agricultural policy has been inadequate. This is stated explicitly in the global plan and in the SAM itself. In addition, Mexico was influenced by a changed attitude about development worldwide—agriculture is now accepted as important, indeed crucial, in the development process, whereas earlier the emphasis was placed almost wholly on industrial output.

The evidence that the López Portillo administration was sincere in its goals for agriculture was the increased budgetary allocations for agriculture. According to the global plan, about 18 percent of public-sector investment was devoted to agriculture and rural development when López Portillo entered office. The figure exceeded 20 percent in 1979, and the target for 1982 was 25 percent. The SAM contemplates decentralization to the states of the resources devoted to the Programa Integral de Desarrollo Rural (PIDER), an integrated rural development program involving hundreds of millions of dollars in which Mexico is being supported by the World Bank and the Inter-American Development Bank. PIDER was started under the Echeverría administration and continued in the López Portillo administration.

The SAM's goals are to minimize the risk of experimentation by small farmers who barely support themselves and who work nonirrigated land; provide technical assistance to these farmers; help organize them; invest more heavily in the commercialization system by building more roads and other transport services; provide adequate guaranteed prices for outputs and subsidies for key inputs; promote integrated agro-industries; strengthen the food distribution system; and reorient eating habits by reversing the publicity promoting expensive and not very nutritious food. Subsidies to producers and consumers, including a special interest-rate subsidy for producers of corn and beans—the staples of the Mexican diet—are the principal means for achieving the SAM's objectives.[69]

The political rhetoric surrounding the SAM repeated endlessly the

69. CONASUPO (Compañía Nacional de Subsistencias Populares) already is a major outlet for food sales at subsidized prices to many Mexicans. This is augmented by the activities of COPLAMAR (Coordinación General del Plan Nacional de Zonas Deprimidas y Grupos Marginados), which tries to improve services and food distribution to the poorest areas and people in Mexico.

goal of self-sufficiency in the production of basic foodstuffs, so much so that it makes one wonder why this goal is so greatly emphasized. The program calls for substantial mechanization; in the words of the minister of agriculture, "in general, to mechanize is to modernize."[70] He had in mind mostly the planned mechanization for 860,000 hectares of nonirrigated land for the production of corn, beans, rice, and sorghum. Mechanization may help increase production, but it may also accelerate the rural exodus to urban areas.

An agricultural and nutritional plan cannot be properly evaluated after only a few years of operation since output depends not just on investment and subsidies but also on uncontrollable events, such as weather. In his final state-of-the-nation address, López Portillo claimed great progress for the plan in what he called "unprecedented" and "record-breaking" increases in the production of corn, beans, rice, and wheat. He made much of the achievement of self-sufficiency for most of these products. He addressed the skepticism that has typically greeted Mexican agriculture plans: "Our *campesinos* have given the lie to the fatalists and skeptics who have always doubted the nation's ability to continue progressing in independence and justice."[71] He did not, however, provide any data of how the SAM actually affected nutrition, which is what the program is intended to improve.

Mexico's Goals in Relation to Free Trade

Mexico's four central objectives as revealed by its development plans are to achieve a competitive industrial structure, increase agricultural output, create more jobs, and reduce inequalities in Mexican society. This section will examine whether a gradual movement to free trade with the United States would impede achievement of these objectives or whether such a movement might promote them. First, a word about politics is in order. The plans themselves and public statements by senior officials describing and promoting the plans are highly nationalistic in tone. The Mexican foreign minister referred to this in 1980 as a "healthy

70. Speech of August 5, 1980, regarding SAM, *El Mercado de Valores*, vol. 40 (November 24, 1980), p. 1147.
71. López Portillo, "Sixth State of the Nation Report to the Mexican Congress," pp. 277–82.

and positive nationalism.''[72] The plans embody a nationalism designed to diminish Mexico's dependency, particularly on the United States. This desire is evident in the limitations placed on energy exports to any one country, the wish to strengthen Mexico's bargaining position by extracting concessions, the setting of a high price for oil to develop an efficient capital goods industry, and the goal of self-sufficiency in the production of basic foodstuffs. This nationalism is a fact of life for Mexico, as it is for almost any country with a population and resource base similar to Mexico's. U.S. energy policy, for example, resembles Mexico's basic foodstuffs policy in that it has had national self-sufficiency as its perhaps dubious goal. The question, therefore, is not whether Mexico's nationalistic mood can be overcome to permit a gradual movement to free trade, since this would be as futile as trying to suppress U.S. nationalism, but rather whether Mexico's "positive nationalism" would be compromised by free trade with the United States. The fear in Mexico is that in an unbalanced dyad such as would exist in trade integration with the United States, Mexico would lose its political and cultural identity. A similar concern has also prevented Canada from seeking bilateral free trade with the United States, and in the relationship between these two countries, the economic disparities are less significant than between Mexico and the United States. In fact, if a move toward free trade were to strengthen Mexico's economy and promote industrial efficiency and job creation by encouraging production for an expanded market, Mexico's political and cultural identity would become stronger than it is now. Its national identity is in far greater peril from the need to export a million or more Mexican workers each year to find jobs in the United States. Such dependency must weaken the national pride of those who emigrate to work and their families.

There have been unbalanced dyads between weaker and stronger countries in which the degree of integration extended well beyond free trade. Yet in the case of Ireland and Great Britain, for example, surely no one would seriously argue that the Irish have lost their sense of national identity or their joy in intense engagement in national politics. Although emotional fears are real and cannot be ignored in the formulation of national policy in any country, they do not necessarily reflect what will occur. There is no historical evidence that free-trade movements designed to be concerned only with trade have in fact promoted

72. Castañeda, "Mexico and the United States," p. 2.

political or cultural submersion of one country within one or more other countries.

Would a gradual move to free trade to become effective, say, by the end of the century impede Mexico's efforts to improve its industrial efficiency? The argument against a gradual movement to free trade is that Mexico needs protection for its infant industries—not necessarily for labor-intensive industries such as textiles, apparel, shoes, and television sets, but for automobiles and parts, steel, and capital goods. Protection may be needed now and for the remainder of the 1980s, but it will not be needed forever or even after the next twenty or more years. The inefficiency of Mexican industry has come from the inability to confront vested interests created by past protection. Of the newly industrializing countries, Mexico is perhaps the last, certainly the leading, bastion of continued high protection. It can be argued that a gradual lessening of protection would promote industrial efficiency and that while efficiency was growing for more sophisticated industries, U.S. tariff and nontariff barriers would gradually disappear for labor-intensive industries in which Mexico could compete. Mexicans see the danger that the investment required in the more sophisticated industries would not occur or that these industries would move to the United States. This issue is discussed at length in chapter 7. The danger would be reduced to the extent that the entrepreneurial Mexican state itself would make these investments, but state-run enterprises may not achieve the necessary efficiency to compete internationally.

In terms of Mexico's plans, the issue is really whether the incentives for industrialization—the product, regional, and small business inducements—would be nullified or weakened by a gradual movement to free trade or whether these internal and external subsidies would be compatible with such a move. Nothing in the free-trade area concept prohibits the granting of internal tax incentives for the development and location of industry. Such incentives are bestowed by national governments in other free-trade areas, including the trade integration movement of the European Community. It is also done within countries that have integrated markets. The United States would presumably wish to retain its freedom to offer tax incentives as well, to promote investment.

The issue of compatibility between the industrial plan and a move toward bilateral free trade is more complex in relation to Mexico's buy-national incentives and comparable U.S. incentives. Such national incentives do discriminate against competitors that are not national companies but that theoretically would enjoy equality in a free-trade area. The buy-national incentives should not be a big issue during a transition to free trade, however; the real question is whether they should disappear when the transition is complete, in twenty years or so. In principle, these incentives should disappear, but their disappearance might not even be controversial by then or may be more controversial in the United States than in Mexico. Also, in practice, some slight derogation from free trade should be possible for buy-national policies. These derogations—some overt, some more subtle—exist in other integration movements. However, a buy-national scheme that might be desired by either partner in a bilateral free trade area in a few decades need not be an issue for current decisionmaking.

Compatibility between Mexican plans and free trade is more problematic in relation to explicit export subsidies. Mexican subsidies to promote exports to the United States would not be consistent with a free-trade agreement. Again, there would be flexibility during the transition period, although this is a more sensitive transition issue than buy-national preferences. The key negotiating problem would probably revolve around damage to competing industries in the United States rather than on the extent of Mexican subsidization. If Mexico were to contemplate significant export subsidies in perpetuity, it would be difficult, probably impossible, to contemplate bilateral free trade.[73] On the other hand, use of explicit export subsidies for only a finite period, say, during a transition period, would not prevent the eventual achievement of bilateral free trade. Also, nothing in the bilateral arrangement would compel Mexico to join the subsidy and countervailing duty code of the GATT. However, if subsidies disappeared during a transition period, Mexico would have no reason not to adhere to the code.

A bilateral free-trade agreement between Mexico and the United States would not preclude subsidies by either country for exports to third countries. Third countries, however, would be able to take self-protective measures in accordance with international trade policy. Even without bilateral free trade, U.S. firms would want to protect themselves against damage from Mexican export subsidies. What a free-trade agreement would provide is a framework under which such subsidies

73. Pablo Gonzalez Casanova, ''The Economic Development of Mexico,'' pp. 192–204, attacks the subsidies in the Mexican industrial structure, which he calls transfers from fixed-income groups and the poor to shareholders of corporations.

would be permitted during a transition and a method by which they could be phased out once free trade was achieved.

The energy plan would not conflict with a movement to free trade either. The discovery of vast energy resources no doubt motivated the United States to think seriously about economic integration with Mexico, just as energy was the fulcrum for Mexico's economic planning. But free trade would not oblige Mexico to make available all the energy U.S. buyers demanded, nor would it limit Mexico's ability to determine the price of energy sold to the United States. All that a free-trade area would call for is the removal of artificial barriers to this trade, on both sides. Mexico's energy policy would continue to be under the control of the Mexican authorities. In the European Community, which is not a precise analogy because it is much more than a free-trade area, the United Kingdom retains control over its energy policy. Although Mexico would retain control of its energy policies and prices, the energy subsidy inherent in Mexico's two-price system, that is, its lower price for internal use and a higher one for export, and the energy subsidy provided to carry out the geographic priorities of the industial plan could be problematic. As in industrial protection and subsidies, this would be a problem mainly if Mexico plans to use energy subsidies for twenty or more years, which the industrial plan alleges is not the case. Energy subsidies during a transition period would not affect most bilateral trade, and what might be affected, such as trade of items in which the energy cost is high, would be subject to discussion and negotiation. There is the danger of a subsidy and countervailing duty dispute in this aspect of trade regardless of any move to free trade.

One can conclude that unless Mexico plans to protect its industry and subsidize industrial exports well into the next century, nothing makes a movement toward free trade incompatible with Mexico's goal of industrial efficiency. In fact, the reverse is the case. The more Mexico builds a nonprotective assumption into its industrial planning, the more likely efficiency in production and competitiveness in world markets will follow. The case for compatibility between Mexican goals and movement toward bilateral free trade is even stronger in the agricultural area. Nothing in a free-trade area, whether during a transition or after free trade is achieved, need conflict with Mexico's internal agricultural incentive system, whether this be the provision of credit, the expansion of marketing infrastructure, or the guarantee of remunerative producer prices. The subsidization of inputs might elicit complaints in international trade if it were deemed harmful to U.S. agricultural interests, but this, like subsidies generally, is unrelated to a free-trade agreement. The United States provides similar incentives; indeed, government loan programs, extension services, and information systems are all a form of government subsidy to the agricultural sector. One final point is that there is precedent for excluding agriculture from a free-trade area, namely, in the European Free Trade Association, and this approach could be followed between Mexico and the United States if both sides wished.

For Mexico, and to a great extent for the United States, the most important goal of Mexico's development plans is to create enough jobs in Mexico for those seeking work. This is critical for the health of Mexico's social structure, and the level of employment in Mexico also affects the United States through the migration of Mexican labor. Mexico's plans will probably not contribute much to job creation, either in the short or long term, until declining birth rates are reflected in declining entries into the labor market and until the migration from rural to urban areas runs its course. Past economic policy, particularly industrial production's favoring of a constricted national market, failed to create enough jobs to meet the demand. Excessive future protectionism is likely to fail as well. Past Mexican policy has also failed in that the jobs created during the López Portillo administration were concentrated in the public sector and unsophisticated services,[74] and as the public sector contracts under Mexico's 1982 agreement with the International Monetary Fund, many of these jobs will disappear. Jobs must be created on a more solid base than Mexico has provided if they are to last.

Bilateral free trade would encourage job creation if trade could help expand industrial exports of mass-market consumer goods competitive with those from other sources. Jobs might be created if Mexico's capital goods industry and automotive and steel industries were competitive on a world scale. If this does not occur, the future is apt to be an inexact replica of the past; jobs will be created in industries that need protection

---

74. In his final state-of-the-nation report on September 1, 1982, López Portillo claimed that 4.2 million jobs were created during his term of office and that open unemployment was reduced from 8.1 to 4.5 percent. "Sixth State of the Nation Report to the Mexican Congress," p. 283. In his first economic message to the Congress a few months later (on December 7, 1982), Miguel de la Madrid noted that open unemployment doubled in 1982 and that these unemployed would have to compete for jobs with the 800,000 persons who would enter the labor force in 1983. "Criterios generales de política económica para 1983," p. 1286.

because of their inefficiency and, hence, need perpetual subsidies. Bilateral free trade would probably stimulate job creation to the extent it could stimulate industrial efficiency.

The same conclusion applies to more equitable distribution of income, goods, and services in Mexico. Past policies have failed, and the success of future policies is uncertain. Most of what is proposed in Mexico's plans to improve access to education and health care and to reduce rural-urban disparities is unrelated to a move toward bilateral free trade as such. How bilateral free trade would affect job creation and through this increase the income of Mexico's unemployed and underemployed depends on whether the competition resulting from loss of absolute protection encourages industry efficiency.

It seems clear that Mexico's most profound economic and social aspirations are unlikely to be adversely affected by a movement toward free trade and might even be promoted by such a movement, unless this process were to compromise Mexico's industrial diversification. In addition, it is hard to see why the United States should fear Mexico's achievement of its goals, including those of industrial diversification. Adequate job creation in Mexico might eventually limit the migrant labor available for work in the United States, particularly in the secondary labor market, but it would also reduce the U.S. problem of controlling its own borders. A more equitable society in Mexico would benefit the United States in many ways by promoting stability in Mexico and by increasing the receptivity of the Mexican commercial market to U.S. exports. Although Mexican self-sufficiency in grains, if achieved, would reduce the market for U.S. grain, the remainder of the world market would surely be ample, viewed from the perspective of the twenty-first century. Finally, U.S. interests would not be unreasonably harmed if Mexican industrial competitiveness increased. Some U.S. industries, both in labor-intensive and more sophisticated areas of production, might well decline, but these industries would seek protection just as noncompetitive Mexican industries will. Also, some regions in the United States might suffer, and affected regions would undergo a difficult adjustment. But the dynamic that applies to Mexico, that efficiency and higher productivity promote the general welfare, would apply as well to the United States as a whole. U.S. society would benefit from higher per capita incomes in Mexico generated by free trade.

CHAPTER SIX

Implementing Free Trade

ECONOMIC integration can be formalized in an agreement or can occur in the normal course of events. The Canadian and U.S. economies are more integrated, despite the absence of a comprehensive, formal free-trade agreement, than the economies of the United Kingdom and Germany or even those of France and Germany, which have detailed treaty agreements and an extensive bureaucracy for carrying out the Treaty of Rome among the members of the European Community. Canada in an average year sends about 70 percent of its merchandise exports to the United States. In 1979 more than three-quarters of U.S. imports from Canada entered free of duty.[1] The U.S. capital market serves Canada as though the market were Canada's own. Canada's overall economic growth and its monetary policy cannot be determined except in relation to what is happening in the United States. The integration is so thorough from Canada's viewpoint that the suggestion has been considered in a standing committee of the Canadian Senate that a free-trade area between the two countries be declared to exist under the rules of the General Agreement on Tariffs and Trade and then be expanded over time.[2] Such a free-trade area would be as real and valid as those among countries of the European Free Trade Association.[3]

Although the automotive products agreement of 1965 between the

1. U.S. International Trade Commission (hereafter USITC), *Background Study of the Economies and International Trade Patterns of the Countries of North America, Central America and the Caribbean*, p. 153.

2. In hearings before the Canadian Standing Senate Committee on Foreign Affairs. See Canadian Parliament, Senate, *Canada–United States Relations*, vol. 3: *Canada's Trade Relations with the United States*, pp. 32–34.

3. Intra-EFTA trade in 1979 was between 20 and 23 percent of total EFTA trade. Some of the accomplishments and remaining trade restrictions in EFTA are discussed in European Free Trade Association, *EFTA—Past and Future*.

United States and Canada is responsible for substantial free trade in both directions (more than $12 billion in U.S. exports to Canada in 1979 and almost $10 billion in Canadian exports to the United States), the main impetus for the trade comes from natural interactions fostered by proximity, such as mutual investment, good transportation links, and personal movement back and forth across the border. Despite efforts by various Canadian governments to diversify trade away from the United States, the integration has continued and even deepened.[4]

Integration Options

Mexico is also integrated into the U.S. economy but less so than Canada because of Mexico's lesser degree of economic development. About the same percentage of Mexico's merchandise exports is sent to the United States as Canada's. The duty-free portion of U.S. imports from Mexico is lower than Canada's but was more than 50 percent of total U.S. imports from Mexico in 1979.[5] Mexico had no controls on capital movements before August 1982 and found after the imposition of these controls that it could not effectively contain capital flows because of the ease of movement across the common border. The dollar is often substituted for the peso in Mexico,[6] and the formal reports of the Bank of Mexico used to cover the banking system's participation in the economy in both national money and in dollars.

The periodic opposition to this natural integration by Mexican authorities has had little impact for the same reasons that Canadian efforts to diversity its exports have had so little result. The Mexican government's effort in the early 1980s to halt the integration then occurring by implementing exchange controls predictably showed that governments cannot always control economic impulses. Mexican- and Canadian-U.S. integration is a natural tendency in both cases; forced diversification

4. Canada's "third option" policy adopted in 1972 was precisely such an effort. The third option was defined by Mitchell Sharp, then Canada's secretary of state for external affairs, in "Canada-U.S. Relations: Options for the Future," p. 1: to "pursue a comprehensive long-term strategy to develop and strengthen the Canadian economy and other aspects of our national life and, in the process, to reduce the present Canadian vulnerability."

5. USITC, *Background Study*, p. 153.

6. Leroy O. Laney, "Currency Substitution: The Mexican Case," pp. 1–10.

would require that economic actors not fully exploit the advantages stemming from proximity and past practice.

Integration of the U.S. and Mexican economies is a fact. Although it is still an asymmetrical integration in which Mexico depends more on the United States than the reverse, U.S. dependency is growing more rapidly than is Mexico's. This is happening not only because of the oil trade but also because of the growing relative importance of the Mexican market as a proportion of the total U.S. export market. It may be that this normal integration is the least controversial way for bilateral free trade to proceed, although this natural process is controversial in its own right—as is evident from the constant Mexican efforts at diversification. Still, why sign agreements if integration will take place in any event? The main argument in favor of formalizing the integration process is that the certainty this adds to the process makes it more efficient and thus benefits the growth of income and employment in both countries over any given period. This motivated Holland to formalize integration with West Germany in the European Community. The agreement made existing integration more exact and more certain (but only relatively so, since agreements can be altered or annulled) and structured it within rules likely to benefit the weaker more than the stronger country, because the country with greater power is more able to impose its will on the weaker if there are no rules.

There is a fear and real concern that formal integration can have adverse side effects—political, economic, and social. Consequently, countries sometimes enter into partial integration agreements as a way to test the water without plunging in all the way. The formation of the European Coal and Steel Community (ECSC) before the EC was established is an example of this approach but is also an exception, since partial trade agreements have rarely led to deeper agreements as the ECSC did;[7] in fact, partial agreements are more likely to founder than to deepen. Western Europe wanted to harness Germany's growing power for the economic and perhaps political unification of the region as a whole, so it used the ECSC to further its objective even as it was testing the water. The U.S.-Canada automotive products agreement did not lead to this kind of deepening—though many in the United States who conceived the idea hoped that it would—because Canada was not as

---

7. William Diebold, Jr., *The Schuman Plan: A Study in Economic Cooperation, 1950–1959.*

committed to deepening the agreement as the United States was. The very concept of a free-trade area was devised to escape the political implications of a customs union and its common external tariff, even though nothing in a customs union inexorably leads to its deepening into an economic or political union. These themes will be developed further in the final chapter.

Mexico's in-bond industry arrangement is a modest form of partial integration. This arrangement permits the importation of U.S. products into Mexico, their further processing in Mexico without having to be entered formally into the Mexican customs territory, and the export of the total product out of Mexico. Provisions of the U.S. tariff code that permit reentry into the United States upon payment only of the value added in Mexico are the U.S. counterpart of Mexico's in-bond arrangement. These Mexican assembly plants that process U.S. imports and export them back have prospered because they exploit the advantage of inexpensive labor in Mexico and market availability in the United States. No agreement describes the rights and obligations of each side in this partial free-trade setup, but each country has taken the necessary steps to make this bilateral arrangement function. Although the system has its advocates and critics in both countries, it works.[8]

Along its borders, Mexico has also established a free zone, with its own special incentive system, to stimulate settlement in this area. Mexico has contemplated incorporating the border incentives into its general industrial incentive system over the medium term and maintaining some border incentives as a permanent part of the industrial plan. The motivations are both political and economic, to facilitate Mexican employment and exports. In other words, Mexico, whether it be through its free zone, in-bond industries, or special border incentives, implicitly accepts that it benefits from limited actions to integrate its economy with that of the United States.

It has been suggested that the free zone be expanded to run about 200 miles from the border into each country and, if that proves beneficial after ten years, that it be expanded into the rest of the two countries.[9] This would be a complicated arrangement with three customs areas: one for the United States, one for Mexico, and one for the vast area of 800,000 square miles (200 miles on each side of the 2,000-mile border)

8. Niles Hansen, *The Border Economy: Regional Development in the Southwest*, pp. 97–100, discusses the two views on the *maquiladora*.

9. Abelardo L. Valdez, column in *Texas Business*, vol. 6 (July 1981), p. 11.

that would constitute the free zone. The suggestion is based on the emotional reflex already discussed: if the two countries are not prepared to start a gradual movement to free trade, then why not start a geographically limited free-trade area to try to ease the emotional tension?[10]

The more common suggestion for testing the water is to do so sectorally, industry by industry, rather than by gradually expanding free-trade territories. If a gradual movement to free trade for most goods raises emotional hackles, then maybe free trade in one industry at a time would be more acceptable.[11] This suggestion is based on the theory that one thing inexorably leads to another, so that eventually all trade would be unrestricted. However, not only does history refute this approach, but also the logic that motivates it is not convincing.

In a general movement toward free trade, implicit trade-offs will be made. The expectation might be that industry X in country A will benefit and industry Y in country B will benefit in turn. When the EC was formed, there was some expectation that French agriculture and German industry would be the main sectoral beneficiaries in the two countries. The outcome was actually more complex, since German agriculture maintained its protection and French industry did not suffer. There was no need to make an explicit trade-off in favor of one industry or sector and against another industry or sector in the same country. Such explicit interindustry or intersectoral trade-offs are political anathema, particularly in a democracy. One group of businessmen, farmers, or workers would resist if they were told that they must sacrifice for the benefit of another group. However, trade-offs are accomplished regularly in countries, but rarely this nakedly. Every import tariff and restrictive import license, for example, contains an implicit trade-off. The winners are sometimes identified, but the losers never are. In Mexico, the main loser from the development model was the agricultural sector, since Mexico subsidized its industrial sector; but no leader ever overtly informed the agricultural sector that it had to pay for Mexico's industrialization. Occasionally the suggestion is made in the United States that one way

10. Joel Garreau, *The Nine Nations of North America*, argues that the continent is developing regionally and that the Southwest in the United States, MexAmerica as he calls it, shows cultural and economic influences that transcend the formal U.S.-Mexican border.

11. The United Nations Association of the United States of America, *Relationships in the North American Economic Area*, vaguely recommends common study and problem solving as a current substitute for formal agreements with the hope that this approach will ease emotional tensions over time.

to deal with the problem of undocumented workers coming from Mexico is to work out an explicit trade—the United States will take the workers in exchange for large quantities of oil. The idea of such an explicit trade is naive because it gives the losers no incentive to accept their loss. The idea might not be so naive if the arrangement were implicit.[12] Harmony between the two countries may in fact require separate decisions on migration and oil production that accomplish the above outcome.

In a single industry agreement, both sides must benefit within the framework of that industry. If the industry involved is the petrochemical industry, for example, each country could be allocated some portion of the industry. There could be an implicit or explicit understanding that country A would refrain from producing some products in return for country B's agreeing not to produce some other products. The Latin American Free Trade Association tried this sort of arrangement but with little success. A variant of this technique was used in the Andean Pact, again not altogether successfully. But despite their unsuccessful outcomes, both the Andean Pact and LAFTA approaches had advantages over an individual industry-agreement approach in that they included many industries, thus leaving room for bargaining.

There are occasions when individual industry or sector agreements can work. The ECSC was such an agreement in Western Europe, but this was essentially a government-sanctioned cartel. The U.S.-Canada automotive arrangement was made possible because the same owners and even the same labor union operated in both countries, mostly near each other on either side of the border. Trade-offs were facilitated since the same parties were gaining and sacrificing in the two countries. The automotive agreement has not been without its troubles, however. From time to time, depending on the overall automotive trade balance and developments in separate parts of the industry, one side or the other has suggested renegotiation of the agreement. In general, there is no reason why an agreement in one sector, even if it is successful, must stimulate agreements in other sectors, since each industry or sector has its own dynamic. The automotive agreement, for example, after more than fifteen years of operation, has not stimulated similar agreements in other industries. A single, general agreement that can build in its own implicit

12. Jorge I. Dominguez, in the introduction to the book he edited, *Mexico's Political Economy: Challenges at Home and Abroad*, pp. 9–22, notes the existence of five explicit or implicit bargains between the United States and Mexico regarding Mexico's political, economic, and social structures.

trade-offs seems preferable to the timid industry-by-industry approach, which makes integration more difficult because it tends to build in the seeds of integrative failure.[13]

Free-trade agreements can be compared with international trade negotiations. When the EC and EFTA were formed, the initial agreement was to reduce internal tariffs for all products over a specific period. Exceptions were permitted, but each had to be justified and limited in duration. The LAFTA proceeded differently in that many of the internal tariff reductions had to be negotiated item by item. For the EC and EFTA, exceptions were negotiated; for the LAFTA, inclusions for tariff reductions were. The EC and EFTA technique worked, but the LAFTA system failed. In regular GATT tariff negotiations, the item-by-item technique was abandoned because it created so much frustration. Tariff negotiations in the past two decades have included all goods, and exceptions have to be justified.

Timid integration formulas and complex schemes such as freeing trade in certain territories are likely to fail. General formulas, with incentives against polarization and time for adaptation, have some chance for success, as the EC and EFTA examples demonstrate.[14] However, success in a free-trade movement does depend on outcomes in many specific sectors and industries to ensure that each country gains equally. Thus a negotiation must involve some analysis of probable outcomes, by industry and by sector, for each party to the negotiation, even if one industry is not explicitly traded away for another.

Specific Industry Concerns

Before examining the situation in some specific high-priority industries in Mexico and speculating about their prospects if there were a gradual movement to free trade with the United States, it may be useful to recapitulate the main economic issues at stake. The principal objective

13. Fritz Machlup has made this argument in "Integrationshemmende Integrations-politik" in Herbert Giersch, ed., *Bernhard-Harms Vorlesungen*. He refers to this essay in footnote 1 on p. 3 of his book *A History of Thought on Economic Integration*.

14. J. E. Meade, H. H. Liesner, and S. J. Wells, *Case Studies in European Economic Union: The Mechanics of Integration*, p. 5, observes that although three studies (of the Belgium-Luxembourg Economic Union, Benelux, and the ECSC) are insufficient to "prove" anything, partial unions may create problems avoided in more complete unions.

Mexico would have in any integration movement would be to promote industrial efficiency, particularly as a consequence of the economies of scale that could result from the assurance of barrier-free access to the entire U.S.-Mexican market. In many industries where scale is a less significant factor, Mexico could enjoy a wage advantage that would not be nullified by U.S. import barriers. Although agriculture could be included in a free-trade arrangement, the main motivation for trade integration would be industrial and not agricultural. Mexico's chief misgiving would be that investment in industries that must rely on scale for efficiency would occur in the United States rather than in Mexico and thus promote economic polarization rather than Mexican industrial development. This concern is not germane to labor-intensive activities, such as the manufacture of shoes or apparel, but it might be to the manufacture of automobiles, trucks, and steel. Development in industries on the frontier of technology, such as microprocessing, the newest forms of computer hardware and software, and genetic experimentation, is not really an issue now since leadership in these fields will in the near future continue to be in advanced industrial societies rather than in developing countries that lack the necessary research capacity. This is not to say that Mexico would not want to stimulate these industries, but rather that their development in Mexico depends primarily on government incentives; these could continue with or without a gradual movement toward economic integration.[15] Indeed, industrial efficiency is probably a prerequisite for highly sophisticated research-intensive activities. Government investment in other industries in Mexico could also continue with or without bilateral economic integration, thereby mitigating any polarization.

The Automotive Industry

There is no other industrial group to which the Mexican authorities have devoted more attention and real resources over the past twenty years than the automotive industry. In 1979 alone, fiscal support for this industry amounted to almost 7.5 billion pesos (about $330 million), or more than 100 pesos for every Mexican. This industry reportedly

15. Research and development activities stimulated by the Mexican agency CON-ACYT (Consejo Nacional de Ciencia y Tecnología) are now being conducted. See Dilmus D. James, "La planeación reciente de la ciencia y la tecnología en México," pp. 491–501.

received more than 50 percent of subsidies granted that year to all economic activities combined,[16] in addition to indirect assistance, such as absolute import protection. The automotive industry was expected to contribute 6.2 percent of Mexico's GDP in 1982.[17] Mexico sees the automotive industry as the pioneer for stimulating production to-and-fro between Mexico and the United States and particularly for subcontracting within Mexico for components for fully assembled vehicles and for parts.[18] Integration within Mexico was made mandatory in successive decrees calling for more Mexican components in the manufacture of vehicles and making imports of components more difficult to encourage national production. Authorities have emphasized the development of this industry for some time in Mexico's industrial planning and would not risk its future for trade integration. The total production of 444,426 motor vehicles in 1979 made Mexico the twelfth largest producer in the world that year, manufacturing 1 percent of world production (tables 6-1 and 6-2).[19] The U.S. International Trade Commission estimated employment in the Mexican automotive industry at 40,000, not counting workers in the supplier industries.[20] The Mexican industrial census of 1975 showed employment in the industries supplying automotive components at more than 61,000 (table 6-3). Mexico's minister of national properties and industrial development estimated employment in 1979 at 120,000.[21]

Much has happened since the 1975 employment figures were gathered. Chrysler invested about $300 million into Mexican industry for the production of four-cylinder engines. Ford has entered into various ventures with Mexican partners to produce aluminum cylinder-head castings for engines, automotive glass, and automotive plastic products and on its own is trying to increase production of four-cylinder engines. General Motors is extending its engine production in Mexico as well as

16. Statement by Jesus Silva-Herzog Flores, under secretary of finance and public credit, January 28, 1980, as reported in *El Mercado de Valores*, vol. 40 (February 4, 1980), pp. 97–98.
17. "Views of the Motor Vehicle Manufacturers Association of the United States on the President's Report to the Congress on North American Trade Agreements," p. 9.
18. Albert O. Hirschman, *The Strategy of Economic Development*, p. 100.
19. Motor Vehicle Manufacturers Association of the United States, *World Motor Vehicle Data, 1980 Edition*, p. 8.
20. USITC, *Background Study*, p. 117.
21. "Views of the Motor Vehicle Manufacturers Association of the United States," p. 9.

Table 6-1. *Passenger Car Production in Mexico, 1970, 1975, and 1979*

Units

Manufacturer	1970	1975	1979
Chrysler de México	25,027	33,518	50,653
Ford Motor Company	22,526	33,335	35,281
General Motors de México	13,487	16,576	24,778
Nissan Mexicana	11,957	23,727	35,744
Renault de México	. . .	. . .	14,366
Vehículos Automotores Mexicanos[a]	11,857	21,960	20,309
Volkswagen de México	39,166	88,851	98,918
Diesel Nacional[b]	12,336	19,151	. . .
Total	136,712[c]	237,118	280,049

Source: "Views of the Motor Vehicle Manufacturers Association of the United States on the President's Report to the Congress on North American Trade Agreements," table 2.2, based on data from the Asociación Mexicana de la Industria Automotriz (AMIA).
a. A Mexican-owned firm in which American Motors is a minority shareholder.
b. A joint venture between the Mexican government and Renault.
c. Total as given, although detail totals 136,356.

Table 6-2. *Commercial Vehicle Production in Mexico, 1970, 1975, and 1979*[a]

Units

Manufacturer	1970	1975	1979
Chrysler de México	14,096	31,514	40,067
Fabricas Autocar Mexicana	121	391	1,115
Ford Motor Company	14,446	22,437	39,040
General Motors de México	12,874	19,710	29,640
International Harvester Mexico	591	1,439	965
Kenworth Mexicana	452	1,452	1,885
Mexicana de Autobuses	345	934	1,151
Nissan Mexicana	3,978	7,144	15,123
Vehículos Automotores Mexicanos	1,713	2,185	4,420
Volkswagen de México	. . .	15,719	10,546
Diesel Nacional	6,798	16,187	19,893
Trailer de Monterrey	694	197	100
Victor Patron	. . .	. . .	432
Total	56,108	119,309	164,377

Source: Same as table 6-1.
a. Trucks, tractors, and integral buses.

its production of other parts and fully assembled passenger cars. American Motors and Renault plan to produce front-wheel-drive Renault vehicles with Vehículos Automotores Mexicanos (VAM), which will produce transmission units for American Motors cars in the United States. International Harvester entered into a new joint venture in 1978

Table 6-3. *Firms and Employees in the Mexican Automotive Components Industry*

Firm type	Number of firms	Labor employed
Body parts	223	7,269
Engines	46	12,700
Transmissions	26	7,098
Suspensions	80	4,276
Brakes	48	4,006
Electrical parts	42	5,005
Other parts and accessories	263	13,001
Aircraft components	12	233
Tires and inner tubes	14	7,595
Total	754	61,183

Source: Mexican Industrial Census, 1975, cited in "Views of the Motor Vehicle Manufacturers Association of the United States," table 2.1.

to manufacture heavy-duty diesel trucks and engines, Nissan expanded its Mexican manufacturing facility, and Volkswagen expanded its facilities there to increase its export capacity.[22] In 1982, there was a pause in all this growth. Sales volume, after increasing at an annual rate of 19 percent from 1978 to 1981, declined almost 12 percent during the first nine months of 1982 compared with the same period of 1981.[23] Overall, motor vehicle production declined in 1982 by between 15 and 18 percent.[24] Further production declines are anticipated for 1983.[25] The industry was hurt by the general decline in economic activity in Mexico and a shortage of inputs because of the import restrictions imposed on balance-of-payments grounds.[26] Mexican authorities expect that production and sales will resume their growth in 1984 and thereafter.

Mexico's motor vehicle industry started in the 1920s with the assembly of completely knocked down (CKD) automotive kits imported from the United States.[27] The first major decree to develop a more extensive

22. Ibid., table 2.5.
23. American Chamber of Commerce of Mexico, "Automotive: Sales Slump, Import Restrictions Have Reversed Industry's Prospects," p. 16.
24. "Report on the Economy: The Industrial Sector," p. 428.
25. From a report by the Secretaría de Patrimonio y Fomento Industrial and the Secretaría de Programación y Presupuesto on expectations for the automotive industry in Mexico from 1982 to 1986, summarized in *El Mercado de Valores*, vol. 42 (November 29, 1982), pp. 1230–33.
26. American Chamber of Commerce of Mexico, "Automotive: Sales Slump," p. 16.
27. "Views of the Motor Vehicle Manufacturers Association of the United States," p. 2.

automotive manufacturing industry was in 1962. This was modified in 1972 and again in 1977.[28] The decree sought to augment the performance requirements regarding national procurement of automotive parts, improve the automotive trade balance by limiting imports to no more than a firm exports (a zero-net-import rule), and further nationalize the industry. The zero-net-import rule is really a net-export rule in that any firm that does not meet the minimum local content requirement must compensate for imports by exports of 110 percent of the import value. Minimum local content requirements are based on a cost formula and escalate over time. For 1981 these were 75 percent for passenger cars and 85 percent for trucks; if the minimum requirements are not met, export requirements are increased. Certain imports are limited to companies with majority local ownership. Parts manufacturers must be at least 60 percent Mexican owned. The regulations concerning the decree provide formulas for the interrelationships of national ownership, national procurement, and export performance.[29] The formulas, which are explicit and complicated, contain both compulsion and incentives; fiscal and other benefits are conditional on meeting performance requirements. The incentives relate to duty exemption on imported inputs as well as other tax exemptions.

Despite the performance requirements, the United States retains a positive balance in automotive trade with Mexico. U.S. automotive exports to Mexico in 1980 were $1,067 million and imports were $245 million, a difference of $822 million. Of the total trade, auto parts accounted for $937 million of U.S. exports and $242 million of U.S. imports.[30] Trade between affiliated companies, what in U.S. terminology is referred to as related-party transactions, is significant in the automotive trade between the United States and Mexico.[31]

28. *Diario oficial de la federación*, June 20, 1977. This decree, the "Decreto para el fomento de la industria automotriz," was distributed widely again when the industrial plan was published in 1979. Hector Vazquez Tercero, *Una decada de política sobre industria automotriz*, covers the development of the automobile industry before the 1977 decree.

29. "Acuerdo que establece las reglas de aplicación del decreto para el fomento de la industria automotriz," *Diario oficial de la federación*, October 19, 1977. The incentives available were amplified in regulations published in the *Diario oficial* of January 24, 1979, "Acuerdo por el que se otorga subsidio en favor de las empresas de las industrias terminal automotriz y de autopartes."

30. "Views of the Motor Vehicle Manufacturers Association of the United States," table 2.4. According to *El Mercado de Valores*, November 29, 1982, the overall automotive trade deficit was $526 million in 1976, almost $1,500 million in 1980, and $2,148 million in 1981.

31. USITC, *Background Study*, p. 162. See also Douglas Bennett and Kenneth E.

Managers of the U.S. motor vehicle industry have made their peace with the requirements of Mexico's automotive policy, judging from the input they gave to the executive branch in connection with the study on possible trade agreements in North America.[32] The report cites Mexico's energy resources as a "sufficient" basis for the United States not to take retaliatory measures against Mexico and asserts that, while Mexican policy in this field is "perhaps less than perfect," it does permit U.S. industry to participate in Mexico's growth in the motor vehicle field.[33] The evidence is clear that the U.S. industry has participated and is doing so increasingly. The report notes that the potential motor vehicle market in Mexico is substantial and advises the U.S. government not to take any action that might prejudice participation of the U.S. industry in this market.[34]

The U.S. government has been reluctant to accept Mexican policy because it creates precedents for other countries—that is, reinforces performance requirements elsewhere—and other industries. The performance requirements contradict half a century of U.S. trade policy since they make reciprocity impossible unless it is retaliatory or restrictive. Thus far, all the U.S. government has been able to do is complain, which may be its only viable option. However, continued tension between the two governments because of Mexican automotive policy is inevitable. The interests at stake for the United States as a whole are much greater than for just those who manage the U.S. motor vehicle industry, since Mexican practices also affect U.S. labor, U.S. parts manufacturers, and U.S. trade policy generally. Tensions between the countries in the automotive sector will remain, with or without a movement to free trade.

Those who manage the U.S. automotive industry are also influenced by worldwide trends that now dominate the industry. These include internationalized motor vehicle manufacture in which components are produced in many countries for what may be final assembly in the United States or elsewhere. Global production and hence trade in parts and components rather than in finished vehicles makes economies of scale

---

Sharpe, "Transnational Corporations and the Political Economy of Export Promotion: The Case of the Mexican Automobile Industry," pp. 177–201.

32. The executive branch study was mandated in section 1104 of the *Trade Agreements Act of 1979*, Senate Hearings, pt. 1, p. 371.

33. "Views of the Motor Vehicle Manufacturers Association of the United States," pp. 22, 24.

34. Ibid., p. 57.

more feasible, in fact crucial for competitiveness in automotive production and trade.[35] A second trend is that sales prospects in this industry are more substantial in developing countries, particularly the more advanced, than in the United States or industrial countries generally. The growth in motor vehicle sales in industrial countries, about 2 to 3 percent a year, comes mainly from the replacement market, whereas the developing countries are apt to provide a new growth market. Using data from the Organization for Economic Cooperation and Development (OECD), one expert estimated that two-thirds of the overall growth in the number of vehicles sold in the remainder of this century will occur in developing countries.[36] Mexico plays an important role in this growth prospect. Motor vehicle registration for passenger cars, trucks, and buses in 1978 was 4.2 million, about 16 persons for each vehicle. In the United States that year, there were 1.5 persons for each vehicle registered.[37]

If free trade in automotive vehicles and parts were under consideration now—something along the lines of the U.S.-Canada automotive agreement—Mexico would have no reason to abandon its current automotive policy. Despite U.S. complaints, Mexico's policy has stimulated national growth in the industry. This growth seems to be accelerating as facilities are expanding in Mexico for the production of components with which to assemble cars in the United States and elsewhere. Stimulating this growth has been expensive for Mexico, and Mexico would not now abandon the vast sums already sunk into subsidies and import restrictions. However, the expense for subsidies and the continuing bilateral trade deficit with the United States did lead to modifications in the regulations in September 1983, which presage a reduction in the level of subsidies.[38] The issue, however, is not free trade now but free trade twenty years or so hence. It is conceivable but not probable that Mexico will continue its subsidy-protection policy at a high level for twenty more years. The necessity of such subsidies for so long would indicate the failure of policy, however.

It seems reasonable to make the following assumptions about the probable situation twenty years from now. The trend toward worldwide com-

35. Robert B. Cohen, "Brave New World of the Global Car," pp. 28–35; Marina v. N. Whitman, *International Trade and Investment: Two Perspectives*.

36. C. Kenneth Orski, "The World Automobile Industry at a Crossroads," p. 4.

37. *World Motor Vehicle Data, 1980 Edition*, p. 27.

38. *El Mercado de Valores*, vol. 43 (September 19, 1983), pp. 961–70.

ponent production in large plants will continue, and Mexico will supply many of these components. Production costs in Mexico will be increasingly competitive as a result of scale production, relatively modern plants, and cheaper unit labor costs than in the United States or other industrial countries. If these assumptions are accurate, then it will be Mexico that is likely to seek free trade in the automotive industry in the year 2000 and groups in the United States, such as labor, that will probably resist.

If Mexico needs to keep subsidizing its automotive industry twenty years hence to keep it alive, it will probably do so. Nor will the United States abandon its automotive industry after the year 2000. The official bailout of Chrysler is indicative of what would happen if the entire U.S. industry were at stake. There is a small risk that bilateral free trade would be fatal to the industry either in Mexico or the United States. However, the likely demise of the industry in either country would elicit derogations from free trade or tolerance of national subsidies to prevent this outcome. The existence of separate automotive industries in member countries was not compromised by the formation of the EC. A similar outcome could be expected in bilateral free trade between the United States and Mexico, particularly after a protracted transition.

To be successful, free trade in the automotive sector would have to bring gains for both countries, particularly through specialization in the industry. Such specialization is already taking place, and industry planning for free trade is likely to stimulate even more specialization. The real negotiation in a free-trade agreement would focus not on free trade two decades hence but on the transition to free trade. Such negotiation would be difficult since it would require the United States to accept Mexico's subsidization of its industry, with performance requirements fostering national production. The United States will probably have to accept these conditions even without a formal agreement. The negotiating issue, then, would focus on the duration of Mexico's subsidy and protection policy and whether it could be phased out during a transition period. This is a hard but not an impossible negotiation. Mexico might try to obtain in such a negotiation some assurance of an open market for what is almost certain to be an extensive national industry that will be part of a worldwide network for automotive production. During the next twenty years, Mexico will probably benefit regardless of whether free trade is sought. It is the U.S. government and U.S. labor that will be most resistant to a move to free trade in the automotive industry because of the inevitable benefits Mexico will reap.

Table 6-4. *Mexican Steel Capacity and Production, 1979*
Millions of metric tons a year unless otherwise specified

Company	Installed capacity	Percent of total	Production
AHMSA	3.2	. . .	. . .
Fundidora	1.5	. . .	. . .
SICARTSA	1.2	. . .	. . .
SIDERMEX	5.9	64	4.4
HYLSA	1.5	16	1.5
TAMSA	0.4	5	0.3
Nonintegrated companies	1.4	15	1.0
Total	9.2	100	7.2

Source: U.S. Embassy, Mexico City, "Department of State Airgram A-106," October 25, 1979, p. 13, based on industry sources.

The Steel Industry

The Mexican government is deeply involved in the production and marketing of steel. As with the automotive industry, Mexico has devoted substantial resources for increasing steel production and plans to allocate even more. There are five vertically integrated steel producers in Mexico, twenty-six semi-integrated producers, and about forty rolling companies.[39] Three of the vertically integrated companies are wholly owned by the government: Altos Hornos de Mexico, S.A. (AHMSA), currently the largest producer; Fundidora Monterrey, S.A., the third largest of the five integrated producers; and Siderurgica Lázaro Cárdenas–Las Truchas S.A. (SICARTSA), the newest firm and expected eventually to become the largest. The other two firms are HYLSA (formerly Hojolata y Lamina, S.A.), the steel division of the Alfa industrial group of Monterrey and the larger of the two private-sector companies, and Tubos de Acero de Mexico, S.A. (TAMSA), the smallest of the big five and Mexico's only producer of seamless steel pipe. More than 80 percent of TAMSA's production is sold to PEMEX.

In January 1978 the three government-owned companies were organized into a single unit, SIDERMEX, for central management of production and marketing. SIDERMEX owns 51 percent of the privately owned TAMSA.

Table 6-4 gives 1979 production data for the five big companies. In

39. U.S. Embassy, Mexico City, "Department of State Airgram A-106," October 25, 1979, p. 11.

1980 steel production declined to about 6.8 million tons and was expected to increase to 8.0 million tons in 1981.[40] Capacity is expected to rise from 9.3 million tons a year in 1979 to 28.0 million tons by 1990.[41] It is projected that domestic demand in 1990 will be 23.5 million tons.[42] Electric and basic oxygen furnaces account for the largest proportion of steel production, while production of less efficient open-hearth furnaces is declining (table 6-5). Open-hearth products are expected to disappear over the coming decade.[43] As table 6-5 shows, Mexican production of steel and finished products did not meet domestic demand in 1979. The main reason for this shortfall was the large need then of PEMEX for flats and pipe and the automotive industry's need for flats.

Because Mexican authorities are as committed to expanding the steel industry as they are the automotive industry, it is inconceivable that they would sacrifice its future for trade integration. It is in this light that one must look at the potential consequences to the steel industry in Mexico, and in the United States, of free trade some twenty years from now. Currently, the Mexican steel industry has some serious problems. The government-owned firms have a history of mismanagement; it was this, in part, that led to the formation of SIDERMEX. Transportation facilities, particularly rail, do not meet the industry's needs. Mexican steel prices have been controlled since 1956, and they were about 20 percent below international levels in mid-1981.[44] Even if Mexico had excess steel products not needed for domestic use, an overvalued peso would make exportation difficult without subsidization. Of the five integrated companies, and assuming viable exchange-rate relationships, HYLSA would be most able to compete internationally today. HYLSA

40. "The Industrial Sector," p. 189, gives 1981 billet steel production as 7.6 million tons. "Report on the Economy: The Industrial Sector," p. 430, gives billet steel production for January–October 1982 as 6 million tons, down 6.5 percent from the January–October 1981 production of 6.4 million tons.

41. Jerry Brady, ed., *Mexican Industrial Development Plans: Implications for United States Policy*, p. 83.

42. *El Mercado de Valores*, vol. 41 (May 11, 1981), p. 502. This figure comes from estimates made, product by product, by the Mexican Coordinating Committee on the Steel Industry, which is advisory to the government. The figure involves an average annual increase of 10.2 percent in steel demand from 1981 to 1990. Brady, in *Mexican Industrial Development Plans*, estimates steel demand in 1990 at 26 to 28 million metric tons (p. 82).

43. U.S. Consulate, Monterrey, "Department of State Airgram A-12," July 14, 1980, p. 2.

44. Brady, *Mexican Industrial Development Plans*, p. 82. The investment planning figures that follow also come from this report, pp. 83–84.

Table 6-5. *Mexican Steel Production, 1977–79, and Apparent Consumption, 1979*
Metric tons

Product	Production 1977	Production 1978	Production 1979	Apparent consumption, 1979
Primary products				
Ferroalloys	151,998	170,732	176,216	182,200
Pig iron	3,009,036	3,507,448[a]	3,519,969	3,520,000
Sponge iron	1,320,125	1,627,966	1,502,789	1,520,000
Steel	5,601,297	6,775,443	7,041,238	8,300,000
Open hearth	1,627,585	1,505,962	1,473,874	. . .
Electric furnace	2,469,972	2,793,424	2,966,076	. . .
Basic oxygen furnace	1,503,740	2,476,057	2,601,288	. . .
Nonflats	2,025,486	2,392,690	2,676,300	2,587,300
Rod	432,454	537,544	592,600	451,600
Rebar	966,061	1,134,092	1,256,500	1,256,000
Other bars	180,907	177,245	201,800	212,700
Commercial shapes	239,156	256,269	297,100	319,000
Structural shapes	155,170	222,051	251,600	298,600
Castings	39,130	53,383	62,600	n.a.
Forgings	12,210	11,555	14,300	n.a.
Flats	2,056,656	2,422,200[a]	2,633,300	3,228,500
Plate	555,711	687,800[a]	775,200	1,012,000
Hot-rolled sheet	402,399	672,900[a]	726,500	726,900
Cold-rolled sheet	1,098,546	1,061,600[a]	1,131,600	1,186,700
Seamless pipe	220,166	252,400	255,000	323,200
Derivative products				
Galvanized sheet	133,763	181,155	195,258	n.a.
Tinplate	193,021	183,100[a]	174,900	n.a.
Wire	320,880	397,575[a]	441,000	n.a.
Seamed pipe	362,892	565,558[a]	571,750	1,040,750

Sources: U.S. Embassy, Mexico City, "Department of State Airgram A-106," p. 3; U.S. Consulate, Monterrey, "Department of State Airgram A-12," July 14, 1980, p. 5 of enclosure.
a. Preliminary figures.

also has been innovative in developing a direct-reduction process that has become an important technological export for Mexico.

SIDERMEX plans to invest more than $17.2 billion during the 1980s to increase production from 4.5 million metric tons in 1979 to 21.0 million metric tons a year by 1990. About half of this would be produced by SICARTSA, in plants next to port facilities. Both private firms, HYLSA and TAMSA, also are expanding significantly. By 1990, therefore, and definitely by the year 2000, Mexico will have a modern young steel industry. It is probable, though not certain, that the Mexican industry will be more modern than the U.S. industry by the time free trade would be implemented. Certainly the surest road to resolution of the Mexican steel industry's management and transportation problems is the expectation of a more competitive environment by the year 2000. And although it is unclear whether Mexico will have excess supply for export by then, it will probably have an industry that could compete in world markets and certainly in the Mexican market, in terms of plant modernity.

Finally, as in the case of the automotive industry, it is more likely to be the U.S. steel industry than the Mexican industry that resists free trade. The Mexican steel and automotive industries reinforce each other to some degree, since the output from the steel industry is an important input for the automotive industry. There is good reason to expect that each industry will help the other become more competitive.

Petrochemicals

Official investment in recent years has stressed the production of basic petrochemicals to help Mexico become relatively self-sufficient in these products and eventually a primary exporter, especially of ammonia, polyethylene, and aromatics. Petrochemical production is highly capital intensive,[45] and Mexico is devoting substantial resources to this industry. Production of basic petrochemicals in 1980 was 83 percent greater than in 1976, the final year of the Echeverría administration.[46] Before the onset of the 1982 economic crisis, the Mexican government also supported secondary petrochemical plants.

Mexican law gives PEMEX the exclusive right to produce basic petrochemicals. A national petrochemical commission, which is chaired by the minister of national properties and industrial development and includes the director general of PEMEX, must grant permission for new investments or expansion of existing plants or secondary petrochemicals. Table 6-6 shows the relative importance, by value and volume, of

45. Data on value added per worker in various Mexican industries are shown in A. Nowicki and others, *Mexico: Manufacturing Sector: Situation, Prospects and Policies*, p. 98.
46. Report by the director general of PEMEX, Jorge Díaz Serrano, March 18, 1981, on the forty-third anniversary of the Mexican petroleum industry, *El Mercado de Valores*, vol. 41 (March 23, 1981), p. 304.

Table 6-6. *Volume and Value of Principal Basic Petrochemical Products in Mexico, 1978*

Percent of total production

Product	Volume	Value
Ammonia	27.3	21.4
Polyethylene	1.7	10.7
Ethylene	4.5	9.1
Meta- and paraxylene	1.3	4.0
Ethane	8.6	3.9
Toluene	2.1	3.9
Dodecylbenzene	1.1	3.7
Benzene	1.4	3.5
Vinyl chloride	1.0	3.5
Styrene	0.6	3.4
Methanol	1.8	3.4
Paraxylene	0.6	3.2
Ethylene oxide	0.5	3.1
Dichlorethane	1.7	3.1
Carbonic anhydride gas	34.2	1.6
All others	12.6	19.5
Total	100.0	100.0

Source: Secretaría de Programación y Presupuesto, *La industria petrolera en México*, pp. 184, 187.

the main basic petrochemicals produced in Mexico in 1978.[47] Since then, the industry has expanded significantly and will continue to do so. Six new basic petrochemical plants began operations in 1980, making a total of 81.[48] By the end of 1986, Mexico plans to have 157 basic petrochemical plants in operation.[49] The most ambitious new venture is the petrochemical complex at La Cangrejera, near the Gulf port of Coatzacoalcos, Veracruz, which contains 20 plants and will eventually include 36, making it the largest petrochemical complex in the world operated as a single project. Basic petrochemical production was 7.2 million metric tons in 1980; by the end of 1986, the projected production will be 28.4 million tons a year.[50]

Mexico enjoys some natural advantages in this industry over potential competitors, including the United States. The most important advantage

47. "Basic" production, as used in Mexican data, includes both primary products and lower derivatives, such as styrene.

48. Report by Jorge Díaz Serrano, March 18, 1981, *El Mercado de Valores*, vol. 41 (March 23, 1981), p. 304.

49. Statement by José Luis García Luna, subdirector of PEMEX for ecological and social protection, *El Mercado de Valores*, vol. 41 (May 11, 1981), p. 497.

50. Ibid.

is the easy availability of feedstocks. Also, the newer basic petrochemical plants are in port cities to reduce export transportation costs from what they would be if the industry had to rely on the inadequate Mexican rail system. By the year 2000, Mexico will probably be making a profit in basic petrochemical trade and seeking more markets. If there is any industry in which one can expect intra-industry specialization to develop under free-trade conditions, it is the petrochemical industry. Twenty years from now the Mexican interest will most likely not be in the production of primary products, since the major goals in this part of the industry will have been achieved, but will be in greater participation in trade of derivative products. The multipliers for value added and job creation are substantial in these derivative products, by as much as a factor of 250 for job creation and 20 for cumulative value added. It is precisely in these derivative products that U.S. tariff protection is high and in which free trade could be of enormous potential benefit for Mexico.

The petrochemical industry does not seem to be one in which the weaker economic country—Mexico—is apt to fall behind the stronger country—the United States—if there is a gradual movement to free trade. In basic petrochemicals, Mexico will probably become the stronger country. The outcome is more uncertain for secondary products, but there is no reason to expect polarization in favor of the United States.[51]

Labor-Intensive Products

In the automotive, steel, and petrochemical industries, substantial capital investment is required to develop products that will be competitive on the international scene. In each of these industries, major investment has been taking place in Mexico for some time. Each has been important in Mexico's industrial planning even before a formal, comprehensive plan was instituted, and the emphasis on these industries will undoubtedly continue after current plans are superseded by later ones.

Mexico's planning also emphasizes the need for growth in durable and nondurable consumer goods industries, both for domestic consump-

---

51. Data on the petrochemical industry are available in USITC, *Study of the Petrochemical Industries in the Countries of the Northern Portion of the Western Hemisphere.*

tion and for augmenting exports of these products. These are the kinds of products that traditionally have been in the vanguard of market penetration for newly industrializing countries. There is no reason why they cannot play a comparable role for Mexico, particularly if they receive preferential treatment as part of a bilateral free-trade area with the United States. Mexico's textile and apparel industry already is substantial, although exports are still relatively low compared with those of other newly industrializing countries, particularly those in Asia. In 1979 Mexican exports not partially duty-free under U.S. tariff provisions amounted to about 1 percent of the value of domestic shipments of these items.[52] In 1979 fully dutiable Mexican textile and apparel exports amounted to $83 million;[53] partially dutiable exports, for value added, amounted to $170 million, but only $53 million of this constituted Mexican value added before reexport.[54] What this means is that the part of the industry that is Mexican owned pays scant attention to the export market while the part that is American owned—the assembly plants that reexport U.S. imports—processes U.S. textiles and apparel more extensively than it adds value in Mexico. Although Mexico's textile and apparel exports are constricted by the multifiber arrangement (MFA) and the U.S.-Mexican bilateral agreement pursuant to the MFA, this does not fully explain Mexico's relatively low level of exports. U.S. textile and apparel imports from developing countries were about $6.5 billion in 1980,[55] and Mexico's share constituted less than 5 percent. Most of this 5 percent was the reimport into the United States of textile and apparel products shipped to Mexico for further processing.

Under bilateral free trade, the potential for Mexican export growth in the U.S. market for textile and apparel products would be high. Contributing to this potential would be Mexico's stress on producing consumer nondurables and the gradual elimination, just for Mexico, of U.S. tariff and nontariff barriers. For these reasons, the U.S. textile and apparel sector would probably resist bilateral free trade.[56] The U.S.-based

52. USITC, *Background Study*, p. 89.
53. Ibid.
54. Data provided by USITC, "Tariff Items 807.00, U.S. Imports for Consumption, from Mexico by Commodity Groups, 1978–1981," February 1983. The textile and apparel figures in 1980 were $199 million in total exports and $58 million for Mexican value added.
55. Data are from the U.S. Bureau of the Census.
56. One bit of evidence of the intensity of opposition in the United States to free trade in textiles and apparel is the deliberate omission of these products from the one-way free trade for beneficiary countries in the Caribbean Basin proposed by President Reagan on February 24, 1982.

industry under bilateral free trade would presumably have to further specialize in manufacturing high quality textiles, leaving the lower quality goods and more labor-intensive parts of the industry to Mexico.[57] (According to Mexican sources, 255,000 workers are employed in Mexico's textile and apparel industry, and value added to U.S. imports contributes 1.7 percent to Mexico's GDP.)[58]

The same reasoning applies for other consumer-goods industries in which wage costs make up a large part of total product cost (wage costs are more than half of the total cost of apparel production)[59] and for Mexican industries that can compete in the U.S. market. These twin conditions exist for television receivers and parts, parts of telecommunication and sound reproduction equipment, insulated electric conductors, electric motors and generators, many electric household appliances, and furniture. Mexico now exports significant amounts of those and similar products to the United States (see table 3-6). Many of these exports are products assembled from imported U.S. parts, but the value added in Mexico tends to be much higher than for apparel products. In 1980 the dutiable value of U.S. imports (that is, that portion of the import whose value was added in Mexico) for textile products was 29 percent; for metal products it was 54 percent. For television parts, which is included in metal products and was the largest single item imported in 1980 by the United States after assembly in Mexico ($618 million in total value), 68 percent of the value was added in Mexico ($418 million).[60]

The proportion of value added in Mexico is important because it represents mostly labor and therefore addresses what may be Mexico's most troublesome socioeconomic problem.[61] Trade of items manufactured in both Mexico and the United States fosters the placing of operations that will provide the most advantages to both countries. This type of intra-industry cooperation and resulting trade between parts of the same company or related parties will probably increase in a free-

57. *El Mercado de Valores*, vol. 41 (August 1981), p. 836, provides data on the character of Mexican production. The National Textile Industry Chamber published much material on the development of the Mexican textile industry between 1970 and 1980 in its *Memoria estadística, 1981*.

58. The article cited in note 57 reports that the degree of automation is quite high in the Mexican textile industry, which ranks sixth in automation after the United States, Japan, Switzerland, Poland, and East Germany.

59. USITC, *Background Study*, p. 90.

60. USITC, *Imports under Items 806.30 and 807.00 of the Tariff Schedules of the United States, 1977–80*, pp. B-26, B-27.

61. The number of workers involved in the electronics industry in Mexico is estimated at 30,000. USITC, *Background Study*, p. 111.

trade area since it facilitates specialization within an industry. The ability to produce parts of a final product anywhere in the two countries, without regard to tariff or nontariff barriers, would be one of the main benefits investors would derive from free trade. The United States has already chosen Mexico as a desirable place to specialize further the industries cited in this section, and this attraction for production in Mexico should increase as free trade is achieved.

It would be a while before Mexico could produce enough of many of these products to satisfy both domestic demand and demand in export markets, particularly that of the United States. Mexico wants to do this over the next decade in any event. But the goal is more likely to be attained if planning could be based on reasonably assured barrier-free access to the U.S. market, to be achieved gradually over the next two decades, than under conditions of uncertainty about trade barriers.

Conclusions

It would seem that trade integration between Mexico and the United States would be simpler to achieve if it were across-the-board rather than approached through one industry at a time or by gradually expanding "free" territories. Also, for many of the industries Mexico most wants to stimulate, industries that are both capital and labor intensive, a gradual movement to free trade would probably be in Mexico's long-term interest.

Assuming that both countries would want trade integration, there may be individual industries in which integration can be achieved in isolation from other industries or from trade in general, just as trade in the automotive industry evolved between the United States and Canada. Such integration would probably not lead much further.[62] It might also be possible to set up geographically limited free-trade zones that cut across both countries. However, this is harder to envision than integration of a single industry because it entails a more basic departure from sovereignty. A free-trade zone within a country is a relatively simple technique; it is usually designed to promote industrial processing and a

62. Such isolated integration would also be a violation for the United States of the GATT if integration in one or a few industries favored Mexico. Discrimination in favor of Mexico for substantially all trade, on the other hand, would be consistent with the GATT.

base from which products can be exported out of the country or into the customs territory of the country. On the other hand, a free-trade zone that cuts across national lines sets up a new customs entity, and its very purpose would be to remove from both countries economic sovereignty in that area in order to attract investment and labor. It is a complex concept and would be difficult to implement. Also, as with integration of a single industry, even its achievement would probably not stimulate more extensive trade integration between the two countries.

The industries discussed in this chapter were chosen because they are seen by Mexico as crucial and are industries in which Mexico has invested heavily, ones whose future no Mexican government is likely to endanger by experimenting with bilateral free trade. However, it seems clear that these industries in Mexico will not be endangered by a movement toward bilateral free trade. Indeed, the evidence is that it would probably be the managers, shareholders, and employees of these industries in the United States who would be most reluctant about bilateral free trade with Mexico. The outcome of free trade would be acceptable in both countries if entire industries as crucial as these were not prejudiced and if intra-industry specialization took place in both countries. Such specialization is a reasonable prospect in a free-trade area between the two countries.

CHAPTER SEVEN

Questioning the Divergence Theory

THE PRINCIPAL economic issue Mexicans would raise about any proposal to move to free trade with the United States is that the United
States would benefit more than Mexico. Even if one argues that certain
Mexican industries might fare quite well in a gradual movement to free
trade (as was done in chapter 6), this will not allay Mexico's concern
about the effect on its economy and industry as a whole. This chapter
examines the theory of backwash—that free trade benefits only the
richer country and leaves the poorer country a backwater—and how
well it has stood up in other contexts, to reach tentative conclusions
about possible outcomes of U.S.-Mexican bilateral free trade.

Divergence Theory

The theoretical basis for the contention that there will be divergence
in production and incomes between more- and less-developed countries
was set forth lucidly in the writing of Myrdal.[1] Others subsequently
embellished Myrdal's theorizing, and dependency theorists, particularly
in Latin America, put it in a political context. The essence of Myrdal's
argument is that the forces that led to the original divergence reinforce
later divergence as well. Industries are formed that improve efficiency
by regular capital infusions and in some cases by scale, more possible in
richer countries; transportation networks develop in richer areas and
remain inadequate or nonexistent in backward areas; people in better

1. Gunnar Myrdal, *Economic Theory and Under-Developed Regions.*

154

developed countries are trained to participate in industry but those in poor countries are likely to remain uneducated; and so on. Production processes in the countries that develop early become mutually reinforcing and links among industries producing products for each other (for example, a steel industry producing for an automobile industry) become established within the country.[2]

Tendencies toward convergence among countries are swamped by these natural divergent developments. Convergence normally results from migration of persons and capital to produce goods under least-cost conditions and the transfer of technology among countries to make this least-cost production effective. The unequal-development theorists contend that these convergent tendencies do not function effectively, in part because of natural obstructions to factor and technology movements among countries and in part because of deliberate restrictions placed on the migration of people and the transfer of technology. The conditions in backward countries also become less congenial for industrialization as divergence progresses. Once the natural process of divergence gets started, its circular causation, to use Myrdal's term, is reinforced by various oligopolistic practices in the more developed areas.

Prebisch contributed much to the divergence theory with his thesis of unequal exchange in international trade.[3] Prebisch argued that the terms of trade naturally tend to move in favor of manufactures and against primary products, mainly because higher income elasticity of demand for manufactured products tends to raise their prices in relation to raw material prices. According to the Prebisch model of international trade, the "center" is the main producer of manufactured goods in the world and the "periphery" participates in international trade mostly through the export of primary products. Such a delineation intensifies the divergent tendencies in the international economy. The terms-of-trade thesis and the center-periphery characterization of the world have greatly influenced the thinking of economists in developing countries, particularly in Latin America, including Mexico.

The theorists cited and many others writing on the twin themes of unequal development and unequal exchange present their analyses

2. Albert O. Hirschman, *The Strategy of Economic Development*.

3. United Nations Economic Commission for Latin America, *The Economic Development of Latin America and Its Principal Problems*. A well-documented article on the development of Prebisch's thinking is Joseph L. Love, "Raúl Prebisch and the Origins of the Doctrine of Unequal Exchange," pp. 45–72.

mostly in economic terms. The dependency theorists build on the theses of Prebisch and his collaborators as well as on the evident disparities in the levels of development among countries to push the theme one step further. They propose that divergence has been deliberately perpetuated by the center for both economic gain and political hegemony.[4] The writings of these theorists have had great impact in Mexico, where concepts like *dependency* and *hegemony* are part of intellectuals' everyday vocabulary.[5]

Theories on unequal development attempt to explain not only what happens internationally among nations but also internally among different regions of a country. Mexico is a particularly egregious example of disparate levels of regional development that have persisted despite attempts to stimulate convergence.[6] Mexico's industrial plans show that Mexican authorities are concerned about regional disparities. One would assume that disparities within a nation would be easier to correct than those among nations since factors of production, particularly labor, theoretically can move more freely internally. Yet regional disparities have probably widened in Mexico over the past twenty-five years.[7] Mexicans would be concerned about the possible effect of a bilateral movement to free trade on internal regional development as well as on unequal development at the national level.

The theories of unequal development and unequal exchange implicitly demand correctives to promote national development. They contradict neoclassical ideas of free trade or even a movement to free trade, that is, until the economic divergence has been eliminated. Myrdal, for example, labeled as "intellectually false" the commercial policy doctrine of the developed countries that argues for progressive reduction of

4. The Winter 1978 issue of *International Organization*, vol. 32, is devoted to the theme of "Dependence and Dependency in the Global System." The lead essay by the editor of the volume, James A. Caporaso, "Dependence, Dependency, and Power in the Global System: A Structural and Behavioral Analysis," pp. 13–43, provides the theme for the analysis and a brief review of the literature.

5. My observation is that the term *dependency* and its counterpart *hegemony* are used mainly by political scientists, whereas words like *backwash, polarization, unequal development,* and *unequal exchange* are used more by economists.

6. See David Barkin and Timothy King, *Regional Economic Development: The River Basin Approach in Mexico.*

7. Data on gross domestic product by person and by activity among Mexican states, 1960 to 1970, appear in the publication of the Economic Commission for Latin America, *Distribución regional del producto interno bruto sectorial en los países de América Latina*, pp. 34–36, 61–63.

import barriers.[8] He categorized import restrictions as one means of bypassing natural divergence in that they create demand for new industry and recommended their use. This recommendation was also made by economists of the Economic Commission for Latin America (ECLA) working with Prebisch who propounded the thesis of import-substituting industrialization (ISI). This is what Mexico and other Latin American countries began practicing in the 1950s and 1960s. Two statements by proponents of ISI characterize widely held conclusions.

Prebisch wrote: "Industrialization is not an end in itself, but the principal means at the disposal of those [periphery] countries of obtaining a share of the benefits of technical progress and of progressively raising the standard of living of the masses."[9] And according to Dell, "it is simply not true that free trade and greater competition have much to contribute to the economic growth of underdeveloped countries."[10]

The corrective for unequal development need not have been ISI as extreme as that practiced in Mexico and the rest of Latin America, but the level of development of these countries did require some government action to stimulate industrial production. Some import substitution was practiced in all post–World War II cases of industrialization, but there was a marked contrast in the direction of the bias between Asian countries, such as Taiwan and South Korea, and Latin American countries. Latin America favored import prevention and Asia favored export promotion.[11] It seems significant that dependency theory, which refers to the center's deliberate prevention of industrial development in the periphery, originated in Latin America, where the government bias led to industrial inefficiencies. It did not originate in Asia, where the export-promotion bias led to a highly competitive industrial structure. Geographic separation makes impractical any consideration of a movement toward bilateral free trade between the United States and South Korea, but if the two countries were neighbors, it is inconceivable that U.S. labor would accept a movement to free trade with South Korea. The latter's industry is too competitive. The issue in this case would not be one of unequal development leading inevitably to unequal benefits in free trade, but rather of the competitive conditions under which Korea's

8. Gunnar Myrdal, *An International Economy: Problems and Prospects*, p. 223.
9. U.N. Economic Commission for Latin America, *The Economic Development of Latin America*, p. 2.
10. Sidney Dell, *Trade Blocs and Common Markets*, p. 215.
11. See Anne O. Krueger, *Liberalization Attempts and Consequences*.

industrialization flourished. Those who contend that disparities in the degree of industrialization between countries must lead to the kind of circular causation and backwash posited by Myrdal obviously overstate their argument. The outcome clearly depends on the nature of the industrialization process and its efficiency in the poorer country.

The ECLA theorists who asserted the inevitability of unequal exchange between the center and the periphery did advocate trade integration among the countries of Latin America. Because of the unequal development of Latin American countries, various schemes were devised to counteract the unequal benefits that would flow from free trade. Many of these schemes are similar to trade integration efforts elsewhere, including those in Europe. They involve financial assistance from the stronger to the weaker countries, a slower reduction of tariffs by the weaker country, and actual preferences for exports by the weaker into the stronger countries in the period before internal tariffs are completely eliminated. Latin America also sought to override unequal benefits in free-trade areas by negotiating on which country would obtain which industry or segment of industry.

In practice, unequal benefits existed in the Latin American Free Trade Association; this fact was one reason it failed. This was also true in the Central American Common Market (CACM). Wionczek has since asserted that "Latin American economic integration will most probably remain an empty dream for some time to come" because of the inevitable outcome of unequal benefits.[12] The formation of the Andean Group by the countries in the western part of Latin America was designed to escape from the unequal-benefit implications of free trade with Argentina, Brazil, and Mexico. Dell, in arguing that planned joint development of specific industries in Latin America is essential, insisted that "market forces will tend to concentrate development in the richer areas of the continent, bypassing the poorer areas."[13] Such planning for location of industries was embodied in the agreements for LAFTA, the Andean Group, and the CACM. The effort was not generally successful and was one of the reasons for Chilean withdrawal from the Andean Group.

The question of whether decisions about the location of specific industries should be left in the hands of private corporations and governments acting alone or be made in government-to-government negotiation would also arise in any movement toward free trade between

12. Miguel S. Wionczek, "The Rise and the Decline of Latin American Economic Integration," p. 66.
13. Sidney Dell, *A Latin American Common Market?* p. 122.

Mexico and the United States. This issue could be handled precisely as industrial development is now handled—by leaving unaltered the two countries' laws and practices regarding foreign investment. Nationalization of Mexican industry need not be tampered with in a free-trade area. However, the whole issue undoubtedly would enter into the bilateral negotiation. Mexican intellectuals deeply distrust the influence of U.S. transnational corporations. On the other hand, U.S. labor would resent Mexican compulsion about industry location, since it believes that Mexican performance requirements ultimately deprive U.S. workers of jobs. The issue would almost certainly make for difficult negotiation, particularly for the transition period to free trade.

Vaitsos has asked whether free trade can be said to exist, even in the European Community, when there is so much internalization of trade among affiliated parts of transnational corporations.[14] (Related-party imports by the United States made up 46 percent of total imports from Mexico in 1979.)[15] Vaitsos contends that transnational enterprises operating this way preempt and even negate the meaning of markets. It is not apparent how such corporations, even as they internalize operations, can escape competition from other internalizing corporations. Nor is it clear which country—the United States or Mexico—would benefit more if tariffs and other trade barriers were eliminated over time, or even if the trade barriers were not eliminated.

The literature on U.S. and other foreign investment in Mexico is extensive, and the issue of Mexican control over its own destiny in the face of this investment is still a sensitive one.[16] It is not an issue that can be resolved in a single bilateral negotiation dealing with free trade, nor

14. Constantine Vaitsos, "Corporate Integration in World Production and Trade," in Dudley Seers and Constantine Vaitsos, eds., *Integration and Unequal Development: The Experience of the EEC*, pp. 24–25.

15. U.S. International Trade Commission, *Background Study of the Economies and International Trade Patterns of the Countries of North America, Central America and the Caribbean*, p. 163.

16. Some of the relevant literature includes John M. Connor, "A Qualitative Analysis of the Market Power of United States Multinational Corporations in Brazil and Mexico"; John M. Connor and Willard F. Mueller, *Market Power and Profitability of Multinational Corporations in Brazil and Mexico*, Committee Print; Richard S. Newfarmer and Willard F. Mueller, *Multinational Corporations in Brazil and Mexico: Structural Sources of Economic and Noneconomic Power*, Committee Print; Fernando Fajnzylber and Trinidad Martínez Tarragó, *Las empresas transnacionales*; Bernardo Sepúlveda Amor and Antonio Chumacero, *La inversión extranjera en México;* Bernardo Sepúlveda Amor, Olga Pellicer de Brody, and Lorenzo Meyer, *Las empresas transnacionales en México*; Miguel S. Wionczek, *El nacionalismo mexicano y la inversión extranjera.*

is there any compelling need to determine in advance the outcome of practices that have been evolving in recent decades. If there were a free-trade agreement, investment practices could become part of the continuing dialogue. The issue is raised here because Mexico sees extensive and still growing U.S. direct investment in Mexican industry as benefiting U.S. industry more than Mexico.[17] In some industries, such as the automotive industry, the trade inequities resulting from U.S. investment may lean in Mexico's favor by the year 2000.

In summary, there is a strong body of belief that there will be progressive economic divergence among nations, as the rich get richer and more diversified in their economic and industrial structure and the poor grow much less rapidly and assume a peripheral role in the world economy. According to those who believe this theory, this outcome can be mitigated or averted only by government action to foster industrialization and economic diversification in the backward countries. Since unequal development is intensified by unequal exchange, avoidance of unequal development entails rejecting the neoclassical model of international trade. It is not clear just how long infant industry protection is required. The extreme ISI model incorporating these ideas was tested most intensively in Latin America but was slowly abandoned during the 1970s in favor of a model that embodied far less export pessimism and that therefore stressed export promotion more than import substitution. Mexico has come late to export promotion and, indeed, remains an uncertain adherent to the philosophy of import liberalization. This was evident from the national debate in Mexico about entry into the GATT. The combination of unequal development and unequal exchange, for those who subscribe to this theory, applies directly to integration theory since free trade among unequals curtails the ability of the weaker country to manipulate its commercial and industrial policies to protect itself against imports from the stronger country. The LAFTA experience is seen as confirming this outcome of unequal benefits in a free-trade agreement among economic unequals. The outcomes in the LAFTA were unequal despite its efforts to stimulate development in the weaker countries.

17. The U.S. direct investment position in Mexico at the end of 1979 was $4,575 million, 2.4 percent of U.S. direct investment abroad. USITC, *Background Study*, p. 30. In 1980 U.S. direct investment in Mexico was $1.1 billion and estimated at $1.2 billion in 1981. American Chamber of Commerce of Mexico, "U.S. Investment Here Seen Increasing 13% in '81," p. 11.

All these arguments would carry great force in any debate in Mexico over the idea of moving to free trade with the United States. The possibility that Mexico could be granted privileges not allowed to the United States during a transition to free trade (such as a longer transition period, degressive permission to use export subsidies, or financial assistance for development of backward regions) might be seen as a way to mitigate the unequal outcome but not likely to eliminate it.

Divergence Facts

There are enough facts to support almost anything about the unequal development and unequal exchange theory. During the 1960s the annual average growth in gross domestic product per capita for all developing countries was 3.4 percent; the same measure of growth was 3.8 percent for the industrial countries. By this measurement, divergence occurred during that decade. During the 1970s, however, the annual average GDP growth rates per capita were 2.8 percent for developing countries and 2.7 percent for industrial countries. To argue that divergence occurred in the 1970s requires using absolute amounts of growth rather than percentages. The former were obviously higher for industrial countries because of their higher base.[18]

Measurement at this level of aggregation is useful mainly for making debate points that pit the third world against the so-called first world. When the developing countries are separated into groups with different characteristics, much of the ambiguity disappears. During the 1960–78 period, what the World Bank calls the middle-income developing countries (MICs) had an increase in GDP per capita of 3.7 percent, precisely the same as that of the industrial countries. Since the former had annual population growth of 2.4 to 2.5 percent a year and the latter between 0.7 and 1.0 percent a year, the gross growth rate was substantially greater in the MICs, although again absolute growth was lower. If the most rapidly growing MICs, the so-called newly industrializing countries

18. This and the following data come from the World Bank, *World Development Report, 1979*, pp. 126–131; and *1980*, pp. 109–13. The groupings used by the World Bank are: thirty-eight low-income countries, whose per capita income was $360 or less in 1978; fifty-two middle-income countries, with per capita income of more than $360 in 1978; eighteen industrial countries; five capital-surplus oil-exporting countries; and twelve centrally planned economies.

(NICs), are singled out, what emerges are spectacular annual rates of GNP growth per capita over this period: Singapore, 7.4 percent; South Korea, 6.9 percent; Taiwan, 6.6 percent; Greece, 6 percent; Yugoslavia, 5.4 percent; Spain, 5 percent; Brazil, 4.9 percent; and Israel, 4.2 percent. Of the three main industrial countries the only one that matched these figures was Japan, which had a GDP growth rate per capita of 7.6 percent. West Germany's was only 3.3 percent and that of the United States was 2.4 percent.

Using more detailed growth data and looking further back into history, Rostow concluded precisely the reverse of what Myrdal hypothesized. Rostow concluded that poor countries tend to get richer and rich countries tend to slow down. He ascribed this effect mainly to the ability of the countries at the developmental stage of the NICs to absorb existing knowledge and technology, whereas growth in high-income countries depends on the rate at which new knowledge and technology is developed.[19]

The divergency theorists make a good empirical case when they choose the low-income countries (LICs) and compare their growth performance with either that of the MICs or the industrial countries. Between 1960 and 1978 the annual average rate of real growth in GNP per capita of the LICs was 1.6 percent, substantially lower than the 3.7 percent growth of both the MICs and the industrial countries. What has become clear during the past twenty-five years is that phrases like *developing countries* or *third world* have little economic meaning. Lumping together all countries other than the industrial and communist countries masks economic differences and, more significantly, obscures the differential treatment needed from the world community to mitigate divergence. The growth of the MICs and particularly the NICs is converging with that of the industrial countries; essentially they require equal treatment from the world economy. It is the LICs that need special privileges, such as concessional aid.

A similar pattern emerges when one examines unequal exchange, namely, that the performance of some (but not all) MICs has tended to converge with the industrial countries over the past twenty-five years, whereas the LICs are diverging from both. The world trading system underwent a profound shock in 1974 and again in 1979–80, when oil

19. W. W. Rostow, "Growth Rates at Different Levels of Income and Stage of Growth," in Rostow, *Why the Poor Get Richer and the Rich Slow Down*, pp. 259–301.

Table 7-1. *Real Annual Growth of Merchandise Trade, 1960–70*
and 1970–78

Percent

	Exports		Imports	
Country type	*1960–70*	*1970–78*	*1960–70*	*1970–78*
Low-income countries	5.0	−0.8	5.0	3.2
Middle-income countries	5.5	5.2	6.8	5.8
Industrial countries	8.7	5.7	9.4	5.1
Capital-surplus oil exporters	9.5	−1.2	11.1	21.1
Centrally planned economies	n.a.	n.a.	n.a.	n.a.

Source: World Bank, *World Development Report, 1980*, table 8, pp. 124–25.
n.a. Not available.

prices increased sharply. To examine oil trade performance, then, would require grouping countries according to those that import oil, those that are mostly self-sufficient, and those that export a lot of oil. This is not the place to do that in any detail, but it is worth mentioning that the terms-of-trade shock faced by developing-country oil importers and the continuing high cost of oil did deeply affect trade patterns and economic growth prospects. Some countries adjusted better than others, but all in fact had to change their prior thinking and planning. Even the partial combination of LICs and MICs is too aggregative for analyzing trade performance.

One way to see the complexity of possible outcomes is to look at trade performance by both broad and narrow groups of countries. Table 7-1 shows trade performance of all groups of countries, using the World Bank breakdown. The LIC-MIC divergence emerges clearly for the 1970s. Table 7-2 shows the data for the same NICs cited earlier as fast-growing countries, plus Mexico. Their export performance has tended to match their spectacular GDP growth and clearly does not reflect an inability to participate effectively in world trade. Some industrial countries had real export growth rates comparable to those of some of the NICs, but the average performance of the NICs exceeded that of the industrial countries.

In view of the stress early proponents of unequal exchange theory placed on industrial growth in developing countries and the stress on manufactures in most trade integration efforts, it should be pointed out that manufactures are the fastest growing category of exports of developing countries. This growth has been so substantial in some sectors—

Table 7-2. *Real Annual Growth of Merchandise Trade of Selected Developing Countries, 1960–70 and 1970–78*
Percent

Country	Exports		Imports	
	1960–70	*1970–78*	*1960–70*	*1970–78*
Brazil	5.0	6.0	4.9	6.6
Greece	10.7	13.1	10.9	5.9
Israel	10.9	10.6	8.7	4.5
Mexico	3.3	5.2	6.4	4.0
Singapore	4.2	9.8	5.9	8.1
South Korea	35.2	28.8	20.1	13.5
Spain	11.6	11.0	18.4	3.3
Taiwan	23.7	9.3	17.9	9.1
Yugoslavia	7.8	4.8	9.0	4.9

Source: Same as table 7-1.

mostly but not exclusively in labor-intensive goods—that it has stimulated protectionism in industrial countries. The protectionism is directed primarily against Japan and the NICs already listed, plus a few others.[20]

In its pure form, the theory of inevitable divergence based on the twin concepts of unequal development and exchange clearly cannot be sustained from the record. It cannot be sustained for Latin America, which consists mostly of MICs, and it clearly is not valid for the Asian NICs. The thesis of unequal development and unequal exchange does hold up, however, for the poorest countries, particularly those in sub-Saharan Africa and Asia. The theory is not a useful generalization for describing relations between developed and developing countries, even though that is why it was born and how it is often still used today. Mexico, for example, falls in the category of MIC and NIC but is a NIC that has fallen somewhat short in its trade performance compared with others.[21] But it is hard to blame Mexico's relatively poor performance on inevitable tendencies in the world system since other NICs have shown how the world system can be used to their benefit. Mexico's shortcoming must be explained by internal Mexican policies.

The real economic issue is not unequal development and unequal exchange in the abstract but whether fewer benefits would fall to Mexico

20. See discussion of this theme in World Bank, *World Development Report, 1979,* pp. 20–28.
21. Mexico's export growth rate improved for a few years after 1978, but because of oil exports, not competitiveness in manufactures.

than to the United States if the two countries moved over time to free trade. As already indicated, many Mexican economists assume that this will happen. However, as with unequal development and unequal exchange, the evidence from other examples of trade integration is ambiguous, despite the extensive literature on this subject. Efforts at trade integration in Latin America and Africa generally have not flourished, which is not to say they brought no benefits. Segal has pointed out that the political preference for sharing industrial production in East Africa, which is what motivated the common market among Kenya, Tanzania, and Uganda, did not succeed.[22] In addition, Fagan has written: "Even before the July war [between Honduras and El Salvador in 1969], the Central American Common Market was on the verge of collapse, primarily because of its inability to deal satisfactorily with the problem of unbalanced development."[23] That is, Honduras and Nicaragua were unable to attract as much industrial investment as the other members.

On the other hand, the LAFTA was able to expand intraregional trade. Between 1962 and 1977 such trade increased from 7.1 to 14.1 percent of the region's total trade.[24] According to one comprehensive study, intra-LAFTA trade was such a large factor in the region's total trade that it helped increase the region's total exports in the few years after a slump in 1974.[25] The reason for the collapse of the LAFTA was not its failure to promote trade but its failure to equally distribute the benefits of trade expansion.[26] The big three countries—Argentina, Brazil, and Mexico—tended to accumulate trade surpluses. Compared with most other LAFTA members, they had larger proportions of sophisticated manufactures in their exports, whereas the less developed countries barely participated in the export of complex manufactures.[27] Of the 110 bilateral trading relationships possible among LAFTA countries, 11 of these, or 10 percent, accounted for 52 percent of the value of all intra-

22. David Segal, "On Making Customs Unions Fair: An East African Example," pp. 115–60.
23. Stuart I. Fagan, *Central American Economic Integration: The Politics of Unequal Benefits*, p. 1.
24. Comision Económica para América Latina (CEPAL), "ALALC: El programa de liberación comercial y su relación con la estructura y las tendencias del comercio zonal," table 11. The absolute level of intra-LAFTA exports was $547.0 million FOB in 1962 and $5,685.4 million FOB in 1977.
25. Ibid., p. 32.
26. ALADI (Latin American Integration Association) was founded in 1980 to succeed LAFTA, but without the latter's emphasis on free trade.
27. CEPAL, "ALALC," p. 41.

LAFTA trade. These 11 bilateral trading relationships involved trade generated by the oil price increases in 1973 and 1974 and the trade of the three biggest countries, which were exporters, importers, or both in 10 of the 11 cases.[28] The LAFTA experience did demonstrate the proposition that there will be unequal benefits in free trade among economic unequals, or, as I have argued in this chapter, that there will be unequal benefits among unequals when one or more countries have an industrial capacity in place and the others have barely begun industrialization. This is not Mexico's situation; Mexico does have an industrial structure in place.

There is no doubt that in integration schemes involving developing countries, unequal benefits have been a problem, indeed, the central obstacle to success. Hansen has pointed out that what is involved is the sharing of benefits, not the question of absolute benefit. "But the major issue there [in the CACM], as in East Africa, is that of gains *relative* to those of one's partners, not as measured against any absolute standard."[29] These integration efforts among developing countries may have been useful despite their collapse. Hansen's observation highlights the importance of the word *unequal* when calculating the distribution of benefits among partners in an integration scheme.

There are contrary examples, however. In a book that seems to be dedicated to demonstrating the thesis of unequal benefits in integration schemes, Seers admits: "If one just looks at figures of economic growth, Ireland does not fit the picture of unequal development [in the EC]. Although a relatively poor country when it joined the Community, it has since been experiencing faster growth than the Community as a whole."[30] The chapter of the book on Ireland seeks to explain this by the big jump in livestock prices to the EC level, but there is an admission that Irish industry was dynamic as well.[31] This book argues that Italy, the poorest of the original six countries in the EC, has fallen further behind the others in income and technology, particularly with respect to Germany,

---

28. Ibid., pp. 35–36.
29. Roger D. Hansen, "Regional Integration: Reflections on a Decade of Theoretical Efforts," p. 259. Emphasis in original.
30. Dudley Seers, "Conclusions: The EEC and Unequal Development," in Seers and Vaitsos, eds. *Integration and Unequal Development*, pp. 307–08.
31. Anthony Coughlan, "Ireland," in ibid., pp. 121–35. This industrial growth is denigrated in the concluding comments of the book (written by Seers) because "the capital has been predominantly foreign in origin" (p. 308).

the wealthiest of the original six.[32] Yet the income data provided show that between 1958 and 1977 average annual GDP growth in Italy was at a slightly higher rate than in Germany when measured by current prices and current purchasing power parities (10.8 versus 10.3 percent). Growth was also higher between 1963 and 1977 when measured by 1970 prices and 1970 exchange rates (3.9 versus 3.8 percent) or 1970 prices and 1970 purchasing power parities (3.87 versus 3.79 percent).[33] This shows that Italy's fractionally higher growth rate was lower in absolute terms than the absolute growth of German income when measured from a higher base. This is hardly a demonstration of unequal benefits.

The performance of Portugal in the European Free Trade Association (EFTA) is another example contradicting the unequal benefits hypothesis. In 1959, the year before EFTA began operating, Portugal's income per capita in current prices was $260, or 10 percent of that of the then richest EFTA member—Iceland. In 1979, Portugal's GDP per capita was $2,050 in current dollars, or 14 percent of that of the then richest member—Switzerland.[34] (Portugal's GDP per capita was 20 percent of Iceland's by then.) Between 1959 and 1979, Portugal had the highest average annual GDP growth rate of any of the EFTA members, whether measured on a per capita or a total basis. It also had the highest annual growth rate in industrial production—6.7 percent compared with an EFTA average, including Portugal's performance, of 4.9 percent. Portugal rated third in growth of total employment, that is, 1.2 percent a year—lower than Iceland's 2 percent and Norway's 1.3 percent but well above the weighted EFTA average of 0.7 percent.[35] Portugal's intra-EFTA exports increased from 12 percent of its total exports in 1959 to 19 percent in 1978, while its imports from other EFTA members increased from 13 to 16 percent.[36] In other words, Portugal's reliance on EFTA trade increased but not to the exclusion of trade outside the EFTA.

Machlup has summarized the arguments on unions between weaker and stronger nations as follows:

32. Massimo Roccas, "Italy," in ibid., pp. 100–20.

33. Seers and Vaitsos, eds., *Integration and Unequal Development*, "Statistical annex," tables A.10 and A.11, pp. 346–47.

34. European Free Trade Association, *EFTA—Past and Future*, p. 35. As a basis for comparison, Mexico's per capita income in 1979 ($1,590) was 15 percent of that of the United States ($10,820), according to the *World Bank Atlas, 1980*, p. 18.

35. European Free Trade Association, *EFTA—Past and Future*, tables 1–5, pp. 35–39.

36. Ibid., p. 15.

Everything is conceivable and nothing can be said with any degree of certainty. . . . One can without undue imagination conceive of circumstances in which the development of a backward country would be helped and accelerated by its association with more advanced areas. But one can just as easily conceive of circumstances in which the backward country would be held back by such an integration, and its economic development retarded.[37]

The Seers-Vaitsos book already cited gives much attention to unequal regional development within and among countries in the EC as well as to unequal development between entire countries.The studies in this book make several conclusions useful for purposes here, including that disparities between the poorer and wealthier regions within countries grew in the late 1970s, despite an overall slowdown in economic growth.[38] The study on Italy found, however, that the north-south disparity in per capita incomes had not appreciably changed between 1951 and 1971,[39] British membership in the EC was found to have had a small or negligible impact on Britain's regional disparities.[40] Perhaps the most important conclusion is that "the redistributive power of a national economy is stronger than that of any other form of association or group of countries."[41] This merits emphasis when considering the desirability of a gradual movement to U.S.-Mexican free trade. Although such an agreement might include financial assistance from the United States to help Mexico overcome its regional disparities, such assistance could not be expected to be more than a small percentage of what Mexico would have to devote from its own resources to this end. Trade integration is, after all, a far less ambitious goal than an economic union or common fiscal policies.

To some extent, the trade integration that has already taken place at the border through the establishment of in-bond assembly plants has helped reduce the economic disparities between Mexico's northern frontier and its other high-growth areas, such as the federal district, Monterrey, and Guadalajara. Mexican development plans are intended to further reduce these disparities through continued incentives for industrial location at border areas. However, this is at best a partial

37. Fritz Machlup, *A History of Thought on Economic Integration*, p. 84.
38. See especially Marja-Liisa Kiljunen, "Regional Disparities and Policy in the EEC," in Seers and Vaitsos, eds., *Integration and Unequal Development*, pp. 199–222.
39. Roccas, "Italy," p. 112.
40. Martin Fetherston, Barry Moore, and John Rhodes, "Britain," in Seers and Vaitsos, eds., *Integration and Unequal Development*, p. 151.
41. Kiljunen, "Regional Disparities and Policy in the EEC," p. 219.

response to the disparities among Mexico's regions. Yet nothing in a movement toward a free-trade area or its eventual accomplishment need diminish a national regional policy. Mexico would be able to promote regional convergence with or without bilateral free trade.

Divergence in a Movement to U.S.-Mexican Free Trade

Assertions about unequal development, unequal exchange, and unequal benefits vary in validity as far as trade integration between Mexico and the United States is concerned. If Mexico were to move toward free trade with Bolivia, which is really what it did in the LAFTA, one might expect unequal benefits. Bolivia is a desperately underdeveloped country without the infrastructure and trained people to take advantage of technology that has been developed elsewhere, whereas Mexico possesses these assets. One cannot really talk of trade integration when such economic disparity exists at the outset. The more logical relationship is one of aid from the more developed to the less developed country; in its way, the LAFTA tried to incorporate such a relationship into its programs.

What seems to emerge from the facts examined in this chapter is that convergence is just as likely as divergence, indeed more likely, inside or outside a trade integration scheme, when the economically weaker country has the necessary infrastructure and human skills to take advantage of existing and emerging technology. The relationships between per capita incomes, often used to measure the potential of the weaker country to converge with the stronger, is not the relevant measurement.[42] What seems to be necessary for convergence is that the weaker country must have crossed some technological, savings, educational, and infrastructural threshold.[43] The NICs have crossed this threshold and seem to be converging on the industrial countries, just as Japan crossed this threshold a few generations ago and overtook countries that had industrialized earlier. Ireland and Portugal, despite sub-

---

42. See J. S. Nye, "Comparing Common Markets: A Revised Neo-Functionalist Model," pp. 796–835, for this kind of use of relative per capita incomes.

43. This essentially is the argument used by W. W. Rostow, *The Stages of Economic Growth: A Non-Communist Manifesto*, pp. 36–58, as the preconditions for the start of self-sustained economic growth.

stantial disparities in per capita income with other members of the EC and the EFTA, seem to be converging on their wealthier partners. Greece, by entering the EC, is betting that it has crossed the threshold.

Whether Mexico has crossed this threshold is the appropriate question to ask. In my view, Mexico has crossed it, judging from the development of many of its industries. Mexico is still a dual society, where there is a sharp contrast between highly educated persons able to handle the latest technology and a substantial undereducated and functionally illiterate population. The argument in favor of a movement to free trade is that it could help break down this dualism by promoting industrial expansion and efficiency. Free trade would ensure Mexico a larger market and some degree of consistent liberalization of import policy.

Many of the government programs Mexico has used and intends to carry out in the future would be consistent with both a transition to bilateral free trade and its achievement. Regional policies, investment tax incentives, tax incentives to stimulate employment, subsidized research, nationalization of Mexican industry, direct government involvement in industry, and limitations or expansions of oil production or concentration of oil exports are examples of Mexican policies that need not be compromised by a movement to free trade and its accomplishment. Whether all these government practices, such as price controls on steel or subsidized energy sales within Mexico, are in fact efficient or valuable from Mexico's standpoint can be questioned, but even in a free-trade area, the decisionmaking would rest with Mexicans in Mexico.

In other respects, Mexico would have to give up some national discretion if it began to move toward bilateral free trade. The use of export subsidies, the curtailment of imports from the United States by means of import licensing, and the degree of national content and performance requirements in different industries are examples of practices Mexico would have to temper in a free-trade area, at least in relation to Mexico's free-trade partner. The degree of constraint on Mexico presumably would be less in the transition to free trade than it would be after free trade were achieved. In any event, these practices would be proper subjects for negotiation in reaching and implementing the initial agreement. To some extent, Mexico will be limited in the use of protective practices with or without free trade. This is particularly true for export subsidies.

By the same token, the United States would be constrained in its use of marketing agreements imposed against Mexico or of limitations on apparel imports if it entered into free trade with Mexico. U.S. export subsidies would also have to be constrained in trade with Mexico. The U.S. constraints would be fewer than Mexico's—although not negligible, particularly for imports of labor-intensive products—because these practices are used less by the United States. Each country would have to make political and economic adjustments under free trade, but Mexico's would be more extensive because of the greater protection it now affords its industry. By the same token, however, the potential benefits of bilateral free trade would be greater for Mexico.

In summary, gradual achievement of free trade between Mexico and the United States would not inevitably result in fewer advantages for Mexico and more for the United States. It is just as likely that Mexico would benefit more than the United States, especially in a transition period extending to the twenty-first century. In addition, many of the industrial encouragements granted by the Mexican government or those comtemplated in Mexico's plans need not be affected by a bilateral free-trade agreement. Some practices, however, would be affected. These would be measures under which the Mexican government either subsidizes exports or arbitrarily curtails imports from the United States. Constraints or the lack of constraints for many national industrial policies would apply for the United States as well as for Mexico.

CHAPTER EIGHT

Summary

THIS CHAPTER summarizes the arguments for and against U.S.-Mexican free trade, separates the real from the false issues, discusses the possibility of trilateral free trade with Canada, and draws conclusions from this analysis.

Arguments Favoring U.S.-Mexican Free Trade

The arguments in favor of U.S.-Mexican free trade are based on three considerations: the adverse consequences to Mexican industry (and to employment and incomes in Mexico) of continuing past and current protectionist policies; the desire to eliminate U.S. protection that Mexican exports face, and might face, in entering the U.S. market; and the issue of whether explicit trade integration might enhance Mexican influence on mutual policies rather than reduce it. The last point is relevant because the trade and financial integration that already exists makes independent Mexican macroeconomic policies infeasible in any event.

Costs of Mexican Protectionism

Mexico's use of import-substituting industrialization (ISI) was extreme by any standard, in that protection for most industries was absolute. Import policies began to be liberalized in 1976 when some import licenses were converted to tariffs to permit some price competition, but this did not go far and the experiment did not last long. One consequence of this extreme form of ISI is that Mexican industry generally is noncompetitive in world markets and Mexico must rely on special concessions by others, particularly the United States, to gain markets for its industrial products.

Since about 60 percent of Mexico's imports are made up of intermediate industrial goods (table 4-1), the burden of its protective import policies can be substantial. Another third of Mexico's imports are capital goods; to foster industrialization and at the same time not penalize potential exporters, duties on these imports frequently are waived. This encouraged capital-intensive production rather than procedures that would use Mexico's ample labor supply.

The problem of noncompetitiveness has been aggravated by the periodic overvaluation of the Mexican peso, bringing on abrupt and substantial devaluations in 1954, 1976, and 1982 and 1983. This combination of substantial import protection and an overvalued exchange rate has made it more or less mandatory for Mexico to subsidize industrial exports in order to penetrate foreign markets. The use of subsidies, a pervasive feature of Mexico's industrial practice and planning, was made possible by a combination of massive external debts and, during the late 1970s, a quantum increase in oil revenue. Debt limits may now have been reached, and oil revenue is not growing. Even in the heyday of Mexico's oil boom, until 1982, use of this revenue to subsidize industry was expensive because a nonrenewable resource was being depleted by the development of noncompetitive industries that would continue requiring subsidies to survive.

Mexico's industrialization model is mostly to blame for the high unemployment and underemployment of Mexico's economically active population and for the great inequities that persist in Mexican society. This pattern of development also prejudiced the agricultural sector, which had to bear a large part of the cost of subsidizing industry. Despite high overall economic growth rates for three decades after World War II, many of Mexico's young men and some women have needed to emigrate to the United States to find jobs. Some people have emigrated legally and others without documents, some permanently, and others come and go with the seasons. The beneficiaries of the Mexican industrialization model have not been most of the 40 percent of the population that still lives in nonurban areas and certainly not the unemployed and underemployed. The beneficiaries of this economic development model, in other words, are only a minority of the Mexican population.

Reversing these consequences of protectionism does not necessarily call for bilateral free trade. These consequences do suggest, however, that changes in Mexico's protectionism are required, a point on which most Mexican economists agree, even if most of Mexico's small-business community does not. Mexico has three options: it can maintain the present system with such modifications as the balance-of-payments situation permits to eliminate its worst effects; it can seek substantial trade liberalization on a multilateral basis; or it can seek closer economic ties with the United States, since this is where Mexico's natural advantages lie. Multilateral liberalization might reduce Mexican trade reliance on the United States, but it might not because of the natural links between the two countries. Canada found that its pursuit of trade diversification did not alter Canada's trading pattern. The advantage of the bilateral free-trade option is that it would go further over time toward free trade with one country (or in all North America, if Canada were included) while still permitting protection against imports generally for as long as this was desired. Bilateral free trade would also do this within a definite time schedule that would facilitate planning and investment decisions by private entrepreneurs.

The initial advantage Mexico would enjoy in a movement to free trade with the United States would result from Mexico's lower wages, compensating many industries for lower Mexican productivity. Over time, if the free-trade arrangement worked, wages in Mexico and the United States would tend to equalize, but this is decades away at best and, if it occurs, would signify that the free-trade arrangement had succeeded. The investment in assembly plants, most of which are along the U.S.-Mexican border, demonstrates the attraction of low wages for labor-intensive industries such as apparel and electronics. In addition, because of the abundant availability of oil and natural gas, Mexico has a resource advantage as well as a labor-cost advantage in the production of basic petrochemicals. Much of Mexico's steel industry is younger than that in the United States and will be modernized further. Finally, the investment taking place in Mexico's automotive industry already contemplates export of components to the United States and elsewhere.

Mexico is not a thoroughly underdeveloped country but rather possesses a substantial and growing technically educated population with the capacity to originate ideas and adapt research done elsewhere to the Mexican scene. Therefore it is not necessarily true that movement toward one large, barrier-free market would lead to the concentration of complex industrial production in the United States, leaving raw material and simple processing in Mexico, particularly if trade integration were phased in over a sufficiently long time. There would, however, be impediments to achieving efficiency in industrial production if Mexico continued to circumscribe industrial investment by non-Mexicans. Although bilateral free trade does not require the free flow of capital, the effects of integration would be more pervasive if capital could flow freely into Mexico. However, even without complete freedom for foreign direct investment, massive industrial investment has taken place in Mexico, some by foreigners but mostly by private Mexicans and the Mexican government. Industrial development would proceed in any case.

Just as a free-trade area does not require the free movement of capital, neither does it require the free movement of labor. However, the free movement of goods is an imperfect alternative to free movement of labor and capital. A bilateral free-trade arrangement would be more efficient if labor, like capital, could move freely, but this is not essential, nor is it usual in other free-trade areas.

It is possible that these conclusions are inaccurate and that greater benefits would flow to the United States. In this event, the integration process could certainly be stopped, as it was in the Latin American Free Trade Association. Bilateral trade integration does entail risk for Mexico, as it does for the United States, but the potential benefits are substantial. If political conditions in Mexico permitted, a gradual movement to a large bilateral (or North American) free market for goods is one way Mexico could begin to resolve its most pressing problems of employment and income distribution. It is by no means the only way, nor is it a sure-fire panacea, but it is a feasible option for Mexico.

Escaping U.S. Protectionism

The United States employs both tariff and nontariff measures to protect its market against some imports from Mexico at the same time that it extends nonreciprocal benefits to help Mexico export to the United States. Both types of restrictive measures in their present forms would gradually disappear during a transition to free trade. Thus, assuming that U.S. restrictions on textiles and apparel imports from all sources will remain, their gradual and discriminatory disappearance for Mexico under bilateral free trade would substantially boost this Mexican industry. If agriculture were part of the free-trade arrangment, seasonal duties on tomatoes and other fresh vegetables would disappear. Mexican shoes, television, other electronic equipment, furniture, consumer durables, and other labor-intensive goods on which U.S. restrictions tend to be highest would also diminish gradually and discriminatorily. Some of these benefits could be quite substantial.

The U.S. general system of preferences would become moot since all Mexican goods, or most of them if there are exclusions from free trade in the agreement, would enjoy duty-free entry into the United States, again in a discriminatory fashion. U.S. tariff provisions allowing duty only on value added in Mexico would lose their relevance since no duty would be paid on any product produced or assembled in Mexico, not even on Mexican value added.

The more salient Mexican concern may be the fear that future export success will bring U.S. protectionism in its wake. This probably would not be traditional tariff protectionism but rather nontariff measures. In a free-trade agreement, the United States would have to treat Mexico differently from other countries. Any U.S. requests for voluntary export restraints, the negotiation of orderly marketing agreements, or efforts to exclude foreign producers from bidding on government-procured goods could not be the same for a free-trade partner as for others. In this respect Mexico would have more influence on U.S. policy than it has now and could exert this influence before decisions were made. When President Richard M. Nixon imposed a temporary surcharge on dutiable imports from all countries in August 1971, Mexico was able only to complain, to no avail, after the fact. Under a free-trade agreement, the United States could not have imposed these surcharges on imports from Mexico.

Too much should not be made of this Mexican advantage from a movement to bilateral free trade since restraints on protection would be reciprocal. In addition, despite Mexican fears of potential U.S. protectionism, the record for Mexican access to the U.S. market has been reasonably good. However, Mexico's ability to consult before the United States took protectionist action and its exemption from most of this action would allay a Mexican fear that has been perennial in trade relations between the two countries over the past twenty-five years.

Mexican Influence on Mutual Policies

In a free-trade agreement, not only would Mexico have to be consulted in advance regarding proposed U.S. trade actions, but the United States would have to be consulted about Mexican trade actions. The balance of benefits in this mutual consultation process would depend on the competitive situation that developed during a transition period. Each side would lose some national trade sovereignty and gain some bilateral influence.

This mutual influence on trade policies would not cover other vital aspects of national policy. Mexico's decisions on the pace of its oil and gas exploitation, the marketing of resulting products, or on internal industrial and agricultural incentives need not be affected by free trade. This is an important argument in favor of a free-trade agreement from the Mexican standpoint: Mexico's influence on U.S. trade decisions would increase while its influence on vital national decisions in other fields would remain mostly unaffected. The same, of course, would be true for the United States. Mexico would lose some national sovereignty over trade policy and be compensated by the addition of sovereignty in the two-country area. In such circumstances, rules or prior consultation are more likely to protect the weaker than the stronger partner, since actions by stronger countries affect the weaker more than the reverse.

Arguments against U.S.-Mexican Free Trade

The arguments in Mexico against bilateral free trade are both political and economic. The political opposition is formidable, so much so that it almost certainly would preclude any concurrence in Mexico now about a free-trade agreement. Such opposition is deeply rooted in Mexican history and in the Mexican psyche and can be changed only with time or as the result of cataclysmic events that transform attitudes. In Europe, it took several wars to change German and French attitudes from animosity to cooperation. This transformation was helped along by intellectual debate stimulated by people like Jean Monnet, Robert Schuman, and Konrad Adenauer. Current political views in Mexico need not preclude intellectual debate on the economic merits (and defects) of free trade.

The economic opposition in Mexico to bilateral free trade is also deeply interwoven with political attitudes. By itself the economic argument against free trade is based on the polarization or unequal-benefits hypothesis—that the rich country will get richer and the poor country poorer. Chapter 7 questioned whether this backwash effect would apply in a free-trade area between the United States and Mexico that would evolve gradually over about twenty years. However, the outcome is admittedly uncertain, so free trade would involve a gamble for Mexico. By the same token, the benefits could be great.

One political and economic concern Mexico might have is that under bilateral free trade, loyalties in northern Mexico could drift from Mexico City, where jobs are scarce and incomes are low, to the United States. This drift need not follow from free trade, which has not weakened national sovereignty in the smaller countries of the European Community that rely on larger member countries for goods and in some cases even for jobs. The drift would be more likely to occur if the center in Mexico did not distribute national benefits broadly.

The U.S. Interest

Most of the discussion in this study has concentrated on the Mexican interest in a movement to free trade. What is the U.S. interest? Does it coincide with Mexico's or does it diverge? Is the U.S. interest simply a matter of maintaining political hegemony and economic dominance and acquiring easy access to Mexican oil and natural gas? It is hard to see why political and economic dominance over Mexico would interest the United States. This would not be a durable accomplishment, nor would U.S. incomes benefit unless Mexican income and employment similarly benefited. There are economic interests in the United States that do profit from the elastic supply of relatively cheap labor from Mexico, but in general the United States would prefer that Mexico be able to provide enough jobs for its own people, so that the United States could control its immigration.[1] At one time people believed that political dominance of other countries benefited the mother country, but it has become abundantly clear that former colonial powers prefer to shuck their remaining responsibilities rather than expand them. Colonies or dependencies tend to be economically costly. It would not be in the interest of the United States to transform the U.S.-Mexican relationship into something that existed in the nineteenth or early twentieth century. The manifest destiny period in U.S. history is over.

Any U.S. interest in bilateral free trade must be the same as the Mexican interest, even if viewed from another vantage. If bilateral free trade facilitates investments of optimum scale in the most fitting location

1. "New Immigration Policy," *Newsweek* (August 3, 1981), pp. 25–26, reported a Roper poll in 1980 in which 90 percent of those surveyed favored an end to illegal immigration.

without trade barriers dictating decisions, total welfare should increase. How these benefits will be shared between the two countries is at the heart of the free-trade issue and is not clear. The United States wants Mexico to be prosperous and fully employed for trading, investment, and political reasons. Free trade leading to stagnation would no more benefit the United States than it would Mexico.

The standard analysis of a free-trade arrangement looks at the welfare benefits that result from trade created by the reduction of barriers between members and from diversion of trade caused by discrimination against third countries. Because the United States dominates Mexican imports and exports, the initial scope for diversion away from third countries is limited. Whatever diversion might actually occur for trade in either direction would depend on the levels of the respective tariffs and the nontariff barriers that remain against third countries. The case for free trade from the U.S. standpoint would not rest on increasing U.S. exports by diverting the exports of others but rather on the dynamic effects this would have on Mexico. These would, in turn, stimulate U.S. dynamism, thereby augmenting both U.S. and third-country exports.[2]

The U.S. interest in bilateral free trade thus rests on a combination of efficiency and industry dynamism. In these respects, the U.S. objectives would be the same as those of Mexico. In other respects, the U.S. and the Mexican interests differ. The United States does not need to increase the size of its potential market to achieve scale economics in its manufacturing plants. The United States does need reindustrialization, however, and a larger, fast-growing market should stimulate this process.

That the economic issues at stake for the United States in bilateral free trade may be less important than for Mexico does not mean that there would be no U.S. resistance to free trade with Mexico. Mexico's advantage of low wages implies that its labor-intensive industries, such as textiles and apparel, and its automotive industry would grow at the expense of workers in these industries in the United States. It is precisely such industries—those in which wage costs are a significant proportion of final product cost—that push the hardest for U.S. protectionism. U.S. workers would be concerned that low wages in Mexico would stimulate

2. There is substantial evidence from studies of trade integration schemes that the static effects tend to be small and that the important argument for such integration must be based on the dynamic considerations. See Tayseer A. Jaber, "Review Article: The Relevance of Traditional Integration Theory to Less Developed Countries," pp. 254–67.

industries to leave the United States in order to use Mexican labor. The responses to these concerns by those who favor bilateral free trade would have to be similar to those made in Mexico. They would have to deal with the potential benefit for the entire U.S. society, in which new job opportunities would be created. The point would have to be made that a long period of transition to free trade would permit gradual adjustment. In addition, U.S. industry would not necessarily suffer even in the short term. In the European Free Trade Association, for example, great shifts in industries have occurred, but there has been specialization within industries. And while Portugal's textile industry grew, as expected, the Swiss industry continued to thrive by producing higher-quality textiles.[3] Such specialization within industries would have to occur in both Mexico and the United States if both countries are to be satisfied with a movement to free trade.

False Issues

Mexicans are deeply concerned that any movement toward free trade with the United States would inexorably lead to U.S. political domination. Many Mexicans would not see such a movement as giving Mexico much greater influence over U.S. decisionmaking on trade issues but would expect the reverse to occur, that U.S. authorities would obtain greater influence over Mexican policies. However, the very idea of a free-trade area as opposed to integrating trade by means of a customs union was invented precisely to allow maximum national sovereignty for trade and other economic decisions. Even a customs union does not require its members to sacrifice all national authority on trade issues. In the EC specific decisions were required to go beyond the customs union toward a common commercial policy, and yet commercial policies of the member countries differ. In the same way, to even approach a common commercial policy in a free-trade area, both Mexico and the United States would have to want that outcome and make separate, specific decisions to bring it about. Judging from the history of other free-trade areas, this is unlikely to happen.

Even more remote is the possibility that a movement to and achievement of free trade will lead to economic or political union. The history of free-trade movements shows how difficult it is to achieve even free

3. European Free Trade Association, *EFTA—Past and Future*, p. 18.

trade. There is no precedent of bilateral or multilateral free trade leading to political union except when the countries specifically desired this, for example, in the German *Zollverein* of the last century.[4] There is no inevitable progression from sector agreements, to general free trade, to a customs union, to monetary union, to economic union, to political union. The issue is a false one.

In Mexico, an issue that is perhaps as sensitive as potential political domination or political union is that the United States seeks bilateral free trade mainly as a way to obtain leverage over Mexican oil and gas production and marketing. The United States did, in fact, provoke this suspicion. Several aspiring candidates for the U.S. presidency before the 1980 election as well as many legislators advocated a North American common market for energy, reasoning that Mexico has available supplies and the United States would provide a secure market. But this, too, is a false issue, since nothing inherent in a free-trade area would give the United States authority to dictate the level of hydrocarbon production in Mexico or the markets to which products are sent. Should the two countries wish to reach long-term agreements for the purchase of oil and gas, they can make this decision whether there is bilateral free trade or not. U.S. tariff and nontariff barriers are not at issue in hydrocarbon sales, but they are at the heart of bilateral free trade. Actually, the U.S. interest is served by Mexican oil production no matter where it is exported. Any exports relieve pressure on world supply-and-demand relationships.

A final false issue has already been raised in this chapter: that free trade would involve the free flow of capital and labor between the two countries. This is not necessarily true. In practice, free trade has proved easier to accomplish than free movement of labor and capital.

Effects of Trade Integration on Relations with Other Countries

Mexico is attempting to diversify its trade and economic relations in order to reduce its reliance on the United States, and the United States, of course, has trading and economic interests that are worldwide in scope. To a certain extent, these objectives and interests would be prejudiced if the two countries moved to free trade. Mexico would lose

4. See Jacob Viner, *The Customs Union Issue*, pp. 91-108.

some of its prestige in the third world if it moved toward free trade with the very country that is the target of most third-world demands. The United States would have to explain to other developing countries why they could not be given preferential trade treatment in the U.S. market in the same manner as Mexico. There would be political costs. (Presumably European countries would have no grievance against a free-trade area in North America that covered substantially all trade.)

In other respects, Mexican and U.S. international objectives need not be prejudiced by a free-trade agreement. Both countries would tend to divert some trade away from third countries in favor of bilateral trade, and this could frustrate to some degree Mexico's efforts to diversify its trade. As already stated, however, the existing predominance of the United States in Mexican trade limits the scope for trade diversion in any case. Moreover, if free trade did result in greater efficiency, Mexico's total trade should expand, so that in absolute terms, its trade with third countries need not suffer. The same is true for the United States. The countries of the EC and EFTA have increased their trade with each other since the formation of their trade integration schemes, but they have not ceased to be formidable world traders at the same time.

For both Mexico and the United States, international influence flows primarily from domestic economic strength. Mexico's influence is not based on sponsorship of resolutions in the United Nations, for example, but stems from its economic growth, its size, and, under certain conditions in the world oil market, the possession of oil. Its future influence will depend on the competitiveness of its industries. If free trade did succeed in enhancing economic growth and national welfare in the two countries, their international political influence would be augmented. In short, although free trade would involve some alteration of objectives in each country, these changes need not be drastic, nor should they figure crucially in any decision to move to free trade. If free trade improves the economic efficiency and growth of both countries, third-country trade need not suffer and, therefore, neither would relations of each country with the rest of the world.

Bilateral versus Trilateral Free Trade

The possibility exists to include Canada in a movement to free trade in all of continental North America. Canada is a more congenial free-trade partner for the United States than Mexico in that most of the trade between the two countries is now free of duty,[5] an agreement calling for free trade in automotive products already exists, joint defense production arrangements are in place, and per capita incomes are more or less equal. Trade between the United States and Canada is also greater by a factor of 2.75 than that between Mexico and the United States.[6]

Despite the greater similarities in the economies of Canada and the United States than between either of these two and Mexico, there is substantial reluctance in Canada to join with the United States in a movement to free trade. This reluctance is based on concerns similar to those held in Mexico, such as the fear that the United States will dominate economically, that there will be unequal economic benefits, and that Canada will lose its political identity and even its cultural uniqueness. There is a difference in atmosphere between Canada and Mexico in that many Canadians believe the economic prosperity of Canada requires free trade with the United States. There is also a body of literature by Canadians analyzing the economic implications of trade integration,[7] but there is no comparable literature by Mexicans on trade integration with the United States.

The opposition to North American integration was stated explicitly in a joint statement on behalf of Mexican President López Portillo and Canadian Prime Minister Pierre Trudeau when they met in Ottawa in May 1980: "The President and the Prime Minister exchanged views on current informal proposals for trilateral economic cooperation among Canada, Mexico and the United States and agreed that such an approach would not serve the best interests of their countries."[8] The support for U.S.-Canadian trade integration can be found in the reports of Canada's Senate Standing Committee on Foreign Affairs[9] and in the Canadian studies already mentioned.

5. Seventy-six percent of U.S. imports from Canada and 70 percent of Canada's imports from the United States were duty free in 1979. U.S. International Trade Commission, *Background Study of the Economies and International Trade Patterns of the Countries of North America, Central America and the Caribbean*, pp. 152, 155.

6. According to the U.S. Department of Commerce data, in 1980 U.S. exports to Canada amounted to $34,102 million and imports from Canada, $41,455 million.

7. Some of these studies include Sperry Lea, *A Canada-U.S. Free Trade Arrangement: Survey of Possible Characteristics*; Canadian-American Committee, *A Possible Plan for a Canada-U.S. Free Trade Area*; Ronald J. Wonnacott and Paul Wonnacott, *Free Trade between the United States and Canada: The Potential Economic Effects*.

8. José López Portillo and Pierre Elliot Trudeau, "Joint Statement by the President of Mexico and the Prime Minister of Canada, Ottawa, May 27, 1980," p. 8.

9. Canadian Parliament, Senate, *Canada–United States Relations*, vols. 2 and 3: *Canada's Trade Relations with the United States*.

The idea of trilateral free trade among the United States, Mexico, and Canada both simplifies and complicates the issue of potential free trade between the United States and either of the other two countries. The simplifying aspect is that political sensitivity in either Mexico or Canada might be more attenuated if they were joined together in a trade integration scheme rather than if either negotiated by itself with the economic colossus next door. The complicating feature is that negotiating problems would be multiplied, probably exponentially, as the number of countries increased. If Canada were to opt for free trade, a bilateral negotiation with the United States would be far more manageable than a trilateral one. The Canadian Senate Standing Committee on Foreign Affairs stated its preference for a bilateral approach, using the following reasoning:

The European parallel might suggest that it would be wise to proceed from the first to establish a North American free trade agreement to include Mexico and the countries of Central America. The Committee disagrees. It will be difficult enough to negotiate a free trade arrangement with the United States, without further complicating the task. However, it should be understood that any agreement reached should be open to accession subsequently by third countries, just as the European common market provided for expansion.[10]

The bilateral trading relations between Mexico and Canada are not now significant.[11] This relationship would intensify, of course, if both countries were part of a North American free-trade area. However, expanding the free-trade area to Central America and the Caribbean would be unduly complicating because it would include small countries more disparate economically with either Canada or the United States than Mexico is. These small countries have not crossed an industrial threshold that would permit them to share equally in the potential benefits of free trade.

The United States would gain potentially more in the long term from unifying markets with Mexico than with Canada, while in the present and near term it would gain more from free trade with Canada. In terms

10. Ibid., vol. 2, p. 123.
11. Tables 4-4 and 4-5 use Mexican data; the figures would be different if Canadian data were used. An internal paper of Statistics Canada, "Discrepancies in Reported Statistics Measuring International Trade Flows: The Case of Trade Between Canada and Mexico," April 1978, points out that (1) the total value of trade is much lower when measured by Mexican than by Canadian statistics; (2) trade flows in both directions increased faster when measured by Canadian statistics; and therefore that (3) the statistical discrepancy between the two sets of data is growing over time.

of bargaining power with other countries and regions, a trilateral free-trade area would be more interesting. It may be, however, that the United States could best pursue potential benefits from market unification with Mexico by confining its free-trade negotiations to just Canada, thus allowing the debate on free trade to percolate longer in Mexico. The point made by the Canadian Senate Standing Committee on Foreign Affairs would then be relevant, that any U.S.-Canadian arrangement could be kept open for Mexico (and others), if Mexico showed any interest. It does not seem fruitful to try to resolve the bilateral versus trilateral issue in the abstract. If the free-trade idea prospers, it can take either form, and the precise form an initial negotiation would take need not unalterably prejudice the ultimate agreement.

Conclusions

The purpose of this study has been to analyze the arguments for and against a movement toward free trade between Mexico and the United States. The discussion has focused mainly on arguments favoring such a movement in order to deal with the conventional wisdom that the economics of trade integration would preclude the transition to and accomplishment of free trade between two countries with such disparate economies and per capita incomes. The analysis has dealt more with the situation in Mexico than in the United States because the deepest doubts about bilateral free trade, on political and economic grounds, are held in Mexico rather than in the United States.

The case in favor of starting a movement toward bilateral free trade must rest on the expectation that each country will be better off economically than it would be without free trade and that each will share more or less equally in the benefits. Bilateral free trade is not the only way for each country to resolve its pressing economic problems but would be effective and simpler to implement than other viable approaches. In both countries free trade could help increase employment and improve industrial efficiency, and each would benefit from the process. The argument in favor of limiting free trade in North America to the United States, Mexico, and Canada is based on the assumption that other North American countries would not be prepared to accept global free trade. The three countries could seek free trade on a wider basis once they achieved free trade among themselves. Indeed, they probably would be in a good position to obtain reciprocity from other countries and regions in such a negotiation if they started from a large base of free trade.

The potential benefits of bilateral free trade are substantial for Mexico. Economic advantages would come from trade created by the gradual removal of tariff and nontariff barriers and the ability to plan for investment in plants of optimum size. Such investment could take advantage of a large U.S. market, with assurance that success in that market would not breed protectionism. The potential benefits to the United States from economies of scale are negligible since its market is not as constricted as Mexico's.

There are possible disadvantages of bilateral free trade, and their domination for either country would destroy an agreement. However, these disadvantages have been taken so much for granted until now, particularly in Mexico, that prospective gains hardly get a full hearing.

Any analysis of the potential economic gains and costs of bilateral free trade for either country must take explicit account of the developments taking place in each as well as the adjustments possible over an extended transition period. This adjustment period is necessary to help cushion many of the shocks of free trade and to allow for adjustment not by transfers of industries between the two countries but by specialization of industries within both countries.

The opposition to free trade would be formidable on political grounds in each country, so much so in Mexico that it has precluded any debate until now on the potential economic benefits. Mexico's fear is the political analogue of economic polarization—that formal trade integration with the United States would lead to political dependence. This is an emotional and not an intellectual concern, since dependence does not require a formal free-trade agreement. Indeed, a case can be made that the surest way to avoid dependence is to strengthen the Mexican economy and that bilateral free trade would be a political equalizer if it contributed to this result. The political fear in the United States is just as emotional— that free trade will lead to unlimited migration of Mexican labor and that the United States would then be swamped by cheap, alien labor.

There has been an unspoken attitude among government officials in both countries that the issue of bilateral free trade is so sensitive that it is best not discussed. My hope is that this study stimulates precisely such a discussion, not only or even mainly in governments but among scholars, businessmen, labor leaders, and others.

Bibliography

American Chamber of Commerce of Mexico. "Automotive: Sales Slump, Import Restrictions Have Reversed Industry's Prospects." *Mexico Update*, vol.1 (November 16, 1982).

————."Foreign Trade." *Mexico Update*, vol. 1 (December 27, 1982).

————."Key Economic Indicators." *Mexico Update*, vol. 1 (January 31, 1983).

————."Prior Import Licenses List Increased Sharply." *Mexico Update*, vol. 5 (July 1981).

————."U.S. Investment Here Seen Increasing 13% in '81." *Mexico Update*, vol. 5 (June 1981).

"Anti-Dumping Investigation." Petition before the U.S. Customs Service, Washington, D.C., of Florida Fresh Winter Vegetable Industry under the Anti-Dumping Act of 1921 concerning tomatoes, peppers, cucumbers, eggplant and squash, submitted by Southwest Florida Winter Vegetable Growers Association, Palm Beach–Broward Farmers Committee for Legislative Action, and South Florida Tomato and Vegetable Growers, September 12, 1978.

"Anti-Dumping Investigation: Certain Fresh Winter Vegetables from Mexico." Brief of Union Nacional de Productores de Hortalizas and West Mexico Vegetable Distributors Association, by Arnold and Porter, Washington, D.C., June 5, 1979.

Balassa, Bela. "A 'Stages' Approach to Comparative Advantage." Working Paper 256. Washington, D.C.: World Bank, 1977.

————. *The Structure of Protection in Developing Countries*. Baltimore: Johns Hopkins Press, 1971.

————. *The Theory of Economic Integration*. Homewood, Ill.: R. D. Irwin, 1961.

————, ed. *European Economic Integration*. Amsterdam: North-Holland Publishing Company, 1975.

Baldwin, Robert E. *Nontariff Distortions of International Trade*. Washington, D.C.: Brookings Institution, 1970.

Banco de México. *La distribución del ingreso en México*. México, D.F.: Fondo de Cultura Económica, 1974.

187

————. *Informe Anual, 1980.* México, D.F.: Banco de México, 1981.

————. *Informe Anual, 1981.* México, D.F.: Banco de México, 1982.

————. *Producto interno bruto y gasto, cuaderno 1960–1977.* México, D.F.: Banco de México, 1978.

Banco Nacional de Comercio Exterior, S.A. "Opiniones sobre el ingreso de México al GATT." *Comercio Exterior,* vol. 30 (February 1980).

Barkin, David, and Timothy King. *Regional Economic Development: The River Basin Approach in Mexico.* London: Cambridge University Press, 1970.

Bennett, Douglas, and Kenneth E. Sharpe. "Transnational Corporations and the Political Economy of Export Promotion: The Case of the Mexican Automobile Industry." *International Organization,* vol. 33 (Spring 1979).

Bergsman, Joel. *Income Distribution and Poverty in Mexico.* Working Paper 395. Washington, D.C.: World Bank, 1980.

Berkstein K., Samuel. "México: Estrategía petrolera y política exterior." *Foro Internacional,* vol. 21 (July–September 1980).

Bhagwati, Jagdish N., ed. *The New International Economic Order: The North-South Debate.* Cambridge, Mass.: MIT Press, 1977.

Blair, Calvin P. *Economic Development Policy in Mexico: A New Penchant for Planning.* Technical Papers Series 26. Austin: University of Texas, Institute of Latin American Studies, 1980.

Blasquez, Miguel. "Mexico–U.S. Trade." Speech to the International Trade Club of Chicago, reported in the United States–Mexico Chamber of Commerce publication *Washington Letter,* vol. 3 (November 1977).

Brady, Jerry, ed. *Mexican Industrial Development Plans: Implications for United States Policy.* Prepared for the Departments of State and Commerce and the Office of the U.S. Trade Representative. Washington, D.C.: Ventana Associates, 1981.

Bueno, Gerardo M., ed. *Opciones de política económica en México despues de la devaluación.* México, D.F.: Editorial Tecnos, 1977.

Canadian-American Committee. *A Possible Plan for a Canada-U.S. Free Trade Area.* Washington, D.C.: CAC, 1965.

Canadian Parliament. Senate. Standing Committee on Foreign Affairs. *Canada–United States Relations,* vol. 2: *Canada's Trade Relations with the United States.* Ottawa: Queen's Printer for Canada, 1978.

————. ————. ————. *Canada–United States Relations,* vol. 3: *Canada's Trade Relations with the United States.* Ottawa: Minister of Supply and Services Canada, 1982.

————. ————. ————. *Canadian Relations with the United States.* Ottawa: Minister of Supply and Services Canada, July 8, 1980.

Caporaso, James A. "Dependence, Dependency, and Power in the Global System: A Structural and Behavioral Analysis." *International Organization,* vol. 32 (Winter 1978).

Castañeda, Jorge. "En busca de una posición ante Estados Unidos." *Foro Internacional,* vol. 19 (October–December 1978).

————. *Mexico and the United Nations.* New York: Manhattan Publishing

Company for El Colegio de México and the Carnegie Endowment for International Peace, 1958.

————."Mexico and the United States: The Next Decade." Speech delivered at the forty-second annual conference of the Council on Foreign Relations, New York, June 6, 1980.

Chenery, Hollis B., and Donald B. Keesing. *The Changing Composition of Developing Country Exports.* Working Paper 314. Washington, D.C.: World Bank, 1979.

Chenery, Hollis, and others. *Redistribution with Growth.* London: Oxford University Press, 1974.

Clement, Norris, and Louis Green. "The Political Economy of Devaluation in Mexico." *Inter-American Economic Affairs,* vol. 32 (Winter 1978).

Cline, William R., and Sidney Weintraub, eds. *Economic Stabilization in Developing Countries.* Washington, D.C.: Brookings Institution, 1981.

Cohen, Robert B. "Brave New World of the Global Car." *Challenge,* vol. 24 (May–June 1981).

Comisión Económica para América Latina. "ALALC: El programa de liberación comercial y su relación con la estructura y las tendencias del comercio zonal." Document E/CEPAL/L.195. New York: United Nations Economic and Social Council, 1979.

Connor, John M. "A Qualitative Analysis of the Market Power of United States Multinational Corporations in Brazil and Mexico." Ph.D. dissertation. University of Wisconsin–Madison, 1976.

Connor, John M., and Willard F. Mueller. *Market Power and Profitability of Multinational Corporations in Brazil and Mexico.* Committee Print. Senate Committee on Foreign Relations. 95 Cong. 1 sess. Washington, D.C.: Government Printing Office, 1977.

Cooper, C. A., and B. F. Massell. "Toward a General Theory of Customs Unions for Developing Countries." *Journal of Political Economy,* vol. 73 (October 1965).

Corredor Esnaola, Jaime. "El significando económica del petróleo en México." *Comercio Exterior,* vol. 31 (November 1981).

Cosío-Villegas, Daniel. *El estilo personal de gobernar.* México, D.F.: Editorial J. Mortiz, 1974.

De la Madrid, Miguel. "Documento: Criterios generales de política económica para 1983." *Comercio Exterior,* vol. 32 (December 1982).

————. "President de la Madrid's Inaugural Address." *Review of the Economic Situation of Mexico,* vol. 58 (December 1982).

Dell, Sidney. *A Latin American Common Market?* London: Oxford University Press, 1966.

————. *Trade Blocs and Common Markets.* New York: Knopf, 1963.

Diebold, William, Jr. *The Schuman Plan: A Study in Economic Cooperation, 1950–1959.* New York: Praeger for the Council on Foreign Relations, 1959.

Dominguez, Jorge I., ed. *Mexico's Political Economy: Challenges at Home and Abroad.* Beverly Hills, Calif.: Sage Publications, 1982.

Eckaus, R. S., and P. N. Rosenstein-Rodan, eds. *Analysis of Development*

Problems: Studies of the Chilean Economy. Amsterdam: North-Holland Publishing Company, 1973.

European Free Trade Association. *EFTA—Past and Future.* Geneva, Switzerland: Secretariat, European Free Trade Association, 1980.

Fagan, Stuart I. *Central American Economic Integration: The Politics of Unequal Benefits.* Research Series 15. Berkeley: University of California, Institute of International Studies, 1970.

Fagen, Richard R., and Henry R. Nau. "Mexican Gas: The Northern Connection." Working Paper 15. Washington, D.C.: Woodrow Wilson International Center for Scholars, 1979.

Fajnzylber, Fernando, and Trinidad Martínez Tarragó. *Las empresas transnacionales: Expansión a nivel mundial y proyección en la industria mexicana.* México, D.F.: Fondo de Cultura Economica, 1976.

Felix, David. "Income Inequality in Mexico." *Current History,* vol. 72 (March 1977).

Foreign Investment Review Agency of Canada. Policy, Research, and Communications Branch. "Barriers to Foreign Investment in the United States." Ottawa: FIRA, 1982.

Garreau, Joel. *The Nine Nations of North America.* Boston: Houghton Mifflin, 1981.

General Agreement on Tariffs and Trade. *Basic Instruments and Selected Documents,* vol. 1: *Text of the Agreement and Other Instruments and Procedures.* Geneva, Switzerland: The Contracting Parties to the GATT, 1952.

———. *Basic Instruments and Selected Documents,* vol. 1 (revised): *Texts of the General Agreement, as Amended, and of the Agreement on the Organization for Trade Cooperation.* Geneva, Switzerland: The Contracting Parties to the GATT, 1955.

———. *Basic Instruments and Selected Documents,* vol. 4: *Text of the General Agreements, 1969.* Geneva, Switzerland: The Contracting Parties to the GATT, 1969.

———. "Draft Protocol for the Accession of Mexico to the General Agreement on Tariffs and Trade." L/4849. October 26, 1979. Unclassified.

Gómez Palacio, Roberto Dávila. "Estrategía para el comercio exterior de México." *El Mercado de Valores,* vol. 41 (June 22, 1981).

Gonzalez Casanova, Pablo. "The Economic Development of Mexico." *Scientific American,* vol. 243 (September 1980).

Graham, Thomas R. *The Impact of the Tokyo Round Agreements on U.S. Export Competitiveness.* Significant Issues Series. Washington, D.C.: Georgetown University, Center for Strategic and International Studies, 1980.

Grayson, George W. *The Politics of Mexican Oil.* Pittsburgh: University of Pittsburgh Press, 1980.

Hansen, Niles. *The Border Economy: Regional Development in the Southwest.* Austin: University of Texas Press, 1981.

Hansen, Roger D. "Regional Integration: Reflections on a Decade of Theoretical Efforts." *World Politics,* vol. 21 (January 1969).

Hartland-Thunberg, Penelope. *The Political and Strategic Importance of Exports*. Significant Issues Series. Washington, D.C.: Georgetown University, Center for Strategic and International Studies, 1979.

Hewlett, Sylvia Ann, and Richard S. Weinert, eds. *Brazil and Mexico: Patterns in Late Development*. Philadelphia: Institute for the Study of Human Issues, 1982.

Hirschman, Albert O. *The Strategy of Economic Development*. New Haven: Yale University Press, 1958.

Ibarra Muñoz, David. "The Annual Convention of the Mexican Bankers Association." *Review of the Economic Situation of Mexico*, vol. 57 (June 1981).

Jaber, Tayseer A. "Review Article: The Relevance of Traditional Integration Theory to Less Developed Countries." *Journal of Common Market Studies*, vol. 9 (March 1971).

James, Dilmus D. "La planeación reciente de la ciencia y la tecnología en México." *Comercio Exterior*, vol. 31 (May 1981).

Johnson, Harry G. "An Economic Theory of Protectionism, Tariff Bargaining, and the Formation of Customs Unions." *Journal of Political Economy*, vol. 73 (June 1965).

Katz, Bernard S. "Mexico's Import Licensing Strategy for Protecting Import Replacements: An Aspect of Trade Policy and Planning for Industrial Development." *American Journal of Economics and Sociology*, vol. 33 (October 1974).

King, Timothy. *Industrialization and Trade Policies since 1940*. London: Oxford University Press for the Development Center of the Organization for Economic Cooperation and Development, 1970.

Krause, Lawrence B. *European Economic Integration and the United States*. Washington, D.C.: Brookings Institution, 1968.

Krause, Lawrence B., and Sueo Sekiguchi, eds. *Economic Interaction in the Pacific Basin*. Washington, D.C.: Brookings Institution, 1980.

Krueger, Anne O. *Liberalization Attempts and Consequences*. Cambridge, Mass.: Ballinger for the National Bureau of Economic Research, 1978.

Laney, Leroy O. "Currency Substitution: The Mexican Case." *Voice of the Federal Reserve Bank of Dallas* (January 1981).

Lea, Sperry. *A Canada-U.S. Free Trade Arrangement: Survey of Possible Characteristics*. Washington, D.C.: Canadian-American Committee, 1963.

López Portillo, José. "Sixth State of the Nation Report to the Mexican Congress." *Review of the Economic Situation of Mexico*, vol. 58 (August–September 1982).

Love, Joseph L. "Raúl Prebisch and the Origins of the Doctrine of Unequal Exchange." *Latin American Research Review*, vol. 15, no. 3 (1980).

Lyndon B. Johnson School of Public Affairs. *Growth and Equity in Mexico*. Development Studies Program Case Studies in Development Assistance 5. Washington, D.C.: Agency for International Development, 1979.

Machlup, Fritz. *A History of Thought on Economic Integration*. New York: Columbia University Press, 1977.

Marquez, Javier, ed. *Pensamiento de México en los periódicos: Páginas editoriales, 1976.* México, D.F.: Editorial Tecnos, 1977.

Mead, Donald C. "The Distribution of Gains in Customs Unions between Developing Countries." *Kyklos,* vol. 21, fasc. 4 (1968).

Meade, James E., H. H. Liesner, and S. J. Wells. *Case Studies in European Economic Union: The Mechanics of Integration.* London: Oxford University Press, 1962.

"The Mexican Economy in 1980: The Industrial Sector." *Review of the Economic Situation of Mexico,* vol. 56 (December 1980).

Meyer, Lorenzo. *Mexico and the United States in the Oil Controversy, 1917–1942.* Austin: University of Texas Press, 1977. Translated from *México y los Estados Unidos en el conflicto petrolero, 1917–1942.* México, D.F.: El Colegio de México, 1972.

Meyer, Michael C., and William L. Sherman. *The Course of Mexican History.* New York: Oxford University Press, 1979.

Morawetz, David. *The Andean Group: A Case Study in Economic Integration among Developing Countries.* Cambridge, Mass.: MIT Press, 1974.

Motor Vehicle Manufacturers Association of the United States. *World Motor Vehicle Data, 1980 Edition.* Detroit, Mich.: MVMA, 1980.

Myrdal, Gunnar. *Economic Theory and Under-Developed Regions.* London: Duckworth, 1957.

————. *An International Economy: Problems and Prospects.* New York: Harper and Brothers, 1956.

Nacional Financiera, S.A. *México: Una estrategía para desarrollar la industria de bienes de capital.* México, D.F.: Nacional Financiera and U.N. Industrial Development Organization, 1977.

Newfarmer, Richard S., and Willard F. Mueller. *Multinational Corporations in Brazil and Mexico: Structural Sources of Economic and Noneconomic Power.* Committee Print. Subcommittee on Multinational Corporations of the Senate Committee on Foreign Relations. 94 Cong. 1 sess. Washington, D.C.: Government Printing Office, 1975.

Nowicki, A., and others. *Mexico: Manufacturing Sector: Situation, Prospects and Policies.* Washington, D.C.: World Bank, 1979.

Nye, Joseph S., Jr. "Comparing Common Markets: A Revised Neo-Functionalist Model." *International Organization,* vol. 24 (Autumn 1970).

Ojeda, Mario. *Alcances y límites de la política exterior de México.* México, D.F.: El Colegio de México, 1976.

————. "El poder negociador del petróleo: El caso de México." *Foro Internacional,* vol. 21 (July–September 1980).

Paz, Octavio. "Reflections: Mexico and the United States." *New Yorker,* vol. 55 (September 17, 1979).

Pellicer de Brody, Olga. "Consideraciones acerca de la política comercial de Estados Unidos hacia México." *Comercio Exterior,* vol. 30 (October 1980).

Peñaloza, Tomás. "Mecanismos de la dependencia: El caso de México (1970–75." *Foro Internacional,* vol. 17 (July–September 1976).

"Plan nacional de desarrollo agroindustrial, 1980–1982," drawing on "Programa nacional de empleo." *El Mercado de Valores*, vol. 40 (June 9, 1980).

Poder Ejecutivo Federal. *Plan nacional de desarrollo, 1983–1988.* México, D.F.: Poder Ejecutivo Federal, 1983.

Pomareda, Carlos. "Evaluación de la política comercial de Estados Unidos sobre importaciones de hortalizas." *Comercio Exterior*, vol. 28 (October 1978).

"Primera evaluación del plan global." *El Mercado de Valores*, vol. 41 (May 25, 1981).

Rama, Ruth, and Robert Bruce Wallace. "La política proteccionista mexicana, un análisis para 1960–1970." *Demografía y Economía*, vol. 11, no. 2 (1977).

Ramirez de la O., Rogelio. "Las empresas transnacionales y el comercio exterior de México: Un estudio empírico del comportamiento de las empresas." *Comercio Exterior*, vol. 31 (October 1981).

Rangel, Carlos. "Mexico and Other Dominoes." *Commentary*, vol. 71 (June 1981).

Ranis, Gustav. "¿Se está tornando amargo el milagro mexicano?" *Demografía y Economía*, vol. 8, no. 1 (1974).

"Report on the Economy." *Review of the Economic Situation of Mexico*, vol. 58 (April 1982).

"Report on the Economy: Foreign Trade." *Review of the Economic Situation of Mexico*, vol. 58 (December 1982).

"Report on the Economy: The Industrial Sector." *Review of the Economic Situation of Mexico*, vol. 58 (December 1982).

Reynolds, Clark W. "Labor Market Projections for the United States and Mexico and Their Relevance to Current Migration Controversies." *Stanford University Food Research Institute Studies*, vol. 17, no. 2 (1979).

————. *The Mexican Economy: Twentieth Century Structure and Growth.* New Haven, Conn.: Yale University Press, 1970.

Rico F., Carlos. "Las relaciones mexicano-norteamericanas y los significados de la 'interdependencia.' " *Foro Internacional*, vol. 19 (October–December 1978).

Robson, Peter. "The Distribution of Gains in Customs Unions between Developing Countries: A Note." *Kyklos.* vol. 23, fasc. 1 (1970).

Ronfeldt, David, Richard Nehring, and Arturo Gándara. *Mexico's Petroleum and U.S. Policy: Implications for the 1980s.* Prepared for the U.S. Department of Energy. R-2510-DOE. Santa Monica, Calif.: Rand Corp., 1980.

Ross, Stanley R. *Francisco I. Madero: Apostle of Mexican Democracy.* New York: AMS Press, 1970.

Rostow, W. W. *The Stages of Economic Growth: A Non-Communist Manifesto.* London: Cambridge University Press, 1971.

————, ed. *Why the Poor Get Richer and the Rich Slow Down: Essays in the Marshallian Long Period.* Austin: University of Texas Press, 1980.

Secretaría de Comercio. "Concisiones recibidas por México en al GATT." *Comercio Exterior*, vol. 30 (February 1980).

Secretaría de Patrimonio y Fomento Industrial. *Plan nacional de desarrollo industrial, 1979–1982.* México, D.F.: SPFI, 1979. Or *Mexico: Industrial Development Plan, 1979–1982.* London: Graham and Trotman, 1979.

Secretaría de Programación y Presupuesto. *La industria petrolera en México.* México, D.F.: SPP, 1979.

———. *Plan global de desarrollo, 1980–1982.* México, D.F.: SPP, 1980.

Seers, Dudley, and Constantine Vaitsos, eds. *Integration and Unequal Development: The Experience of the EEC.* New York: St. Martin's Press, 1980.

Segal, David. "On Making Customs Unions Fair: An East African Example." *Yale Economic Essays,* vol. 10 (Fall 1970).

Segovia Canosa, Rafael. *La politización del niño mexicano.* México, D.F.: El Colegio de México, 1975.

Sepúlveda Amor, Bernardo. "Las nuevas reglas del GATT y el marco jurídico mexicano." *Comercio Exterior,* vol. 30 (February 1980).

Sepúlveda Amor, Bernardo, and Antonio Chumacero. *La inversión extranjera en México.* México, D.F.: Fondo de Cultura Económica, 1973.

Sepúlveda Amor, Bernardo, Olga Pellicer de Brody, and Lorenzo Meyer. *Las empresas transnacionales en México.* México, D.F.: El Colegio de México, 1974.

Sharp, Mitchell. "Canada-U.S. Relations: Options for the Future." *International Perspectives* (Autumn 1972).

Simmons, Richard L., James L. Pearson, and Ernest B. Smith. *Mexican Competition for the U.S. Fresh Winter Vegetable Market.* Agricultural Economic Report 348. Washington, D.C.: U.S. Department of Agriculture, Economic Research Service, 1976.

Simons, Marlise. "Mexico: The People Next Door." *Wilson Quarterly,* vol. 3 (Summer 1979).

Solís M., Leopoldo, ed. *La economía mexicana: Análisis por sectores y distribución.* México, D.F.: Fondo de Cultura Económica, 1973.

Trejo Reyes, Saúl, "El sector externo en la economía mexicana: Crecimiento óptima y política de exportaciones." *El Trimestre Económico,* vol. 42 (April–June 1975).

United Nations Association of the United States of America. *Relationships in the North American Economic Area.* North American Economic Area Panel of the Economic Policy Council. New York: UNA-USA, 1981.

United Nations Economic Commission for Latin America. *Distribución regional del producto interno bruto sectorial en los países de América Latina.* Santiago, Chile: Cuadernos de la CEPAL, 1981.

———. *The Economic Development of Latin America and Its Principal Problems.* Prepared by Raúl Presbisch. Lake Success, N.Y.: U.N. Department of Economic Affairs, 1950.

"United States–Mexican Relations." *Texas Business Review,* vol. 53 (March–April 1979).

United States–Mexico Chamber of Commerce. "Countervailing Duty Cases." *Washington Letter,* vol. 9 (January 1983).

Urquidi, Victor L. "Prospects for Further Development of Economic Relations among Mexico, Canada, and the United States." *Mexican Forum*, vol. 2 (October 1982).

U.S. Congress. House. Committee on Banking, Finance, and Urban Affairs. *International Financial Markets and Related Problems*. Hearings. 98 Cong. 1 sess. Washington, D.C.: Government Printing Office, 1983.

———. Committee on Ways and Means. *Report to the Congress on the First Five Years' Operation of the U.S. Generalized System of Preferences (GSP)*. Committee Print. 96 Cong. 2 sess. Washington, D.C.: Government Printing Office, 1980.

———. Joint Economic Committee. Subcommittee on Inter-American Economic Relationships. *Recent Developments in Mexico and Their Economic Implications for the United States*. Hearings. 95 Cong. 1 sess. Washington, D.C.: Government Printing Office, 1977.

———. Senate. Committee on Agriculture, Nutrition, and Forestry. Subcommittee on Foreign Agricultural Policy. *Inspection Standards of Vegetable Imports*, pts. 1–3. Hearings. 95 Cong. 2 sess. Washington, D.C.: Government Printing Office, 1978.

———. ———. Committee on Finance. Subcommittee on International Trade. *Trade Agreements Act of 1979*. Hearings. 96 Cong. 1 sess. Washington, D.C.: Government Printing Office, 1979.

U.S. Department of Commerce. International Trade Administration. "Marketing in Mexico." *Overseas Business Reports*. Prepared by Frederick J. Tower. OBR 81-09. Washington, D.C.: Government Printing Office, 1981.

U.S. Department of Labor. Bureau of International Labor Affairs. *Profile of Labor Conditions: Mexico*. Prepared by Martha R. Lowenstern. Washington, D.C.: Government Printing Office, 1979.

U.S. International Trade Commission. *Background Study of the Economics and International Trade Patterns of the Countries of North America, Central America and the Caribbean*. USITC 1176. Washington, D.C.: USITC, 1981.

———. *Imports Under Items 806.30 and 807.00 of the Tariff Schedules of the United States, 1977–80*. USITC 1170. Washington, D.C.: USITC, 1981.

———. *Study of the Petrochemical Industries in the Countries of the Northern Portion of the Western Hemisphere*, vols. 1–4. USITC 11230. Washington, D.C.: Government Printing Office, 1981.

U.S. Library of Congress. Congressional Research Service. *Mexico's Oil and Gas Policy: An Analysis*. Joint Committee Print. Prepared for the Senate Committee on Foreign Relations and the Joint Economic Committee. 95 Cong. 2 sess. Washington, D.C.: Government Printing Office, 1979.

"U.S.-Mexico Joint Communiqué." *Department of State Bulletin*, vol. 79 (March 1979).

U.S. Select Commission on Immigration and Refugee Policy. *U.S. Immigration Policy and the National Interest*. Staff report and nine appendix volumes. Washington, D.C.: Government Printing Office, 1981.

U.S. State Department. *United States Treaties and Other International*

Agreements. TIAS 9619. Washington, D.C.: Government Printing Office, 1981.

Vazquez Tercero, Hector. *Una decada de política sobre industria automotriz.* México, D.F.: Editorial Tecnos, 1976.

Vernon, Raymond, *The Dilemma of Mexico's Development: The Roles of the Private and Public Sectors.* Cambridge, Mass.: Harvard University Press, 1963.

————, ed. *Public Policy and Private Enterprise in Mexico.* Cambridge, Mass.: Harvard University Press, 1964.

"Views of the Motor Vehicle Manufacturers Association of the United States on the President's Report to the Congress on North American Trade Agreements." Submitted to the Trade Policy Staff Committee, February 6, 1981.

Villarreal Arrambide, René Patricio. "External Disequilibrium and Growth without Development: The Import Substitution Model—the Mexican Experience (1929–1975)." Ph.D. dissertation, Yale University, 1976.

————. *El desequilibrio externo en la industrialización de México, 1929–1975: Un enfoque estructuralista.* México, D.F.: Fondo de Cultura Económica, 1976.

Villarreal, Rocío de, and René Villarreal. "El comercio exterior y la industrialización de México a la luz del nuevo GATT." *Comercio Exterior*, vol. 30 (February 1980).

Viner, Jacob. *The Customs Union Issue.* Lancaster, Pa.: Lancaster Press for the Carnegie Endowment for International Peace, 1950.

Warnecke, Steven J., ed. *International Trade and Industrial Policies: Government Intervention and an Open World Economy.* New York: Holmes and Meier, 1978.

Watanabe, Susumu. "Constraints on Labour-Intensive Export Industries in Mexico." *International Labour Review*, vol. 109 (January 1974).

Weintraub, Sidney. "Fear of Free Trade." *Policy Options* (Canada), vol. 2 (July–August 1981).

————. "Greater Trade Integration in North America: Key Economic Issues." Statement before the Senate Committee on Finance, Subcommittee on International Trade, June 6, 1979.

————. "Mexican Subsidies and U.S. Law: Potential Collision Course." *Mexican Forum*, vol. 1 (April 1981).

————. "North American Free Trade." *Challenge*, vol. 23 (September–October 1980).

"Western Hemisphere: Secretary Vance Visits Mexico." *Department of State Bulletin*, vol. 78 (June 1978).

Whitman, Marina v. N. *International Trade and Investment: Two Perspectives.* Essays in International Finance 143. Princeton, N.J.: Princeton University, 1981.

Wionczek, Miguel S. "Algunas reflexiones sobre la futura política petrolera de México." *Comercio Exterior*, vol. 32 (November 1982).

————. *El nacionalismo mexicano y la inversión extranjera*. México, D.F.: Siglo Veintiuno Editores, 1967.

————. "The Rise and the Decline of Latin American Economic Integration." *Journal of Common Market Studies*, vol. 9 (September 1970).

Wonnacott, Ronald J., and Paul Wonnacott. *Free Trade between the United States and Canada: The Potential Economic Effects*. Cambridge, Mass.: Harvard University Press, 1967.

World Bank. *1981 World Bank Atlas*. Washington, D.C.: World Bank, 1982.

————. *World Development Report, 1980*. Washington, D.C.: World Bank, 1980.

————. *World Development Report, 1979*. Washington, D.C.: World Bank, 1979.

Zepp, G. A., and R. L. Simmons. *Producing Fresh Winter Vegetables in Florida and Mexico: Costs and Competition*. U.S. Department of Agriculture, Economics, Statistics, and Cooperatives Services. ESCS-72. Washington, D.C.: Government Printing Office, 1979.

Index